Proceedings

Computer Security, Dependability, and Assurance: From Needs to Solutions

Proceedings

Computer Security, Dependability, and Assurance: From Needs to Solutions

7-9 July 1998
York, England

11-13 November 1998
Williamsburg, Virginia

Sponsored by
The Office of Naval Research
National Science Foundation

Los Alamitos, California
Washington · Brussels · Tokyo

IEEE Computer Society Order Number PR00337
ISBN 0-7695-0337-3
ISBN 0-7695-0339-X (microfiche)
Library of Congress Number 99-64234
IEEE Order Plan Catalog Number 98EX358

Additional copies may be ordered from:

IEEE Computer Society	IEEE Service Center	IEEE Computer Society
Customer Service Center	445 Hoes Lane	Asia/Pacific Office
10662 Los Vaqueros Circle	P.O. Box 1331	Watanabe Building,
P.O. Box 3014	Piscataway, NJ 08855-1331	1-4-2 Minami-Aoyama
Los Alamitos, CA 90720-1314	Tel: + 1-732-981-0060	Minato-ku, Tokyo 107-0062 JAPAN
Tel: + 1-714-821-8380	Fax: + 1-732-981-9667	Tel: + 81-3-3408-3118
Fax: + 1-714-821-4641	mis.custserv@computer.org	Fax: + 81-3-3408-3553
E-mail: cs.books@computer.org		tokyo.ofc@computer.org

Editorial production by Danielle C. Martin

Cover art production by Joseph Daigle/Studio Productions

Printed in the United States of America by Technical Communication Services

IEEE
**COMPUTER
SOCIETY**

Table of Contents

Preface

By Editors: Paul Ammann, Bruce Barnes, Sushil Jajodia, and Edgar Sibley

These proceedings reflect two invitational workshops supported by the Office of Naval Research and the National Science Foundation. The workshops goals were establishing the state of the art in the three scientific communities of Computer Security, Fault Tolerance, and Software Assurance and setting the course for future research. The first meeting was held July 7-9, 1998 in York, UK, and the second meeting was held November 11-13, 1998 in Williamsburg, VA. The workshops were designed to focus on the practical needs of system development, where security, fault tolerance, and assurance requirements are increasing dramatically with the rapid spread of commercial enterprises into cyberspace. The motivating idea for the workshops was that these three communities face many closely related problems, and consequently solutions from one community were likely to be relevant in all communities. Participants are asked to elaborate the fundamental challenges facing their community, map these challenges to related problems in the companion communities, and identify promising solution paths.

The agenda for the first workshop was designed to promote a true dialogue between the communities, as well as foster collaborations between researchers. Each attendee to the first workshop was asked to bring with them a list of outstanding problems in the area, and also a list of success stories from the area that are potential candidates for application in other areas. Although we cannot share with you the whole list due to space limitations, we would like to share a summary of it.

The Internet offers fundamental security challenges in computer security. An immediate one is the elimination of points of failure in domain name and certificate servers. Replicated software errors, such as the infamous sendmail bug, have proven resistant to eradication. At the policy level, issues such as allocation of trust, responsibility, legal liability, and sharing of control remain. A separate set of outstanding security problems center around the needs of system integration. The challenge is combining software components with varying levels of trust, often from organizations that work in temporary coalitions. Not only do security problems require solution, but customers also want assurance that the problems have been solved. Despite significant progress (see below), evaluating security properties with any formal degree of assurance remains an open problem.

Many of the outstanding problems in the fault tolerance area revolve around the transition of system construction from art form to engineering discipline. For example, participants noted the need for increased agreement on and usage of an adequate set of basic concepts, the need for the development and understanding of meaningful metrics such as 'complexity' and 'diversity', the ability to plan for and budget dependability, and the need for a formal basis for factoring out dependability-relevant design concerns.

Participants in the assurance group identified three related concerns — requirements, development, and assessment that an economic overlay ties together. The requirements concern is the adequate specification of dependability constraints. It is particularly important to identify whether such constraints are feasible, or merely window dressing, and what tradeoffs such constraints inevitably entail. The development concern is the need to be able to design systems for achievement and assessment. Although systems are designed to other criteria, ignoring assurance in system design typically makes meaningful assurance claims infeasible. The assessment concern is that there is often significant disparate evidence that augers well (or ill) for a given system, but currently there is little understanding of how to advance from the unquantifiable instincts of a project engineer to a repeatable scientific exercise. Finally, developers of real systems must consider all three of these concerns in the context of a budget.

Although there are many smaller ideas that can be cited as success stories in computer security, here are some major ones. The Trusted Computer System Evaluation Criteria (TCSEC) is a collection of criteria used to grade or rate the security offered by a computer system product. The TCSEC is sometimes referred to as 'the Orange Book' because of its orange cover. Evaluation process based on the Orange Book has resulted in high-assurance (B3, A1) operating systems of high quality and security, despite their limitation. Private Key Cryptography, such as DES, is a commercial success. Although the 56-bit key size makes it vulnerable to brute-force attacks DES has held up remarkably well against cryptanalysis. Public Key Cryptography is widely studied and well understood, though still based on unproven assumption. The Computer Emergency Response Team (CERT) provides important public services. It alerts the public to new attacks and ways to prevent them, keeps records and statistics, and increases public awareness of need for computer security.

For fault tolerance, one can cite many real systems that can successfully tolerate faults due to physical degradation. Examples are avionics and spacecraft, Tandem nonstop computers, which support enormous, very reliable database systems, and telephone switching systems, which, despite significant difference between voice and data transmission, have adapted remarkably well to dramatic increases in demand for bandwidth. Fault tolerance overlaps security when the faults in question are malicious in origin, and some researchers believe the phases of the fault tolerance model — detection, isolation, repair, and return to service — form a plausible basis for addressing faults that arise from security breakdowns.

Participants broke the success stories from software assurance into three categories: real successes, promising ideas, and surprising and alarming issues. On the theoretical side, success resides in the areas of measuring and understanding. Specific examples are software reliability growth modeling and results, which show explicit limits beyond which it is unreasonable to expect to measure software dependability. On the industrial side, there are significant software-based systems on line with remarkably good performance to date; some examples are nuclear control systems and telecommunications infrastructure, where observed failure rates are very low. Software process improvement and various analysis methods garner partial credit for these successes. A surprising issue is that systems actually work as well as they do, considering how little is understood about how they are constructed. An alarming issue is that developers sometimes repeat simple, avoidable mistakes.

After a working break, the researchers reconvened in Williamsburg, Virginia to present their analyses of the issues raised in York and to plan a research agenda for the three areas, both individually and as a whole. Individual presentations appeared in sessions on formal methods, architecture, security and fault tolerance, and software assurance. Group sessions to develop a research agenda interleaved with the individual presentation sessions. The schedule worked the participants hard but also allocated time for a tour of Colonial Williamsburg and a taste of colonial cuisine.

A research agenda compiled by the editors appears as the first item in these proceedings. Immediately following that Brian Randell argues in 'Dependability — A Unifying Concept' that it is important to realize when different research communities are addressing different facets of the same underlying concept, and that common terminology can be of great aid in this regard. In 'A Symbiotic Relationship between Formal Methods and Security', Jeannette Wing reviews how the security community supported early research in formal methods and suggests how formal methods can help assure the burgeoning security needs of Internet applications. In her paper, 'Multiple Dimensions of Integrating Development Technology', Betty Cheng presents the case that isolated formal methods are of limited use in commercial software engineering, and that integrating techniques in a coherent way is of significantly greater benefit than using each separately. In 'Error Recovery in Critical Infrastructure Systems', John C. Knight, Matthew C. Elder, and Xing Du propose mechanisms that are needed within large networked information systems to provide error recovery, i.e., state restoration and continued service, under circumstances where the application has been subjected to extreme damage. In 'Security and Fault-Tolerance in Distributed Systems: An Actor-Based Approach', Gul Agha and Reza Ziaei use an actor-based meta-architecture to show how different non-functional properties, such as fault-tolerance and security, can be modeled and implemented using separate modules. Naftaly Minsky argues in his paper 'Why Should Architectural Principles Be Enforced?' that architectural models need to be enforced as well as stated to be useful.

Philip Koopman cites the success of the Ballista project in determining operating system robustness in his paper 'Toward a Scalable Method for Quantifying Aspects of Fault Tolerance, Software Assurance, and Security', which argues for the definition and measurement of basic assurance attributes. In 'Practical Techniques for Damage Confinement in Software', David Taylor assembles a promising list of techniques from fault-tolerance, operating systems, distributed systems, and computer security and argues that the dependability community should consider applying them to the damage confinement problem.

In 'Towards a Discipline of System Engineering: Validation of Dependable Systems', Andrea Bondavalli, Alessandro Fantechi, Diego Latella, and Luca Simoncini address the verifiable compositionality of components in the validation of complex systems. In 'Security and Dependability: Then and Now', Catherine Meadows and John McLean survey security research from the point of view of the dependability taxonomy developed by IFIP Working Group 10.4 and discuss changes since a similar survey was performed four years ago. In 'Diversity against Accidental and Deliberate Faults', Yves Deswarte, Karama Kanoun, and Jean-Claude Laprie examine the relationship between the three topics of the workshop: security, fault tolerance, software assurance, and more precisely the possible contributions of fault tolerance to security and software assurance. Victoria Stavridou and Bruno Dutertre visit the intersection of safety and security in 'From Security to Safety and Back', where they examine the application to safety of the noninterference security models.

In 'Certificate Revocation the Responsible Way', Jonathan Millen and Rebecca Wright argue that prompt and reliable distribution of revocation is an essential ingredient in public-key infrastructure and propose research to develop such a mechanism. In 'A Fault Tolerance Approach to Survivability', Paul Ammann, Sushil Jajodia, and Peng Liu argue that since preventive measures are not always successful in thwarting attacks on information systems, research is needed to develop trusted recovery and continued service mechanisms.

It is a pleasure to recognize Bruce Barnes, workshop organizer, Jean-Claude Laprie and Edgar Sibley, general chairs, Sushil Jajodia and John McDermid, program chairs, and Paul Ammann, proceedings editor. Since the author list for these proceedings differs from the attendees, we wish to acknowledge directly all workshop participants, whose efforts made these proceedings possible:

Gul Agha
Ross Anderson
Frank Anger
Paul Ammann
Bruce Barnes
Betty Cheng
Yves Deswarte
Bruno Dutertre
Gerard Eizenberg
Amgad Fayad
Sushil Jajodia
Zbigniew Kalbarczyk
Karama Kanoun
John Knight
Philip Koopman
Jean-Claude Laprie

Bev Littlewood
Cathy Meadows
John McDermid
John McLean
Jon Millen
Naftaly Minsky
Mike Morgan
Brian Randell
Rita Rodriguez
Edgar Sibley
Mukesh Singhal
Luca Simoncini
David Taylor
Rebecca Wright
Jeannette Wing

A special thanks goes to John McDermid for hosting the local arrangements in York.

Csilla Farkas provided excellent support for the workshop's Web site at www.ise.gmu.edu/~csis/conf/fns98.

We are especially indebted to Andre van Tilborg and Ralph Wachter of the Office of Naval Research and Frank Anger and Mukesh Singhal of the National Science Foundation for making the workshops possible.

CSDA'98

The 1998 York and Williamsburg Workshops on Dependability
The Proposed Research Agenda

Compiled by E. H. Sibley and B. H. Barnes

The research agenda represents a distillation of notes from the York and Williamsburg workshops. The intent is to organize the diverse opinions of the attendees into a cohesive document. Please note, this article also an Appendix: a Dependability Matrix indicating what techniques are being used in the various dependability areas. Readers may be interested in scanning this and the matrix for potential research areas.

1. Definitions:

We first provide a set of statements that explain the intent and discussion areas of the workshops.

Dependability comprises three aspects:
- *Attributes*, which describe or limit dependability: these include availability, reliability, safety, confidentiality, integrity, and maintainability.
- *Means*, which refer to the major factors associated with dependability: fault prevention, fault tolerance, fault removal, and fault forecasting.
- *Threats*, which reduce or affect the dependability, including errors, faults, and failures.

Dependable systems, among others, include:
- embedded systems,
- safety-critical systems,
- critical-information systems, and
- electronic commerce.

The pair of workshops was initiated to discuss the means available and research to be accomplished in order to establish sets of scientific principles and practical engineering techniques for developing, maintaining, and evaluating dependable computer-based systems. Participants started by assuming that this could be initiated by concentrating on the integration of methods and disciplines used in the fields of security, fault-tolerance, and high-assurance, especially by concentrating on those techniques that enable measurement of their attributes. Emphasis was therefore placed on techniques that enable integration, composability, reuse, and cost prediction of dependable systems.

2. Categories of Research

The discussion in the workshops can be split into five major categories:

1. Formal methods and models, involving
   - Application of known methods to dependability,
   - A calculus of change for dependable systems, and
   - Development of better tools.

2. Architectural aspects, especially for performance aspects, such as
   - Concurrency and
   - Compatibility to other connected or related systems.

3. Assessment of dependability attributes, including
   - Measurement of attributes,
   - Quantitative techniques, and
   - Models and methods that can be developed from measurements of attributes.

4. Engineering and system building methods, analysis, and techniques for
   - Defining processes,
   - Making economic tradeoffs,
   - Determining performance of single and interconnected systems, and
   - Learning new engineering rules-of-thumb.

5. Multi- or Cross-attribute aspects of systems, involving
   - Security Policy Composition,
   - Enforcement mechanisms,
   - Security economics (performance *versus* affordability),
   - Secure assembly of non-secure components,
   - Identification and authentication protocols,
   - Intrusion detection and response,
   - Secure remote security administration, and
   - Assurance methodologies and tools.

6. Information Assurance, including
   - Fault tolerance perspective of protect, detect, and respond
   - Assurance issues in electronic commerce applications
   - Data protection and privacy

These categories are now used to structure discussion of research topics in these areas of dependability. However, it is important to note that some of them overlap – e.g., the validation and building of systems depends on an analyst's ability to measure important attributes and interpret how they affect overall system performance.

The availability of *challenge systems* is an important research need that cuts across all of the dependability categories. Such a system provides a common example for workers within a research community to use as a vehicle for developing new ideas and as a test bed for comparing different approaches. Funding agencies play a pivotal role in such an endeavor by encouraging the development of and convenient access to challenge systems. They have proven enormously effective in the past. Ideally, the challenge system is large enough to avoid the so-called *toy problem syndrome*. A good example of a currently available challenge system is the generic but realistic *Flight Guidance System* (FGS) specification made available by Rockwell Collins to the formal methods and high assurance systems communities. Availability of the FGS system has resulted in published evaluations and specifications in PVS, Z, SPIN, and the SCR toolset. In terms of the dependability aspects discussed here, the Dependability Challenge System should include target attributes, appropriate means, and potential threats.

2.1 Research in Formal Methods and Models of Dependable Systems

In general, software and systems engineering must include formal methodology [FM] in all its levels, combining techniques using models and theorem proving in systems analysis and SW development/analysis methods (simulation, test, etc.). It should cover not only the requirement level and system's implementation but also involve policy formulation and the more esoteric parts of the system definition. This could, ultimately, result in a system development interface where wishes and politics could be included as requirements, intents, or needs that can only be partially satisfied due to some contradictions in the set of requirements. We must also incorporate a calculus into formal methods to deal with change; i.e., move FM from analysis to calculus to address change. This probably also requires serious work in making formal methods less brittle. Incremental changes in software architecture imply an incremental change to formal analysis (e.g., it is modular with respect to security and fault tolerance properties). As an example, there must be models of concurrency for interaction between security and fault tolerance.

Possible avenues of research here include:
- Revisiting fault methodology, including examining the appropriateness of fail-stop and Byzantine models for security,
- Considering formalization of techniques that could provide better interfaces between building blocks: e.g., the adversary often exploits weaknesses at the boundary when attacking a system. The effort would need to concentrate on different blocks both at the same and different levels of abstraction, especially above the crypto and protocol levels,
- Integrate the formalism with other analyses, such as: risk and hazard analysis; fault and intrusion detection, isolation, and recovery; and simulation, testing, and debugging, and
- Develop better ways of inserting formal methods into the testing area so that it helps in detecting bugs in systems, especially early in the development process.

2.1.1 Short time-frame research issues
A short-term approach should include the examination and analysis of some case studies (previously termed a Dependability Challenge System). Typical problems that may be topics for such analysis include:
- Systems and applications involving major integration of technologies and disciplines, such as electronic commerce,
- Problems in protocols, such as SET, SSL, and Mobile Ipv6, and
- Languages and systems, such as Java, Active Networks, etc.

2.1.2 Medium time-frame research
In the medium term, there is a need to:
- Provide "certified building blocks,"
- Develop an increased understanding of where Formal Methods can be applied effectively and where they are not useful,
- Determine what methods are applicable to the different phases of the software development life cycle, and
- Decide whether any applications areas are better suited for employing Formal Methods than others.

2.1.3 Long time-frame research topics
There is a need for long term research leading to fundamental breakthroughs in:
- The use of techniques in Database Management in providing better data structures, algorithms, and techniques in the tools available for solutions using formal methods,
- Compositional reasoning methods, and
- New tools, such as
- Better interfaces for theorem-prover and model-checking systems, with solution of many of the really hard problems adapted for dependable systems
- Semantic based program analysis, and
- Integration of approaches through new "logic coupling interfaces."

2.2 Research in Architectural and Process Aspects of Dependable Systems

Architecture is a Constraint. It is therefore necessary to enforce architectural principles automatically; e.g., if the requirement is made that the "system is layered" then this must be automatically enforced. Similarly, it must be possible to perform formal reasoning about a system, and this involves the designer considering architectural principles in all system life cycle phases. Moreover, the choice of process aspects must be better understood; e.g., the quote of Peter Neumann: "What are the mechanisms that would enable us to have much more reliable, secure, etc. infrastructure? What process is viable for doing things better than what we are doing? Probably the almost accidental process connected with "open source" software may be such a model (e.g. Linux, server software, Apache, Halloween documents [annotated internal Microsoft documents expressing concern about this]). This appears to create significantly higher quality software than other processes. Can we redirect the movement to create the appropriate set of high quality components needed for the infrastructure we want?

2.2.1 Short time-frame research issues
The above argument suggests a need to provide:
• Robust ways of obtaining components,
• Ways of trusting that "what you are getting is what you think it is,"
• Better mechanisms to decide what is needed,
• Procedures to assure these mechanisms are produced,
• Ways to ensure dependability following system change or evolution,
• Ways to ensure dependable coordination in open systems that may have been separately developed and are now to be integrated, and
• Policy and system models. Encourage work on development of new models that extend the reach of FM to other factors in dependability.

2.2.2 Medium time-frame research
Continuing effort must amplify most of the initial investigations and also the development of
• Methods to assess the Quality of data, since we are normally working with low-quality data in critical systems and
• Ways to improve system tolerance of imprecise data (data known to be of low quality) in safety-critical systems.

2.2.3 Long time-frame research topics
These include developing
• A practical confinement technique,
• Methods for characterizing and predicting dependability [for achieving dependable services from systems, including COTS, legacy, and mobile code], and
• Methods to compose dependable systems from legacy and COTS.

2.3 Measurement of Dependability Attributes

In the future, it will be even more necessary to provide high dependability systems; this implies a need to be able to measure important attributes [properties] of the systems and use these in assessing the risk of various disasters when the overall system is put to use (c.f., Butler and Finelli. IEEE Transactions on SW Engineering, Jan 1993). There are obviously fault tolerance aspects to this, especially in continuous (real time) service while in the presence of malicious faults and intrusions (attacks). The problems will require structuring for fault prevention, tolerance, removal, and forecasting. Techniques for formalization and/or rationalization of this process are also needed. Therefore, we must develop better, well-grounded metrics for characterizing the quality of structures.

2.3.1 Short time-frame research issues

Quantification of the validation process has been used in certain areas, such as the fault tolerance [FT] community. Thus

- It is important to attempt to use quantitative methods to validate the assumptions made about a system and
- It seems particularly reasonable to take techniques from the FT community and apply them to security.

2.3.2 Medium time-frame research
Continuation of the short-term work will be valuable and also
- Incorporation of "diverse evidence" to assure system dependability

2.3.3 Long time-frame research topics
The ultimate result of the work may therefore require the development of a
- "Robustness Testing Machine."

2.4 Engineering and Building of Dependable Systems

There is a need to produce a new method of making an economic justification for dependable systems. This need applies to the entire systems life cycle (though the overall requirements are often defined by other than design or build people (such as politicians, high level public officials, or upper management). At present, what little analysis is done is either at a very high macro level (dealing only with a few "guestimates" and assumptions) or at an almost trivial but detailed level. The true "engineering" of large critical and similar systems (and the IS that are supposed to aid in their control) is still in its infancy, though there has been some "safety engineering" work in the past years.

There are many kinds of composition. From a standpoint of design and cost, there are a few data points but seldom has any real experiment been performed to validate the results; IBM researchers have made this argument. We need dependable coordination in open systems that includes the way untrusted components interact; e.g., Lehman & Belady have provided statistics on IBM360 releases – these show an escalation in the number of errors due to lack of modularization, where correcting one bug often introduced at least one more bug. ATT data also shows that each time a fix is made, there is a rise in failures for a few hundred hours of service—then the error rate is reduced or becomes entirely zero for a long time.

Dependability specification must be made for the *entire* system. One way that works is look at an existing system and say: "What does NOT work?" Quantification of the validation process is needed here; e.g. a movement that applies quantitative methods from the software into the security domain.

Assuring the public that a complex computer controlled system is safe from serious malfunction and will not result in lose of life and property is a significant and challenging problem. There are many methods for providing some assurance that a system is safe. These would include testing and applying Formal Methods to component parts. The software development process employed in the system's development and the level of education and experience of the developers could also provide useful information. Providing a set of arguments that will convince a reasonable set of individuals, such as government regulators, that a given computational system is safe is frequently referred to as a safety case.

2.4.1 Short time-frame research issues

We must develop and determine
- A set of practical engineering techniques for building dependable systems with focus on what we *do* know about building systems -- preferably not by using a "standards" method,
- Measures assessing the impact of programming language design on dependability; e.g. Java,
- Ways to combine disparate evidence to build a safety case, and
- Methods that show how much each evidence stream contributes to building confidence.

2.4.2 Medium time-frame research

Verifiable composability is needed for any attribute or property of interest. This requires:
- Methods for determining the composability of dependability properties,
- Ways to perform process modeling that specifically supports dependability and the development of real dependable systems (including all fault detection, removal, etc.),
- Efforts to develop a means for stating requirements [in *any* language] so that "real" people understand the specifications that have been developed based on the discussions but written into a set of requirements by systems analysts. With good tools it should be possible to have the users agree with the developers on what they expect to obtain (and not be disappointed at delivery),
- Mechanisms for determining the dependencies that exist between different evidence streams, and, having recognized the dependencies, determining how the different evidence streams can be combined, and
- Finding ways to combine the different evidence streams in different ways to meet the needs of the different shareholders (e.g. developers and certifiers).

2.4.3 Long time-frame research topics

In continuing the above, it will be necessary to
- Develop a framework for reasoning about system properties. Generic models are required to allow people to analyze a variety of [general] systems and to integrate different frameworks [Models are frameworks],
- Provide means for technology transfer. This implies research aimed at getting tools out into the user community, getting people to use them, and finding out what works and what does not, then feeding this back to the research community for action. Of course, formal methods can be specific but this applies to other areas too,
- Develop a set of methods to argue that systems are, in fact, dependable,
- Develop a methodology for certification; e.g. of security and safety cases, and
- Develop models of concurrency for interaction of security and fault tolerance.

2.5 Multi- or Cross-attribute Aspects of Systems

Some areas of dependability cut across other dependability issues—as an example a system can seldom be safe unless it is secure against attacks, etc. This issue is therefore given a special section. Many are discussed here with respect to security, and most are being researched in their own right, but probably the important dependability issues involve another factor as an integral part of the overall system; i.e., they are intricately interlaced with one-another.

Particular issues include changing the concept of security from a single point of tackling the problem to a real engineering effort involving the tradeoffs needed to allow reasonable cost but effective levels of risk, etc. Moreover, as with safety, the problems of lack of security are often caused by poor operational mechanisms (poor controls over enforcement and monitoring of secure systems, etc.). The question of composing policy also is difficult when there are many nations and agencies within them all having slight or major differences in the definition of levels of security and policies that they *should* be following. Obviously, there are overlaps here between the methods being developed in formal methods and the models that may be used to provide verification of the system security.

2.5.1 Short time-frame research issues

In conjunction with the formal methods researchers, it is necessary to develop better methods for using the current tools

- Determine requirements for the next generation formal methods and theorem provers to solve problems of security and other dependability factors,
- Develop better meta-data mechanisms and tagging schemes for all dependability issues
- Develop and specify better enforcement mechanisms,
- Develop good identification and authentication protocols, and
- Develop means of certifying all dependability issues.

2.5.2 Medium time-frame research

Continue the efforts by
- Producing policy workbench designs and determine ways of implementing them to deal with security and other issues,
- Developing better ways of composing policy between different "cultures,"
- Experimenting with and develop new languages for risk and policy specification. Apply this to all dependability attributes, and
- Developing means for the secure assembly of non-secure components (e.g., wrappers, pumps, diodes, proximity devices).

2.5.3 Long time-frame research topics

Continue to develop and experiment with new means to define Policy and its Composition for all dependability areas, including developing
- Cross-domain certification methods,
- Generalized models that can analyze the relationship between policies, regulations, and requirements involving dependability issues,
- Means for calculating the economics of all dependability factors, including mechanisms for trading off affordability versus performance and risks, and
- Methods to analyze legal requirements across regions (e.g., forensics; evidence development and preservation).

2.6 Information Assurance

Information security focuses primarily on prevention: putting controls and mechanisms in place to protect confidentiality, integrity, and availability by stopping users from doing bad things. For the most part, these bad things are those for which the user is unauthorized. However, experience has shown that we cannot be completely successful in preventing problems. Hackers continually surprise us by finding new ways to break into or interfere with computer systems. Moreover, most mechanisms are powerless against misbehavior by legitimate users performing functions for which they are authorized, the so-called "insider threat."

Information security does everything possible to prevent attacks from succeeding, but it must be assumed that not all attacks will be averted at the outset. This fact places increased emphasis on the system's ability to live through and recover from successful attacks. Information security must consider the whole process of attack and recovery, which requires recognition of the multiple phases of information assurance process. These phases and activities that occur in each of them are a refinement of the protect, detect, and respond model:

- Prevention - the defender puts protective measures into place.
- Detection - the defender observes symptoms of a problem and determines that an attack may have taken place or may be in progress.
- Confinement - the defender takes immediate action to try to eliminate the attacker's access to the system and to isolate or contain the problem to prevent further spread.

- Damage assessment - the defender determines the extent of the problem, including failed functions and corrupted data.
- Reconfiguration - the defender may reconfigure to allow operation to continue in a degraded mode while recovery proceeds.
- Repair - the defender recovers corrupted or lost data and repairs or reinstalls failed system functions to reestablish a normal level of operation.
- Fault treatment - to the extent possible, the weaknesses exploited in the attack are identified and steps are taken to prevent a recurrence.

Information assurance is a key aspect of electronic commerce applications as well as traditional data repositories. Malicious activity aside, competing interests have conflicting perspectives of data protection and data privacy. Consumers want to keep some patterns of activity remain anonymous and retain control of records.

A diverse array of opposing interests want to mine the data for commercial and legal purposes. Technologies for tracking, such as unique identifiers embedded in software applications and hardware devices, are being deployed without comprehensive consideration for their effects. Methods and structures for managing data protection and privacy are not available in standard packages suitable for generic use.

Most implementations of end-to-end extensible secure systems are composed and instantiated from components. These components might be protocols, policies, environments, crypto-systems and implementations from the highest levels to fully realized implementations. It is expected that these would provide private communications between groups or individuals. They should also provide reliable and authenticated communications as well as being easy to use and customize.

2.6.1: Short time-frame research issues
These include
- Assessing possible attributes, means, and threats for information assurance,
- Development of detect and response models for information assurance,

- Developing better understandings and characterizations of classes of adversaries, including computationally limited and unlimited attackers, passive eavesdroppers, active failures, and crash failures, and

- Developing methods and tools for creating and validating secure system, especially in an adversarial setting.

2.6.2: Medium time-frame research issues
Continuing issues above also requires
- Integration of protection methods with detect and response models,
- Development of protection and privacy models for electronic commerce applications, and
- Defining and modeling composition and instantiation in such a way that it is not intuitively appealing and useful for proving properties of components and instantiations.

2.6.3: Long time frame research issues
These lead to the question
- How can we successfully implement detect-and-response capabilities in real information assurance applications?

Appendix 1: A Dependability Matrix

Notes:

1. The material presented here is compiled from the papers in the book. However, due to the publication schedule it was not possible to read all papers or ask authors to check the validity of our comments. Thus we apologize for any errors or omissions.

2. There seems to be much work on Fault prevention, Tolerance, and Removal, but little on Fault Prediction. Also there is less work on Malicious Faults than Accidental ones.

3. Some of the elements seem to be protected only by external controls (managerial in nature) -- these are so designated in the matrix.

Means	Attributes		Accidental or Deliberate Non-Malicious Faults	Malicious Faults
Fault Prevention	Reliability and Availability	CS	Formalism 8; Certificates 12; Design 14; Model 9	Formalism 8; Certificates 12; Model 9
		FT	Design 6 and 14; Model 10	Design 6
		SA	Requirements 6, Model 9 and 10; Design 14	Requirements 6; Model 9
	Safety	CS	Minimal 4	Minimal 4
		FT	Design 6 and 14; Model 10 and 15	Design 6
		SA	Requirements 6, Model 10	Requirements 6
	Confidentiality	CS	Formalism 8; Certificates 12; Modeling 15	Formalism 8;Certificates 12; Modeling 15
		FT	Model 10; Design 5	
		SA	Design 6 and 14	Design 6
	Integrity	CS	Formalism 8; Certificates 12	Formalism 8; Certificates 12
		FT	Model 10	
		SA	Design 6	Design 6
	Maintainability	CS	Minimal 4	None 4
		FT	Design 6; Model 10	Design 6
		SA	Requirements 6	Requirements 6
	Reliability and Availability	CS	Design 5; Test 7; Fault isolation 9; Survivability 13, Modeling 15	Design 5; Test 7; Diversity 16; Fault Isolation 9
		FT	Design 5 and 6; Modeling 15 and 16;Test 7; Damage Control 11	Design 5 and 6; Test 7; Diversity 16
		SA	Requirements 5 and 6; Test 7	Requirements 5 and 6; Test 7

	Safety	CS	Design 5; Survivability 13	Design 5; Survivability 13
		FT	Design 5 and 6, Damage Control 11; Diversity 16	Design 5 and 6; Survivability 13
		SA	Requirements 5 and 6	Requirements 5 and 6
Fault Tolerance (confined)	Confidentiality	CS	Major area of work, at present 1, Design 5; Fault Isolation 9	Much work 1; Survivability 13; Design 5; Diversity 16; Fault Isolation 9
		FT	Design 5; Damage Control 11; Survivability 13	Survivability 13
		SA	Requirements 5 and 6	Requirements 5 and 6
	Integrity	CS	Major effort today 1 and 5; Test 7; Fault Isolation 9	Much work 1 and 5; Test 7; Diversity 16; Fault Isolation 9
		FT	Test 7; Damage Control 5 and 11	Test 7
		SA	Design 5 and 6; Test 7	Design 5 and 6; Test 7; Survivability 13
	Maintainability	CS	Little 4; Design 5; Diversity 16	None 4; Design 5
		FT	Design 5 and 6; Damage Control 11	Design 5 and 6
		SA	Requirements 5 and 6	Requirements 5 and 6
Fault Removal (detection)	Reliability and Availability	CS	Controls; Test 7	Controls; Test 7
		FT	Design 6; Test 7	Design 6; Test 7
		SA	Requirements 6; Test 7	Requirements 6; Test 7
	Safety	CS	Little 4	Little 4
		FT	Damage Control 11	
		SA	Requirements 6	
	Confidentiality	CS	Controls; Formalisms 8	Controls; Formalisms 8
		FT	Damage Control 11	
		SA		
	Integrity	CS	Controls	Controls
		FT	Damage Control 11	
		SA		
	Maintainability	CS	Little 4	None 4
		FT	Design 6; Damage Control 11	
		SA	Requirements 6	

	Reliability and Availability	CS	Improving, but some limitations 2	Little 3
		FT	Damage Control 11	
		SA		
	Safety	CS	Little 4	None 4
		FT	Damage Control 11	
		SA		
Fault Forecasting (prediction)	Confidentiality	CS	Improving 2	Little 3
		FT		
		SA		
	Integrity	CS	Especially in databases 2	Little 3
		FT	Damage Control 11	
		SA		
	Maintainability	CS	Little 4	None 4
		FT		
		SA		

Legend:

CS =Computer Security, FT=Fault Tolerance, SA=Software Assurance

----

Notes on the Dependability Matrix Entries with their Source Identified

*My Note on the paper by **Randell, Dependability - a Unifying Concept"***
Contains good definitions that show that dependability has incorporated the major concepts of *Safety Engineering*, as taught in some Universities today. *Dependability* is also equated directly to *trustworthiness*. Randell also points out the disadvantage of multiplicity of terms meaning the same thing, especially if the separate domains do not recognize the overlap.

*A: See the paper by **Meadows and McLean: Security and Dependability: Then and Now***
(following from Meadow's paper: "Applying the Dependability Paradigm to Computer Security" in the Proceedings of the 1995 New Security Paradigms Workshop, IEEE Computer Society Press, 1996)

Point 1: Fault Tolerance
Fault tolerance is divided into *error processing* (error recovery and error compensation) and *fault treatment* (fault diagnosis and fault passivation). This area has shown major growth recently in security and integrity areas; particular issues addressed include:
- Intrusion detection (detecting an erroneous state and possible failure), and
- Recovery from database failure, but surprisingly little work on general error recovery, even for IW.
- Fault masking by using majority voting or self-checking components and
- Mobil agent voting on a trusted platform.
- Crypto-techniques to compensate for errors–such as division of a message into incomprehensible parts and ultimately authentication of the transmission.

It must be noted that counterattacking is often limited by legal or treaty issues.

Point 2: Fault Forecasting: non-Malicious
For non-malicious human-induced faults, likelihood of failure can be assessed (e.g., choosing poor passwords, spread of viruses). Implementation faults also are measurable (Software reliability). The forecast is divided into two: probabilistic (e.g., mean time to failure) and non- probabilistic. Generally the measure of fault forecasting is for failure (calculating risks of known bugs) rather than predicting their advent.

Point 3: Fault Forecasting: Malicious
For malicious faults, measure resources available to the attacker, decision to use them, and payoff expected. [Capability to attack, wish to do so, effect of attack] -- but seldom if ever reported. Little work has been performed, because motives and capacities of intruders are difficult to assess and also prediction of the consequences are difficult to determine.

Point 4: Fault Prevention and Removal and Computer Security
Prevention and removal often involve the same processes, therefor they are put together here. The three steps are: verification, diagnosis, and correction. There is a new focus today: the main methods still exist (e.g., design, formal verification, and testing), but their use has changed to certifying or convincing another person that the software is fault-free. Today some software is not bought but run by the system after being downloaded from some other source. This involves trust and checks before acceptance. Digital certificates are an obvious technique to answer such problems. However, the problem often consists of errors in several ways: a malicious person puts a virus on a bulletin board and a neglectful person uses it.

*B: See the paper by **Knight, Elder, and Du: Error Recovery in Critical Infrastructure Systems***

Point 5: Architectural Methods to Provide Fault Tolerance
Due to the high cost of proving systems, industry tends to concentrate on *survivability* after a fault occurs rather than insisting on proven reliability, etc. The possible failure is then "contained" or "masked" and sometimes also offset by insurance and legal mechanisms. Thus the system becomes "fault tolerant." Methods to retain operation under faulty or attack situations can be applied at many levels of abstraction in distributed systems from software through process and date resiliency, atomic actions, etc. Various authors have shown how to do this; indeed the old OS techniques of restart and recovery and checkpoints in DBMS are examples of this approach, with some manual efforts needed but much capable of being automated. Architectures and ADL (architectural description languages) can be used in analysis and proofs of correctness may result. Re-configurability in the face of attack or error should be possible for many complex systems, but modularisation is obviously an important part of the process.

*C: See the paper by **Chen: Multiple Dimensions of Integrating Development Technology***

Point 6: Formal Methods and Reliability
The areas of system design and maintenance can be improved by the use of formal methods. There have been attempts to ensure both security and safety by using formal methods in the requirements and implementation phases, and these same methods (once recorded for a system) could be used to check problems in maintainability). However, the techniques have not proven easy to apply and there is a substantial feeling on the part of many research funders that the methods are still in their infancy and this nowhere near as close to being useful or economically applied today. Harel's Statechart method (with his StateMate system using finite automata notations and ideas) is used by her to model the data flow and performance. These are used to integrate Object Oriented Techniques (OMT) with a formal method. Obviously, this implies domain analysis.

A major point was also made: it is necessary to use "different formal languages appropriate for each perspective" (different parts of the design and development cycle and the modeling method). Moreover, it is possible to use existing tools (at least in the current research phase) and different tools have limitations and strengths. For example, simulation can validate behavior, but model checking returns a counter-example if a constraint is not satisfied. Formal methods can reduce testing time.

D: See the paper by Koopman, Toward Quantifying Aspects of Fault Tolerance, Software Assurance, and Computer Security

Point 7: Quantification of Testing for robustness
He has been attempting to determine measures for CS, FT, and SA using *robustness testing* methods. Originally the Ballista project concepts were developed for Quality Assurance in highly dependable designs, also dealing with *robustness* of the API. The paper notes that perfection is impossible and requires **less-than-perfect alternatives** that can be measured (not just termed *defective*). Examples include structural, behavioral, and domain *testing* outside-the-envelope of normal operation; it also involves defect-rate-monitoring. This approach may show problems in buffer overflows, etc. Test failure can then be categorized as catastrophic (corrupted conditions), hung (requiring restart), aborted (abnormal termination), silent (no error shown but obviously in trouble), and hindering (such as wrong error code returned).

E: See the paper by Wing, A Symbiotic Relationship Between Formal Methods and Security

Point 8: Formal Methods and Security
Need for a balance between *need* and *cost* of solution. Can never be 100% secure. Problems occur due to the environment – and these cannot always be predicted. Need to pay for better security. Formal methods can help by careful delimiting of the system boundary, its behavior, its properties, and its specification. There are model checking , theorem proving, and hybrid approaches today, mostly in areas of protocol analysis. We need better ways of guaranteeing the applications and language areas.

F: See the paper by Stravridou and Dutertre, From Security to Safety and Back

Point 9: Security and Safety Research Interaction
Security models deal primarily with confidentiality. Early models were limited. However, these techniques could add to safety. In contrast, fault tolerance techniques could lead to better security means – particularly to malicious attacks. An example is given for non-interference in deterministic systems, which could be absolute protection but is often too expensive: less secure systems are still useful. Composability is another factor, especially in safety critical environments; the implementation of secure systems from insecure components is an obvious need (fail-silent or fail-stop is possible in non-deliberate security fault prevention. Probability models are not valuable in realistic secure-systems design. Fire-walls and anti-virus software are examples of ways to protect, here. Unfortunately, the use of duplication/replication to reduce the risk of failure adds to security risk. *Fault isolation* techniques may help in security intrusion solutions.

G: See the paper by Minsky, Why Should Architectural Principles be Enforced?

Point 10: Architectural Modeling
Require a model and enforce compliance through it. Sets of laws (theorems, etc.) about the system are to be enforced on the architecture and thus tied to the system. There must be an implied *immutability* in the laws.

H: See the paper by Taylor, Practical Techniques for Damage Confinement in Software

Point 11: Software Isolation and FT methods
Damage control by ensuring that the fault is detected and then confined (stopped from spreading). The level of confinement depends on the degree of dependence needed. Sharing of resources makes this a difficult problem. Strongly typed languages, separation of components (sand-boxing), use of OS capabilities (such

as backup and recovery), constrained kernal extensions, etc. are means to reduce error proliferation. The degree of fault tolerance depends on the system needs. Proof-carrying code is expensive.

I: See the paper by **Millen and Wright, Certificate Revocation the Responsible Way**

Point 12: Trust and Certificates
Current revocation list techniques are inadequate. There are several reasons for revoking keys: loss, corruption, it is compromised, withdrawal of privileges, etc. Need for trust of both the server and person. But: How can we ensure the integrity of the agent who attempts the revocation?, etc. Also is there a need to notify the revoked user? Should there be both push and pull systems? Obviously, the scheme must be reliable!

J: See the paper by **Ammann, Jajodia and Peng Liu, A Fault Tolerance Approach to Survivability**

Point 13: Survivability in all its phases under security threats
Deals with attack detection followed by damage confinement, assessment, repair, and avoidance. Consider a data integrity scheme involving "colored" data that allows it to be classified as red (potentially dangerously wrong) through green (correct) with several shades in between. A similar scheme could be used for the security or safety of transactions. Recovery from malicious activities may require redesign of the system – however, isolation or wrapping of the parts may be possible.

K: See the paper by **Bondavalli, Fantechi, Latella and Simoncini, Towards a Discipline of System Engineering: Validation of Dependable Systems**

Point 14: Systems Engineering (SE) Approach
Need for verifiable composability. Verifiability and the consequent preservation of properties while using COTS products are also needed. The paper discusses formal and semiformal approaches to validation and includes a set of *Pragmatic Principles* of SE as an appendix

L: See the paper by **Agha and Ziaei: Security and Fault-Tolerance in Distributed Systems: An Actor-Based Approach**

Point 15: Architecture Modeling for Fault Tolerance and Security
Current techniques, like Corba and Java's Remote Methods Invocation, for developing distributed applications deal effectively with distributive interactions. They are not, however, effective in handling higher level requirements, such as fault tolerance and security. An Actor-based meta-architecture is employed to show how non-functional properties, such as fault-tolerance and security, can be modeled and implemented using separate modules. The paper describes an Architecture Description Language (ADL). An ADL specification defines architecture in terms of components, which encapsulate computations and connectors, which describe how components are integrated into the architecture.

M: See the paper by **Deswarte, Kanoun, and Lapri: Diversity against Accidental and Deliberate Faults**

Point 16: Meta-architecture for Fault Tolerance and Security Modeling
The paper examines the relationship between: security, fault tolerance, software assurance, particularly fault tolerance for security and software assurance. Fault classification identifies three major classes of faults: physical, design, human-machine interaction, with the latter two either accidental or deliberate. Faults that occur when considering security, fault tolerance and software assurance are due to design and human-machine interaction errors. Diversity can take place at a number of levels in a system: execution support, design of the application software, human-machine interface, operators, etc. However, some faults can defeat fault-tolerance techniques (e.g., those resulting from tradeoffs between security and usability). It is thus necessary to evaluate risk incurred.

Dependability - a Unifying Concept

Brian Randell

Department of Computing Science, University of Newcastle upon Tyne

Brian.Randell@newcastle.ac.uk

Abstract

This paper discusses the need for a clear set of system dependability concepts and terminology, adequate for situations in which there are uncertainties about system boundaries, the very complexity of systems (and their specifications, if they have any) is a major problem, judgements as to possible causes or consequences of failure may need be very subtle, and there are only fallible provisions for preventing faults causing failures. It then relates this terminology to that in use in the survivability, critical infrastructures, information warfare, and intrusion detection research communities, before describing the European Dependability Initiative, a contribution to the planning of the European Union s Information Society Technologies (IST) Programme.

1. A basic conceptual framework

In the early 1970s I and colleagues at Newcastle started research on what is now known as design fault tolerance . We found that one of the problems facing us was the inadequacy for our purposes of the fault tolerance concepts and terminology that hardware reliability engineers were then using - they were taking various particular types of fault (stuck-at-zero, stuck-at-one, etc.) that might occur within a system as the starting point for their definitions of terms such as system reliability and system availability. But given not just the absence of any useful categorisation of design faults, but also the realisation that in many cases the actual identification of some particular aspect of a complex system design as being the fault might well be quite subjective, we felt in need of a more general set of concepts and definitions. And we wanted these definitions to be properly recursive, so that we could adequately discuss problems that might occur either within or between system components at any level of a system.

The alternative approach that we developed took as its starting point the notion of failure, whether of a system or a system component, to provide its intended services. Depending on circumstances, the failures of interest could concern differing aspects of the services — e.g. the average real-time response achieved, the likelihood of producing

0-7695-0337-3/99 $10.00 © 1999 IEEE

the required results, the ability to avoid causing failures that could be catastrophic to the system s environment, the degree to which deliberate security intrusions could be prevented, etc. [4]

The ensuing generality of our definitions of terms thus led us to start using the term reliability in a much broader sense than was then common. It was a French colleague, Jean-Claude Laprie of LAAS-CNRS, who came to our linguistic rescue by proposing the use of the term dependability [2] for the concept underlying our broadened definition of reliability. The term dependability thus includes as special cases such properties as reliability, integrity, privacy, safety, security, etc.

Summarising the latest published version of the dependability definitions [1]

A system **failure** occurs when the delivered service deviates from fulfilling the system **function**, the latter being what the system *is aimed at*. An **error** is that part of the system state which is *liable to lead to subsequent failure*: an error affecting the service is an indication that a failure occurs or has occurred. The *adjudged or hypothesized cause* of an error is a **fault**.

A failure occurs when an error passes through the system-user interface and affects the service delivered by the system - a system of course being composed of components which are themselves systems. Thus the manifestation of failures, faults and errors follows a fundamental chain :

$$. . . \text{ fi failure fi fault fi error fi failure fi fault fi} . . .$$

A system is **dependable** to the extent to which its operation is free of failures. Then **Dependability** can be defined as that property of a computer system such that *reliance can justifiably be placed on the service* it delivers. (The service delivered by a system is its behaviour *as it is perceptible* by its user(s); a user is another system (human or physical) which *interacts* with the former.)

The development of a dependable computing system calls for the *combined* utilization of a set of methods and techniques which can be classed into:

¥   **fault prevention**: how to prevent fault occurrence or introduction,

¥   **fault tolerance**: how to ensure a service up to fulfilling the system s function in the presence of faults,

---

[1] A revised edition of [2] is curremtly being prepared by Jean-Claude Laprie, Al Avizienis and myself.

¥   **fault removal**: how to reduce the presence (number, seriousness) of faults,

¥   **fault forecasting**: how to estimate the present number, the future incidence, and the consequences of faults.

The notions introduced up to now can be grouped into three classes and are summarized by figure 1:

¥   the **impairments** to dependability: faults, errors, failures; they are undesired but not in principle unexpected circumstances causing or resulting from undependability (whose definition is very simply derived from the definition of dependability: reliance cannot, or will not any longer, be placed on the service);

¥   the **means** for dependability: fault prevention, fault tolerance, fault removal, fault forecasting; these are the methods and techniques enabling one a) to provide the ability to deliver a service on which reliance can be placed, and b) to reach confidence in this ability;

¥   the **attributes** of dependability: availability, reliability, safety, confidentiality, integrity, maintainability; these a) enable the properties which are expected from the system to be expressed, and b) allow the system quality resulting from the impairments and the means opposing to them to be assessed.

(The **Security** attribute involves a combination of availability, confidentiality, and integrity.)

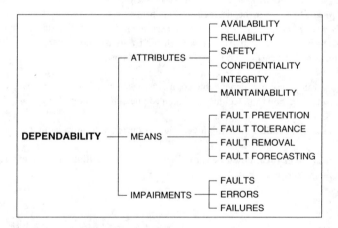

Figure 1

2. Terminology versus concepts

Terminology, such as that introduced above, is important only for communication - it is getting the concepts straight that really matters. Nevertheless, people get wedded to particular terms, especially if they ve helped to invent or popularise them, so this bedevils attempts to discuss concepts.

Clarifying the concepts related to dependability (or any of its aspects, by whatever name you use for them) is surprisingly difficult when one is talking about systems in which there are uncertainties about system boundaries, the very complexity of the system (and its specification, if it has one) is a major problem, judgements as to possible causes or consequences of failure can be very subtle, and there are (fallible) provisions for preventing faults causing failures. Hence it is hardly surprising that many of the attempts at defining terminology in various dependability-related fields are, to my mind, imprecise and indeed simplistic and hence inadequate.

In particular, it is my perception that a number of dependability concepts are being re-invented, or at least re-named, in the numerous overlapping communities that are worrying about deliberately-induced failures in computer systems - e.g., the survivability , critical infrastructures , information warfare , and intrusion detection communities. (The most recent example is the National Research Council Report entitled Trust in Cyberspace [5], which uses the term trustworthiness in exactly the broad sense of dependability .)

Having a multiplicity of terms for essentially the same thing can impede progress. For example, calling a special case of unavailability denial of service , or of error detection intrusion detection (leave alone then arguing that this includes intrusion recovery), can tend to cause confusion and to hamper the search for common, sometimes pre-existing, solutions.

There are, in fact, a number of reasons for using private technical jargon where an adequate well-documented vocabulary already exists: ignorance, the not invented here attitude, the search for academic advantage; the need to tap into new sources of funding, etc. All are understandable but none are very reputable. On the other hand, there can be merit in the introduction and use of appropriately-chosen terms, e.g. for particular classes of impairment, that serve as convenient readily-understood abbreviations of possibly lengthy descriptive phrases, as long as the relationship of these terms to the basic terminology is made clear.

However the issue of whether one uses a common terminology is much less important than whether one realises that the different research communities are concerning themselves with (different facets of) the *same* concept, and are not getting as much advantage from each others insights and advances as they might. Thus, regardless of the terminology employed, I believe it is very important to have, and to use, some term for the general concept, i.e. that which is associated with a *fully general notion of failure* as opposed to one which is restricted in some way to particular causes or consequences. (I also believe it is essential to have separate terms for the three essentially different concepts named here *fault*, *error* and *failure* - since otherwise one cannot deal properly with the complexities (and realities) of failure-prone components, being assembled together in possibly incorrect ways, so resulting in failure-prone systems.)

It then becomes easy to recognise that, even when attention is being deliberately restricted to a situation in which only a particular type of fault or failure is deemed as being of concern, all four of what were termed above dependability means, (i.e., fault prevention, tolerance, removal and forecasting) are likely to be of relevance, even if the particular research community has not been in the habit of employing them all. And one is also provided with a very convenient means of subsuming all the special properties (e.g., safety, availability, confidentiality, etc.), within a single conceptual framework, and of addressing the problem that what a user usually needs from a system is an appropriate balance of several such properties. Such a balance in turn requires a careful determination of how much emphasis should be placed on each of the different dependability means.

3. The European Dependability Initiative

Such concern over concepts that enable the integration of reliability, security, safety, etc., is not just a matter for the academic community. Rather, this sort of thinking is absolutely central to the proposed European Dependability Initiative (EDI), which relates mainly to plans for industrial R&D in Europe, not just at universities. To quote from the EDI Report:

> The different concerns of security, safety, reliability and survivability have, in the past, given rise to different communities of interest. The approach so far has been for each community to invest predominantly in point solutions addressing specific vulnerabilities with little regard for overall system requirements and architectures. Disparate viewpoints emanating from various cultures (nationalities and application domains as well as dependability communities) have to be brought together [6]

The European Dependability Initiative is a contribution to the planning of the European Union s Information Society Technologies (IST) Programme. This

Programme, which subsumes the existing ESPRIT, RACE and Telematics Programmes, is about to begin - with a budget of about $5 billion over the next four years. The crucial significance of dependability, as an integrative concept for, and approach to concurrently solving, problems of reliability, safety, security, etc., is well-accepted at a senior level in the IST Programme. Indeed, the current draft of the 1999 IST Workprogramme [1] states in one of its first sections: the key issues of usability, interoperability, *dependability* and affordability will be addressed ubiquitously throughout the programme . [Emphasis added.]

The Initiative has been formulated in a series of EC-sponsored workshops (during December 1997 - June 1998) in which over fifty organisations, representing industry, academia and public authorities, were involved. The envisioned role of the Dependability Initiative within the IST Programme, is to contribute towards raising and assuring trust and confidence in computing and communications systems and services, by promoting dependability as an enabling technology . This is to be attained by fostering both: (i) R&D into new dependability technologies, and (ii) the better use of available technologies. The plan is to concentrate on the dependability problems of systems that are:

¥   massively networked, interdependent and distributed

¥   constrained by cost and time-to-market

¥   accessible by society at large.

The commitment to a unified approach to the subject is given by the fact that the EDI Report proposes that priority to be given to projects that exhibit:

¥   A combined expertise in multiple facets of dependability (e.g. safety, security) for addressing issues of difficult trade-offs among conflicting requirements/technologies. (The rationale is the need to define procedures and tools for multi-objective synthesis and analysis to produce well-balanced dependability solutions.)

¥   Cross-fertilisation among tools, techniques and communities that can now be seen as dependability-related. (The rationale is (i) the need for more extensive use of complementary techniques that are rarely brought together and (ii) the need for considering dependability as an overall system characteristic.)

In what follows, a number of the specific suggestions made in the EDI Report as to priority topics for research are singled out for quotation, as illustrating points made earlier concerning the advantages of having a unifying dependability concept, and then briefly commented upon from this perspective.

4. Some proposed research topics

(i) Provide improved means of coping with (existing) multiple heterogeneous technical/legal domains.

Most current large distributed systems are, in effect, centrally managed, including even the Internet, at least with respect to some name management issues. Therefore, for example, conflict resolution, whether concerning rival design approaches, uncertain responsibility for repairing or reconfiguring a failing system, or disputes among users or between users and system managers, is comparatively simple. However, particularly in systems that cross national boundaries, there may be essentially no one authority to turn to, and the rival authorities may have differing attitudes regarding the relative importance of different aspects of dependability, and mutually incompatible policies. (Obvious current examples relate to cryptography and personal privacy.) The pre-computer worlds of international trade and diplomacy have long dealt with such situations - however in a globally-interconnected computerised world new problems are arising and new solutions must be found even to many old problems - solutions which will in all probability involving internalising issues that previously could be left external to the computer.

(ii) Develop methods for understanding, recognising and identifying risks and faults in unbounded (emergent) evolutionary systems (systems-of-systems).

Many of the systems that governments, commercial organisations and the public at large, are now finding themselves increasingly dependent upon are in fact systems-of-systems , whose components have been developed, and are being managed, quite independently of each other. The external edges of such systems are typically unknown and unknowable - and the properties that the systems exhibit are more derived from their components and their imprecisely-planned interconnections than from some deliberate attempt at designing to a given functional or dependability specification. (These issues are well-described in [5].) Different users will have differing expectations and needs, and hence will be exposing themselves to different risks, relating to differing aspects of dependability. From day to day, if not minute to minute, the component population will differ, typically will grow, and so various current protocols and strategies that are dependent on complete identification of and knowledge about an overall system state will be of little use. Instead probabilistic algorithms, that make use of just local-state information, will be needed - together with means of assessing the dependability characteristics of such algorithms.

(iii)   Develop methods for characterising and predicting dependability and for achieving dependable services from systems, including COTS, legacy and mobile code.

The computer world seems destined to rush to embrace new technologies without regard to the new dependability problems that they can raise, particularly when deployed in partially malevolent environments. Mobile code is just the latest example of this tendency, especially with respect to security. Similarly, the rush to COTS highlights the problem of the relative dependability, and the relative difficulty of quantifying the dependability, of components whose design is open to scrutiny but which have received relatively little usage, compared to components for which the opposite is true. But COTS, mobile code, and legacy systems are today s reality, and are a challenge to many dependability tools and techniques - in particular those related to characterisation and prediction.

(iv)   Provision of high dependability - perhaps continuous (real-time) service - in the presence of malicious faults.

Most current work in the intrusion detection community assumes that the problems of dealing with detected intrusions can be largely left to humans to sort out. However the very term intrusion detection conceals an important issue. What can, with luck, be detected are the *errors* that result from earlier intrusions, rather than the intrusions themselves. The intrusions are in fact *faults*, whose identification can be slow and uncertain, and often unsuccessful, even after they have caused detected errors. However, without such identification, and/or some already-implemented and robust error containment areas, the problem of determining what other parts of the system state and previous activity are suspect is nugatory, not just difficult. Yet this is essential if the aim is to provide continuous timely service from the system. Indeed the problems of achieving sophisticated levels of tolerance even just to hardware and software faults, leave alone while maintaining adherence to strict deadlines, can be quite severe. Nevertheless, the need to extend this work to cope with malicious faults is evident, and becoming urgent.

(v)   Trade-off of service levels, quality of service, survivability of essential services.

As mentioned earlier, use of an overall conceptual framework facilitates the task of achieving a suitable balance of the various dependability attributes. However, this is but a start, and equally necessary are metrics, even just crude metrics, of the various aspects of dependability, and insights into the various relationships that are likely to hold among them, and between them and various other system parameters. Actual numerical expressions of such relationships are less necessary than knowledge of their form - just as discovery of the high non-linearity of the relationship between memory size and paging rate was crucial to the development of effective paging algorithms.

(vi) Structuring for fault prevention/tolerance/removal/forecasting, and formalisation/rationalisation of this process.

Structuring is our main means of coping with complexity - whether of systems or their specifications. Robust structures in the actual system are needed for purposes of error containment - which is a basis for rational error recovery. Such structures can be spatial or temporal, and enforced by a variety of different mechanisms, including storage protection, transaction managers, cryptography, etc. Well-chosen structure in expression of the design and the specification of a system aid understanding by allowing both the human reader, and various automated tools, to concentrate on just part of the whole at any one time, whether for purposes of fault prevention, removal or forecasting. Yet we do not have any well-grounded metrics for characterising the quality of a given structuring, or for aiding the process of creating a good structuring.

5. Concluding Remarks

The aim of this brief account has been to argue the merits and timeliness of taking a very general notion of failure not just as the basis for a set of underlying concepts but also as a starting point in creating an agenda for future information technology research, within both industry and academia, in and among the various apparently separate fields of reliability, safety, security, survivability, etc., and their respective somewhat overlapping communities. There is, it would seem, good reason to hope that this is what will indeed happen in Europe over the next few years. However, many of the problems to be addressed have global ramifications, and merit collaborative efforts on an international scale. My hope, therefore, is that presently-planned discussions regarding a possible programme of EU-US research collaboration on dependability will reach a similar consensus on these issues and concepts (agreement on terminology is less likely!), and lead to the setting up of a number of appropriately general (and ambitious) projects.

6. Acknowledgements

Evidently, this paper draws heavily on the work of Jean-Claude Laprie, who has also helpfully commented on an earlier draft.

7. References

[1] 1999 IST Workprogramme (Draft 1.0, 23 September), Information Society Technologies (IST) Programme for Research, Technology Development & Demonstration under the 5th Framework Programme, 1998.

[2] J.C. Laprie, (Ed.). Dependability: Basic concepts and terminology in English, French, German, Italian and Japanese, Dependable Computing and Fault Tolerance. Vienna, Austria, Springer-Verlag, 1992, 265 p.

[3] J.C. Laprie. Dependable Computing: Concepts, Limits, Challenges, in 25th IEEE International Symposium on Fault-Tolerant Computing - Special Issue, pp. 42-54, Pasadena, California, USA, IEEE, 1995.

[4] P.M. Melliar-Smith and B. Randell. Software Reliability: The role of programmed exception handling, in Proc. Conf. on Language Design For Reliable Software (ACM SIGPLAN Notices, vol. 12, no. 3, March 1977), Raleigh, ACM, 1977, pp. 95-100.

[5] F.B. Schneider, (Ed.). Trust in Cyberspace: Report of the Committee on Information Systems Trustworthiness, Computer Science and Telecommunications Board , Commission on Physical Sciences, Mathematics, and Applications, National Research Council, Washington, D.C., National Academy Press, 1998.

[6] M. Wilikens, P. Morris and M. Masera. Defining the European Dependability Initiative, (URL: http://ntsta.jrc.it/dsa/Dep-Ini.htm), Joint Research Centre of the European Community, 1998.

A Symbiotic Relationship Between Formal Methods and Security

Jeannette M. Wing*
School of Computer Science
Carnegie Mellon University
Pittsburgh, PA 15213-3890

Abstract

Security played a significant role in the development of formal methods in the 70s and early 80s. Have the tables turned? Are formal methods now ready to play a significant role in the development of more secure systems? While not a panacea, the answer is yes, formal methods can and should play such a role. In this paper we first review the limits of formal methods. Then after a brief historical excursion, we summarize some recent results on how model checking and theorem proving tools revealed new and known flaws in authentication protocols. Looking to the future we discuss the challenges and opportunities for formal methods in analyzing the security of systems, above and beyond the protocol level.

1: Introduction

The formal methods community owes much to the security community. In the United States, the National Security Agency was a major source of funding in the 70s and early 80s for formal methods research and development. Results included the development of formal security models, tools for reasoning about security, and applications of these tools to proving systems secure. Security provided a challenging research application for the formal methods community.

The burgeoning use of the Internet brings security now to the attention of the masses. The success of Amazon.com Inc. and the like suggests that people trust sending their credit card numbers over the wire. People are, however, justifiably hesitant to send their mother's maiden name to an electronic banking system when asked for it on-line. Simultaneous with the increasing desire to perform transactions over the Internet is the maturation of key (pun intended) technology. For example, public-key encryption is no longer an academic exercise. We have fortuitously come to a balancing point between a *need* and a *solution*: People are more willing today to pay the price for increased security.

*This research is sponsored in part by the Defense Advanced Research Projects Agency and the Wright Laboratory, Aeronautical Systems Center, Air Force Materiel Command, USAF, F33615-93-1-1330, and Rome Laboratory, Air Force Materiel Command, USAF, under agreement number F30602-97-2-0031 and in part by the National Science Foundation under Grant No. CCR-9523972. The U.S. Government is authorized to reproduce and distribute reprints for Governmental purposes notwithstanding any copyright annotation thereon. This paper is a contribution to the *Needs-to-Solution* 1998 series of workshops sponsored by the Office of Naval Research and the National Science Foundation. The views and conclusions contained herein are those of the author and should not be interpreted as necessarily representing the official policies or endorsements, either expressed or implied, of the Defense Advanced Research Projects Agency Rome Laboratory or the U.S. Government.

0-7695-0337-3/99 $10.00 © 1999 IEEE

Are formal methods part of this maturing technology? With respect to security, what problems can formal methods help to solve? What problems will formal methods never help to solve?

In an attempt to answer these questions, the remainder of this paper first delimits the bounds of formal methods, and then reviews briefly the historical role of the security community in the early development of formal methods[1]; summarizes recent results in the use of formal methods tools for reasoning about security protocols; and discusses directions for the future role of formal methods applied to security.

2: The Limits of Formal Methods

2.1: What Formal Methods Cannot Do

It is axiomatic that systems will never be made 100% secure. Formal methods will not break that axiom. Moreover, substitute the word "proven" for "made" in the previous sentence, and we have a corollary. It would be foolish for anyone in formal methods to stand up and say "I can prove your system is 100% secure." Why?

Systems do not run in isolation; they operate in some *environment*. The formal specification of a system must always include the assumptions one makes about the system's environment. A proof of correctness is valid only when these assumptions hold. So, if any assumption is violated, all bets are off. Indeed, to break into a system, clever intruders find out how to violate these assumptions.

Moreover, even if one were careful to state these assumptions explicitly, which is often impractical, there would inevitably be conditions missed. And, even if one were comprehensive about stating these assumptions, which is always impracticable, a system could very well be deployed in an environment for which it was not originally designed, perhaps for convenience or lack of an alternative.

These remarks are not particular to security; they apply in general to the process of verifying a system meets its specification.

It is also axiomatic that the more secure one wants a system to be the more one must be willing to pay. This truth implies that security itself is not an either/or property. If you add more locks to your door, you make it harder for someone to break into your house. More locks means more secure.

Requiring passwords, using biometrics, encrypting data, signing messages, setting file access control bits, using firewalls, sandboxing, managing a private network, running secure coprocessors, or hiring a guard are just examples of the collection of "locks" one can use to make a system more secure. In practice, security is a combination of many properties, including data integrity, privacy, entity identification, message authentication, and accountability. Some of these properties are also not either/or, but measured in terms of degree. Also, depending on the application or the user's end goal, some properties will be more important than others. One property may even conflict with another, or achieving one may make it harder to achieve another. For example, both anonymity and accountability are desired properties of electronic payment systems. Achieving some security properties may conflict with achieving other system goals. Requiring passwords for access conflicts with convenience; using a public-key encryption scheme conflicts with performance.

---

[1] This paper does not do justice to either the history of security research or the history of formal methods; rather it focuses on the intersection of the two and even so, only sketchily.

2.2: What Formal Methods Can Do

Formal methods can help us

- Articulate precisely a system's boundary, i.e., the interface between the system and its environment.
- Characterize precisely a system's behavior. Most current methods focus on functional behavior only (What is the correct answer?) but some can handle real-time behavior too (Is the correct answer delivered on time?).
- Define precisely a system's desired properties.
- Prove a system meets its specification.
- Determine under what circumstances a system does not meet its specification; for example, some methods produce counterexamples, such as intruder scenarios, which explain why the system is flawed.

These capabilities of formal methods help the practitioner in two ways:

- Through *specification*, focusing the system designer's attention. What is the interface? What are one's assumptions about the system's environment? What is the system supposed to do under this condition or that condition? What happens if that condition is not met? What are the system's invariant properties?
- Through *verification*, providing additional assurance. Relying on a proof that a system meets its security goals is better than relying on a gut feeling.

It should be emphasized that any proof of correctness is relative to both the formal specification of the system and the formal specification of the desired properties. A system "proven correct" with respect to an "incorrect" specification leaves us with no assurance about the system at all. Finally, there will always be a gap between what is in a person's head and the first codification of the system or desired property. No amount of formalization will eliminate this gap.

3: Past

The early formal methods research funded directly by the National Security Agency, or indirectly through the National Computer Security Center (NCSC), centered on *proving systems secure.*

Addressing the question of what *secure* means, researchers defined models and policies to express Lampson-style [26] access rights of subjects to objects. This work led to the Bell-LaPadula No-Read-Up and No-Write-Down secrecy model [3], the Biba No-Read-Down and No-Write-Up integrity model [5], and the less formal Clark-Wilson integrity model based on a set of nine rules of practice [11]. The Bell-LaPadula model in particular gained notoriety when McLean introduced System Z, which satisfies Bell-LaPadula properties but is clearly insecure [29].

The *systems* of interest to prove secure were operating systems. More specifically, kernels. Given that one cannot prove an entire system secure, better to try to prove a small piece of it. Trust the kernel and nothing else. This approach emphasized the importance of the reference monitor concept: the functionality of the operating system that mediates access by subjects to objects. For example, a user-level process should not have access to the kernel-level stack.

The formal methods community played a fundamental role in fleshing out what *proving* means. The process of proving entails three parts (not necessarily done in this order): First, one must state the property of the system to prove, as expressed explicitly in a *formal specification*. In the security context, this specification might simply be a list of properties such as the so-called *-property (No-Write-Down) of the Bell-LaPadula model. Second, one must model the system so that one can formally prove the property. This mathematical model might be a semantic structure like a state machine or a syntactic structure like a logical expression. Third, the proof. Typically, the proof might rely on induction over traces of the state machine model or it might rely on deduction to show that an implication holds ($SystemModel \Rightarrow SystemProperty$). The proof might be discovered automatically by the machine or require interactive guidance from the human user. *Formal verification* is the process of proving, by hand or machine, that the model of the system satisfies the formal specification. In practice, most theorem proving tools are more like proof checkers; they differ in the amount of human intervention needed to check the proof.

One of the most influential documents of the time, produced by the NCSC, is the U.S. Trusted Computer System Evaluation Criteria, better known as "The Orange Book" [10]. Amoroso [2] summarizes its goals:

- To provide a standard metric for the NCSC to compare the security of different computer systems.

- To guide computer system vendors in the design and development of secure systems.

- To provide a means for specifying security requirements in Government contracts.

In particular for a system to be certified A.1 according to the Orange Book means that one formally specify the system's security requirements, formally model the system, and formally prove that the model meets its specification.

In this context, the major results of the early 80s by the formal methods community in the United States, in particular those funded heavily by the security community, were in the development of theorem proving tools. To get one's system certified A.1, one would use one of these tools to produce the proof.

In fact, these tools were general-purpose theorem provers; they were applied to examples from the security arena, but were applicable in general to all kinds of systems. By 1986, in Kemmerer's landmark Verification Assessment Study [23], four tools were the most mature, known, or used:

- Affirm, developed at the University of Southern California's Information Sciences Institute, best known for its support for reasoning about equational specifications, in particular through its implementation of the Knuth-Bendix completion procedure.

- The Formal Development Methodology (FDM) System, developed at System Development Corporation's Santa Monica Research Center, best known for its support for a non-deterministic state machine model and the Ina Jo specification language.

- Gypsy, developed at the Institute for Computing Science at the University of Texas at Austin, best known for its support for program verification of a subset of Pascal, including a verification condition generator.

- (Enhanced) Hierarchical Development Methodology (HDM), developed at Stanford Research International's Computer Science Laboratory, best known for its SPECIAL specification language and its collection of decision procedures for propositional logic as the heart of its theorem prover.

The general-purpose Boyer-Moore theorem prover [8], also developed during the same time period, was representative of the state of the art in automated theorem proving tools and was applied to many examples, notably the "CLInc Stack" [4].

A few researchers developed tools specific to reasoning about security. The two best known examples are the Interrogator [33] and the NRL Protocol Analyzer [31]. With both of these tools, one specifies an insecure state and the tool searches backwards to determine whether that state is reachable. The Interrogator is based on Prolog, does an exhaustive search (and hence is fully automatic), and has a built-in notion of encryption. The NRL Protocol Analyzer's search is less automatic. It is based on Dolev and Yao's pioneering work on an algebraic term rewriting model for two-party cryptographic protocols [14]. Meadows used the NRL Protocol Analyzer to discover previously unknown flaws in the Simmons Selective Broadcast Protocol and the Burns-Mitchell Resource Sharing Protocol. Kemmerer, Meadows, and Millen's [22] paper summarizes the strengths and weaknesses of FDM, the NRL Protocol Analyzer, and the Interrogator, using the Tatebayeshi-Matsuzaki-Newman (TMN) protocol as the common running example.

In 1990, Burrows, Abadi, and Needham published their work on a Logic of Authentication (aka the BAN Logic) [9], a formal logic designed specifically to reason about authentication protocols. The logic's main construct allows one to reason in terms of *belief*, and in particular the beliefs a principal accumulates during the run of a protocol. One kind of belief a principal might acquire is about the freshness of messages, e.g., through the freshness of message components such as nonces. The lack of proof that a message is fresh suggests a possible replay attack—a well-known vulnerability of the original Needham-Schroeder symmetric-key protocol. The BAN work attracted both praise and criticism. It inspired some to define their own belief logics, e.g., the GNY (Gong, Needham, and Yahalom) logic [16], the SVO (Syverson and van Oorschot) logic [39], and AUTLOG [24]. Unlike the aforementioned general-purpose tools, BAN and its derivatives focused on only authentication protocols, and except for AUTLOG [24], lack tool support. Despite these limitations, the BAN Logic's influence was positive overall: it demonstrates that formal logics have a role in revealing flaws in an important class of security protocols.

One of the criticisms against the original BAN paper was the absence of a semantic model. Solving this problem led to the definition of various state-machine semantic models for authentication protocols, including Abadi and Tuttle's [1], Woo and Lam's [40], and Heintze and Tygar's [18]. Woo and Lam also introduced the need to check not just for secrecy, but also *correspondence*, a property that assures that the authenticating principal is indeed "talking" to the intended authenticated principal.

In their comprehensive 1993 survey report, Rubin and Honeyman [38] use Meadows's four-type classification scheme [30] to categorize twenty-seven different formal approaches to the analysis of authentication protocols. The four types are (1) using general-purpose specification languages and tools, e.g., Ina Jo; (2) using special-purpose rule-based tools, e.g., the Interrogator, to help the protocol designer; (3) using belief logics, e.g., BAN; and (4) using special-purpose algebraic-based tools, e.g., the NRL Protocol Analyzer.

Two international meetings caused the formal methods and security communities to cross paths: the FM'89 [13] and FM'91 workshops, sponsored by the governments of the United States, Canada, and the United Kingdom (in particular by the National Security Agency and its Canadian and UK counterparts). The focus in FM'89 was on the role of formal methods for trustworthy computer systems. Here, trustworthy meant not just security but also safety-critical. The main outcome was the recognition of two different styles of formal methods:

- The UK and European style: The focus was on specification, on the system's high-level design, and on paper-and-pencil analysis.

- The US and Canadian style: The focus was on verification, from the system's high-level design through its code-level implementation down to its bit-level representation in hardware (the "CLInc Stack" approach), and on machine-assisted analysis.

Debate over which style was better subsided by FM'91 where instead there was consensus to embrace all methods, to acknowledge that tools are necessary, and to direct the community's effort to producing more convincing case studies. Another outcome of FM'91 (for the US at least) was the move of mainstream formal methods research out from under the shadow of the security agencies, witnessed by the absence of subsequent workshops sponsored by those three agencies.

4: Present

Since the early 90s the formal methods community has experienced an explosion of new developments: new methods, new tools, and countless large-scaled projects and non-trivial case studies.[2] Clarke and Wing capture the state of the art in their 1996 *ACM Computing Surveys* paper detailing the progress of three threads in the development of formal methods: model checking, theorem proving, and software specification. Model checking, in particular, is a proven success for hardware verification; companies such as Intel are establishing their own hardware verification groups, building their own verification systems, and hiring people trained in formal methods.

In 1996 another convergence of the two communities occurred. Lowe [27] used Roscoe's model checker, FDR, to exhibit a flaw in the Needham-Schroeder public-key authentication protocol, first published eighteen years earlier. Lowe actually discovered the flaw on his own, but used the tool to check both the flawed and the amended protocols. This paper started a flurry of activity in (1) the use of other model checkers to show the same thing, (2) the use of other tools and techniques to show the same thing, and (3) the application of all these tools to other authentication protocols and to simplified electronic commerce protocols. Here is a sampling:

- Model checking approaches

  - Mitchell, Mitchell and Stern [34] use Dill's Murφ model checker (originally designed for hardware verification) on the Needham-Schroeder public-key, TMN, and Kerberos protocols. Current efforts at Stanford are aimed at specifying and verifying SSL 3.0.

  - Marrero, Clarke, and Jha [28] describe a special-purpose model checker, Brutus, which has a built-in model of an intruder. It has direct support for checking correspondence properties. Marrero used it to verify fifteen classic authentication protocols and is currently applying it to examine electronic commerce protocols, including 1KP, 2KP, and Netbill.

  - Heintze, Tygar, Wing, and Wong [19] used FDR to check atomicity properties of Netbill and a simple digital cash protocol.

---

[2] As of 14 May 1999, the Oxford Formal Methods Web page http://www.comlab.ox.ac.uk/archive/formal-methods/ lists 79 different formal methods notations and tools, and 660 "formal methodists".

- Theorem proving approaches

  - Paulson used a general-purpose theorem prover, Isabelle, to show how to use induction to reason about five classic authentication protocols and their variations [37].

  - Dutertre and Schneider embed CSP in the general-purpose theorem prover PVS and used the embedding to verify authentication protocols [15].

  - Bolignano used the general-purpose theorem prover, Coq, to analyze the Needham-Schroeder public-key protocol [6] and is investigating its use for analyzing electronic commerce standards like the Secure Electronic Transaction (SET) protocol [7].

- Hybrid approaches

  - Meadows has recently made improvements to the NRL Protocol Analyzer so that it should best be viewed as special-purpose tool that embodies both model checking (e.g., brute force search) and theorem proving (e.g., lemma generation) functionality. She is currently applying it to analyze the Internet Key Exchange protocol [32] and the SET protocol.

  - Kindred and Wing [25] invented a new technique, called *theory generation*, which automatically generates a finite representation of a protocol's theory, as represented in terms of BAN-like formulae. Kindred has applied this approach to the classic set of authentication protocols and variants of the NetBill electronic payment protocol.

The common theme in almost all of the above recent work is the demonstration of how formal methods can be applied to authentication protocols, particularly Needham-Schroeder's public-key protocol. Indeed at the September 1997 DIMACS Workshop of Cryptographic Protocol Design and Verification many of the speakers presented how their method reveals the flaw discovered by Lowe.

In June 1998, Heintze and Wing [20] ran the well-attended Workshop on Formal Methods and Security Protocols and there are numerous similar workshops scheduled for 1999 worldwide. The interest in the intersection of these two communities remains unabated.

The motivation from the formal methods community is clear: security still remains a challenge. The motivation from the security community is strong too. More and more people place their trust in computing systems today for doing everything from casual shopping to medical recordkeeping; and more and more systems are built out of commercial-off-the-shelf components. It is no longer just the government, the military, or the universities who are the purchasers, users, or conveyors of large, complex computing systems. Thus, system designers and implementers are more willing to pay the price for increasing the assurance that their systems are secure. Formal methods can provide such increased assurance.

5: Future

5.1: The Practice of Building Secure Systems

Figure 1 depicts how we build secure systems. We first and foremost rely on a solid cryptographic base. Out of these primitives for encryption, decryption, signatures, hashing, etc., we define protocols such as for authentication and key-exchange, and we rely on

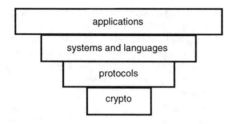

Figure 1. System Layers

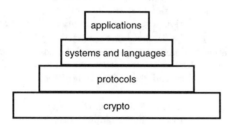

Figure 2. Security Guarantees

standard reliable network protocols like TCP/IP. We rely on these protocols to build security services, some of which we use on a daily basis; for example, I invoke Kerberos's `kinit` every morning to access my files stored remotely. All of these protocols and system services are implemented in general-purpose programming languages such as C or Java. Finally, above the systems and languages level, we have applications which are what the public sees and uses. These applications include on-line shopping, banking, bill payment, and tax forms submission, all of which should provide some guarantees of privacy and protection to the user.

Ironically, the "strength" of what we can guarantee is inversely proportional to the "size" of the layer (Figure 2). There are fundamental and deep results in cryptography that tell us precisely what we can guarantee, what we cannot, and what is still an open question (e.g., the equivalence of the RSA problem and factoring). At the protocol level we have a handful of formal methods, even mechanized ones, that let us provide some guarantees about authentication protocols. At the system/protocol layer, we have protocols like SSL and SHTTP, which provide minimal encryption and authentication functionality for setting up secure channels. At the systems and languages layer, commercial technology such as Authenticode, Active X, Java, and JavaScript provide varying degrees of security, but are subject to widely publicized attacks such as denial of service and spoofing. At the application layer, in terms of security guarantees, we don't have very much at all. What then are the challenges for the future?

5.2: Challenges and Opportunities for Formal Methods Researchers

Below I use N to indicate near-term research; L, long-term.

First, I focus on the *protocol level (N)*. If a protocol has a design flaw, it does not matter if the implementation is correct. The protocol is vulnerable to attack. We know that protocols are notoriously difficult to get right and the more complex a protocol, the harder it is to understand. Good progress has been made in proving or disproving that individual protocols meet certain properties. Progress has also been made in using different mechanized methods like model checking and theorem proving to help with the proof process. This work should continue, as should the more general work of building and integrating formal methods tools and applying them to larger and larger systems.

With respect to security, however, I would like to move the formal methods community to look beyond the protocol level.

- Multiple protocols

  - *Protocol composition (L).* We expect in practice that more and more people will be designing and deploying their own protocols by using existing protocols as building blocks. We should design new and integrated protocols with compositionality in mind. By composition, I mean running protocols interleaved (concurrently), sequentially (back-to-back), and layered (as subprotocols of each other).

    In general we need all composition mechanisms to work together. For example, authentication requires using encryption as a subprotocol; digital cash requires a blind signature scheme; and the SET standard relies on a public-key infrastructure.

    Some newly discovered attacks arise because of multiple, interleaved runs of the same or different protocols. For example, the correctness of the separate runs of two protocols does not imply the correctness of a system where an intruder can participate in both runs at the same time. We need to look at multiple, simultaneous, and possibly interleaved runs of the same *and different* protocols.

- Systems and language level

  - *Program analysis tools (N).* Even if the protocol design is correct, the implementation could be flawed. Many of the Computer Emergency Response Team (CERT) advisories can be traced to a buffer overflow problem, e.g., resulting from using the unsafe `strcpy` C library string routine. From the CERT report the following are given as examples of "weaknesses in how protocols and software are implemented" [12]:

    * race conditions in file access
    * non-existent checking of data content and size
    * non-existent checking for success or failure
    * inability to adapt to resource exhaustion
    * incomplete checking of operating environment
    * inappropriate use of system calls
    * re-use of software modules for purposes other than their intended ones

    We should develop program analysis tools that will help us detect these kinds of weaknesses in the software implementations of protocols and systems. Work such as applying program slicing to do a vulnerability analysis of TCP/IP [17] is a step in this direction.

  - *Certified library components (N).* As more and more systems are built out of off-the-shelf components, it pays to have additional assurance that the components have been certified to meet some degree of security. Since these building blocks will be used multiple times and in different contexts, the cost of certifying them could be amortized over the overall cost of developing the systems in which they are embedded.

These library components might be in hardware too. A milestone was recently achieved when the IBM 4758 PCI Cryptographic Coprocessor, which provides a tamper-sensing and tamper-responding environment to enable secure electronic business transactions, earned the highest certification for commercial security awarded by the US Government. It is the first product to ever meet the Federal Information Processing Standard 140-1 Level 4 [21].

- *Benchmark suite (N).* It would be a great service to the community to have a benchmark suite of intruder scenarios that can be used as a testbed for designing, analyzing, and debugging existing and future protocols and systems. These benchmarks can be used as test cases against source code as well as test cases for formal methods analysis tools.

- *Programming language design (L).* Language designers should investigate incorporating into the programming language more "type" information that would permit some security guarantees to be statically enforced or dynamically checked. Myers's work on JFlow for statically analyzing flow control [35] is one approach based on additional annotations to Java programs. Another approach by Necula and Lee is to use proof-carrying code, allowing clients to execute untrusted remote code safely [36].

• Applications level

- *Case studies (N).* We should do large-scale examples to show the applicability and scalability of our formal methods. Current studies of the SSL, IKE, and SET standards are good examples. Moreover, formalizing a standard has a higher payoff than formalizing a single system. This work takes time, effort, and people power; it also can be extremely tedious. Thus, the case studies need to be chosen wisely; when completed, the targets of these studies must still be relevant.

• Horizontal and vertical slices *(N, L)*

- *Global properties.* At each level and above all levels, we need to reconsider global security properties of systems. We need to understand which properties can be decomposed such that local proofs imply they hold globally, and which do not. We may need new proof techniques to handle global properties that cannot be decomposed.

- *Intruder models.* We need to build a suite of intruder models, each class representing different intruder capabilities (passive, active, etc.). Some intruder models may be protocol-specific; others, more generic. As the taxonomy of protocols of interest expands, e.g., to include electronic payment protocols and secure auction protocols, so must our models of intruders.

- *Crossing abstraction boundaries.* We need to look at slices that cut across the four levels depicted in Figure 1, tracing a property or function from an application at the top all the way down to how it is implemented at the cryptographic level. We should pay particular attention to when we are crossing boundaries between the levels since interfaces often do not match at the boundaries.

Even beyond these layers and slices, we need to take a more *holistic* view of a system. Again, from the CERT report:

Vulnerabilities in the category of system and network configurations are not caused by problems inherent in protocols or software programs. Rather, the vulnerabilities are a result of the way these components are set up and used.

Products may be delivered with default settings that intruders can exploit. System administrators and users may neglect to change the default settings, or they may simply set up their system to operate in a way that leaves the network vulnerable.

An example of a faulty configuration that has been exploited is anonymous File Transfer Protocol (FTP) service. Secure configuration guidelines for this service stress the need to ensure that the password file, archive tree, and ancillary software are separate from the rest of the operating system, and that the operating system cannot be reached from this staging area. When sites misconfigure their anonymous FTP archives, unauthorized users can get authentication information and use it to compromise the system.

Thus, we see that it is not enough to look at just the system or even the system and its intended operating environment. Formal methods need to be integrated with other methods that can address issues—some of which are beyond the scope of formalization—raised by examples like the one above. These analyses include risk analysis, hazard analysis, fault analysis, and intrusion detection analysis. Formal methods also need to be better integrated into the entire software development lifecycle such as during requirements analysis, testing, and simulation.

Finally, we must introduce the human factor, which in principle is part of the system's environment. Human factors cannot be neglected. Research in modeling human behavior, human-computer interaction, and management of processes and organizations can all complement the more formal nature of research of formal methods.

Acknowledgments

Opinions expressed in this paper are my own, not of any of my sponsors or even necessarily of any of my formal methods or security colleagues.

References

[1] M. Abadi and M. Tuttle. A semantics for a logic of authentication. In *Proceedings of the 10th ACM Symposium on Principles of Distributed Computing*, pages 201–216, August 1991.

[2] E. Amoroso. *Fundamentals of Computer Security Technology*. AT&T Bell Laboratories, 1994.

[3] D. Bell and L. LaPadula. Secure computer systems: Mathematical foundations. Technical Report ESD-TR-73-278, The MITRE Corporation, Bedford, MA, 1973.

[4] W.R. Bevier, W.A. Hunt, Jr., J S. Moore, and W.D. Young. An approach to systems verification. *Journal of Automated Reasoning*, 5:411–428, 1989. See also three other articles in the same issue by Young, Moore, and Hunt.

[5] K. Biba. Integrity considerations for secure computer systems. Technical Report MTR-3153, The MITRE Corporation, Bedford, MA, 1975.

[6] D. Bolignano. An approach to the formal verification of cryptographic protocols. In *Proceedings of the Third ACM Conference on Computer and Communications Security*, pages 106–118. ACM Press, 1996.

[7] D. Bolignano. Towards the formal verification of electronic commerce protocols. In *Proceedings of the Tenth IEEE Computer Security Foundations Workshop*, June 1997.

[8] R. Boyer and J. Moore. *A Computational Logic*. ACM monograph series. Academic Press, New York, 1979.

[9] M. Burrows, M. Abadi, and R. Needham. A Logic of Authentication. *ACM Transactions on Computer Systems*, 8(1):18–36, February 1990.

[10] National Computer Security Center. Department of Defense Trusted Computer Security Evaluation Criteria. Technical Report DoD 5200.28-STD, NCSC, 1985.

[11] D. Clark and D. Wilson. A comparison of commercial and military computer security policies. In *IEEE Symposium on Security and Privacy*, 1987.

[12] Computer Emergency Response Team Coordination Center Staff. Security of the internet. In *Encyclopedia of Telecommunications*, 1997.

[13] D. Craigen and K. Summerskill. *Formal Methods for Trustworthy Computer Systems (FM89)*. Springer-Verlag, 1990. Workshops in Computing Series.

[14] D. Dolev and A. Yao. On the security of public key protocols. *IEEE Transactions on Information Theory*, 29(2):198–208, March 1989.

[15] B. Dutertre and S. Schneider. Using a PVS embedding of CSP to verify authentication protocols. In *Theorem Proving in Higher Order Logics*, pages 121–136, August 1997. LNCS 1275.

[16] L. Gong, R. Needham, and R. Yahalom. Reasoning about belief in cryptographic protocols. In *Proceedings of the 1990 IEEE Computer Society Symposium on Research in Security and Privacy*, pages 234–248, May 1990.

[17] B. Guha and B. Mukherjee. Network security via reverse engineering of TCP code: Vulnerability analysis and proposed solutions. In *Proc. IEEE Infocom'96*, pages 603–610, San Francisco, CA, March 1996.

[18] N. Heintze and J. Tygar. A model for secure protocols and their compositions. *IEEE Transactions on Software Engineering*, 22(1):16–30, January 1996.

[19] N. Heintze, J. Tygar, J. Wing, and H. Wong. Model checking electronic commerce protocols. In *Proceedings of the Second USENIX Workshop in Electronic Commerce*, pages 147–164, November 1996.

[20] N. Heintze and J.M. Wing. Proceedings of the workshop on formal methods and security protocols. URL: http://cm.bell-labs.com/cm/cs/who/nch/fmsp/index.html, June 1998.

[21] IBM. IBM Coprocessor First to Earn Highest Security Validation. http://www.ibm.com/security/cryptocards/html/pr_fips.html.

[22] R. Kemmerer, C. Meadows, and J. Millen. Three systems for cryptographic protocol analysis. *Journal of Cryptology*, 7(2):79–130, 1994.

[23] R.A. Kemmerer. Verification assessment study final report. Technical Report C3-CR01-86, National Computer Security Center, Ft. George G. Meade, MD, March 1986. Five volumes.

[24] V. Kessler and G. Wedel. AUTLOG—an advanced logic of authentication. In *Proceedings of the Computer Security Foundations Workshop VII*, pages 90–99. IEEE Comput. Soc., June 1994.

[25] D. Kindred and J. Wing. Fast, automatic checking of security protocols. In *USENIX 2nd Workshop on Electronic Commerce*, 1996.

[26] B. Lampson. Protection. In *Proceedings of the Fifth Princeton Symposium on Information Sciences and Systems*, 1971. Reprinted in *ACMU Operating Systems Review*, Vol. 8, 1974.

[27] G. Lowe. Breaking and fixing the Needham-Schroeder public-key protocol using FDR. In *Tools and Algorithms for the Construction and Analysis of Systems*, volume 1055 of *Lecture Notes in Computer Science*, pages 147–166. Springer-Verlag, 1996.

[28] Will Marrero, Edmund Clarke, and Somesh Jha. A model checker for authentication protocols. In *Proc. of the DIMACS Workshop on Design and Formal Verification of Security Protocols*. DIMACS Rutgers University, September 1997.

[29] J. McLean. A Comment on the Basic Security Theorem of Bell and LaPadula. *Information Processing Letters*, 20, 1985.

[30] C. Meadows. Applying formal methods to the analysis of a key management protocol. *Journal of Computer Security*, 1:5–53, 1992.

[31] C. Meadows. The NRL Protocol Analyzer: An Overview. *Journal of Logic Programming*, pages 113–131, 1996.

[32] C. Meadows. Analysis of the Internet Key Exchange Protocol Using the NRL Protocol Analyzer. submitted to 1999 Securitye and Privacy, 1998.

[33] J.K. Millen, S.C. Clark, and S.B. Freedman. The Interrogator: Protocol Security Analysis. *IEEE Trans. on Soft. Eng.*, 13(2), February 1987.

[34] J. Mitchell, M. Mitchell, and U. Stern. Automated Analysis of Cryptographic Protocols Using Murphi. In *Proceedings of the IEEE Conference on Secuirty and Privacy*, pages 141–151, 1997.

[35] A. Myers. JFlow: Practical Static Information Flow Control. In *Proceedings of the 26th ACM Symposium on Principles of Programming Languages*, January 1999.

[36] G. Necula and P. Lee. Safe Kernel Extensions Without Run-Time Checking. In *Proc. of Second Symp. on Operations Systems Design and Implementation*, October 1996.

[37] Lawrence C. Paulson. Proving properties of security protocols by induction. Technical report, University of Cambridge, December 1996.

[38] A Rubin and P Honeyman. Formal methods for the analysis of authentication protocols. Technical Report 93–97, CITI, November 1993.

[39] P. Syverson and P. van Oorschot. On unifying some cryptographic protocol logics. In *Proceedings of the 1994 IEEE Computer Society Symposium on Research in Security and Privacy*. IEEE Computer Society Press, May 1994.

[40] T. Woo and S. Lam. A semantic model for authentication protocols. In *Proceedings of the IEEE Symposium on Research in Security and Privacy*, 1993.

Multiple Dimensions of Integrating Development Technology*

Betty H.C. Cheng
Department of Computer Science and Engineering
Michigan State University
3115 Engineering Building
East Lansing, MI 48824
chengb@cse.msu.edu

Abstract

Studies have shown that errors are most likely to be introduced in the requirements phase of a development effort. This problem is largely due to prose descriptions that are ambiguous or inconsistent. One potential solution to this problem is to capture requirements information in the form of formal specifications that can be checked for consistency and completeness using automated techniques. However, during the initial phases of a project, it may be difficult to construct formal specifications directly. In contrast, many developers find it more intuitive to create diagrams to model their systems. As a means to bridge the gap between formal and informal approaches to software development, we have investigated the formalization of a commonly used object-oriented modeling notation, Object Modeling Technique (OMT). The formalization of OMT enables the automated generation of formal specifications of the diagrams that can then be analyzed using simulation and model checking, and other types of verification techniques. Lessons from this integration effort can assist in the development of strategies for integrating techniques from the assurance, fault tolerance, and security fields. One key factor to this type of collaboration will be the use of a specific problem domain to focus the integration efforts. Another issue to be addressed is a common framework upon which the researchers from the three fields can build their integrated techniques.

1. Introduction

It is clearly evident that the role of software is significantly increasing. Accordingly, the need to have high assurance in software's correctness increases for systems where correct operation is imperative. Recent studies have shown that the software quality problem is greatest during the early lifecycle phases of requirements and design, which can have a lasting impact on the reliability, cost, and safety of a system [23]. Also, requirements errors are between 10 and 100 times more costly to correct at later phases of the software lifecycle than at the requirements phase [2, 3, 20].

One approach to this problem is to document software requirements and design using a formal language; such a document is called a *formal specification* [39]. This approach is one of the basic elements of the software engineering disciplines referred to as *formal methods*. A formal method is characterized by a formal specification language and a set of rules governing the manipulation of expressions in that language [39]. While the advantages to using formal methods are significant, including the use of notations that are precise, verifiable, and facilitate automated processing [7, 8, 32, 39], attempting to construct a formal specification directly from an informal, high-level requirements document can be challenging. Formal descriptions potentially involve considerable syntactic detail and require careful planning and organization on the part of the

This author is supported in part by NSF grants CDA-9700732,CDA-9617310, CCR-9633391, and DARPA grant No. F30602-96-1-0298, managed by Air Force's Rome Laboratories, and Eaton Corporation.

specifier in order to obtain modular specifications. Minor changes in the natural language description, or the interpretation thereof, can require significant and tedious reorganization of the formal description.

Using formal specification languages facilitates the early evaluation of a software design and verification of its implementation through the use of formal reasoning techniques [6, 7, 32, 39] or static analysis techniques [1, 15, 16]. A formal specification can be rigorously manipulated to allow the designer to assess the consistency, completeness, and robustness of a design before it is implemented. Each step in the development process can be supported by mathematical proof, thus reducing the number of errors due to misinterpretation and ambiguity. This type of approach is supported by many methods [7, 11, 13, 19, 33]. Currently, these methods presume the existence of a formal description of requirements. But, unfortunately, formal descriptions of requirements for large systems are not easy to obtain.

Other approaches to requirements analysis and design include the numerous object-oriented techniques [9, 10, 30, 40]. These "informal" methods enable the rapid construction of a system model using intuitive graphics and user-friendly languages. While such techniques are commonly used, the graphical notations used with these methods are often ambiguous, resulting in diagrams that are easily misinterpreted. In order to determine the correctness of systems developed with these informal approaches, complex validation procedures must be incorporated at every stage of development, and extensive testing methods must be used [29]. The lack of precise definitions for the notations makes it difficult to combine this approach with rigorous, systematic software development methods.

In order to take advantage of the benefits of both approaches, there has been a general movement in the software engineering community towards integrating informal and formal techniques. Several benefits motivate the integration, including the following items:

- Leverage existing technology, from both the informal and the formal languages.
- Leverage existing experience
- Gain benefits from the integrated techniques
- Expand the user community

In short, the sum of the whole is greater than the sum of the individual parts.

This paper gives a summary of a presentation that was given at the *From Needs to Solutions Workshop*, sponsored by the National Science Foundation and the Office of Naval Research, held in Williamsburg, Virginia in November 1998. The objective of the workshop was to bring researchers from academia and industry to discuss how their respective research areas could be integrated in order to address the correct development of critical systems. The three specific fields that were brought together are: assurance, fault tolerance, and security. The remainder of this paper is organized as follows. Section 2 gives background material on an approach to integration that we have developed for integrating OMT with formal specification languages. Section 3 describes the objectives of integration when applied to techniques from the three fields, assurance, fault tolerance, and security, and discusses different approaches to their integration. For discussion purposes, we focus on formal methods, an area within assurance when discussing the integration of assurance, fault-tolerance, and security. Tasks that are relevant to integrating techniques are discussed in Section 4. A summary and potential future investigations are presented in Section 5.

2. Background

One commonly used object-oriented development approach, the *Object Modeling Technique* (OMT) [30], uses three types of models to express important domain-related concepts: object models, functional models, and dynamic models. Each model contributes to the understanding of a system, but the object model is of central importance. Those elements of a system that define its static structure are given by an *object model* using a notation similar to that used for entity-relationship diagrams. An object model determines the types of objects that can exist in the system and identifies allowable relationships among objects. As a result, the object model constrains the set of possible states that the system may enter. A *dynamic model* describes valid changes to system states and indicates the conditions under which a state change may occur. The notation used for dynamic models is a variation of Harel's Statechart notation [14] which, in turn, is an extension to the traditional notation for finite automata [17]. A *functional model* is a data flow diagram that describes the computations to be performed by the system. The main attractive feature of the OMT approach is that by using these three notations in a complementary manner, the system developer can express and refine system requirements into a design and implementation. However, the lack of precise definitions for the notations makes it difficult to combine this approach with rigorous, systematic software development methods.

The original definition for OMT [30] does not have a formal definition of its syntax and semantics, thus preventing rigorous analysis of the modeling diagrams. For example, different aspects of the software requirements are represented in the three different graphical languages mentioned above, but the concepts embedded in these diagrams are interrelated. The semantics of these three graphical notations must therefore be integrated in order to perform a rigorous analysis, but neither the syntax nor the semantics are rigorously defined. Nevertheless, the OMT approach has been widely used because of its simple notation and its multiple views of software requirements, and it is fairly comprehensive in its (albeit informal) treatment of development issues.

In previous investigations [4, 36, 38], we have developed a formalization of all three models of OMT, including a formal definition of the integration of the three models [37]. In order to assist in the understanding of the specifications that are derived from the diagrams, we give a brief overview of the format of the formal specifications. For detailed syntax and semantics of the specifications, please refer to [4, 38, 36]. Figure 1 shows an outline of a specification that describes an object class, including its identity, interface, functionality, and behavior. The words in bold fonts are keywords; the text in "< >" pairs are the components of formal specifications.

```
specification <class name> [<services>] (<essential attributes>)  noexit :=
        ( | *  ......................... * | )
        ( | *  <service specification>  * | )
        ( | *  ......................... * | )
        typedef
              . . . . . .
              <algebraic specification>
              . . . . . .
        endtype
        <starting state> [<services>] (<essential attributes>)
        process <state name> [<services>] (<essential attributes>)  noexit :=
              . . . . . .
              <behavior specification>
              . . . . . .
        endproc
endspec
```

Figure 1. The format of formal specifications

The components of a formal specification include:

- Class name: *identifies a class of objects that share the same interfaces, attribute types, and behavior.*
- Services: *services provided/needed by a class of objects.*
- Essential attributes: *attributes essential to a class of objects.*
- Service specification: *specifies the signatures and pre- and postconditions of the services.*
- Algebraic specification: *specifies the properties that an object may have in terms of algebraic specifications.*
- Behavior specification: *specifies the patterns that an object interacts with other objects.*
- State name: *identifies different states that an object may be in during its life cycle.*
- Starting state: *the state that an object enters after being instantiated.*

A specification depicts four aspects of a class: identity, interface, functionality, and behavior. Class name and essential attributes together contribute to the identity of classes and objects. Services describe the interface of a class. Service specifications delineate the functionalities that the services provide. Behavior specifications, state names, and the starting state capture the behavior of a class. Except for the algebraic specifications that specify the properties of objects and the pre- and postconditions that are based upon the algebraic specifications, all other components of the formal specifications can be automatically generated from diagrammatic models according to our formalization rules. Figure 2 contains a high-level overview of the diagrams and their corresponding formal specifications.

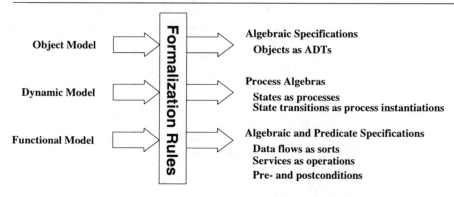

Figure 2. An overview of the formalization rules

2.1. Multiple Dimensions of Integration

In this particular project, integration was performed along multiple dimensions. First, we integrated informal and formal development techniques. OMT (and now its successor UML, the Unified Modeling Language [31]) has been a commonly used development technique among industry as well as in academic settings. Similarly, we identified commonly used specification languages that had similar semantics to the informal notations.

Second, we integrated a number of formal techniques. When initially deciding on how to formalize the OMT notations, we had several criteria for selecting the specific target formal specification language, including reasonably-sized user community, easy to use, tool support, and how well the formal semantics matched the intended semantics of the informal notation. Given the complementary nature of the three OMT models, it was no surprise that it was more straightforward to identify different formal languages appropriate for each perspective. We started with the object model that lent itself to an algebraic formalization given its heavy emphasis on data abstractions and their interrelationships. The Larch Shared Language (LSL) was a good candidate given its support for modular specifications and tool support, including syntax checker [18], Larch Prover [12], and graphical browsing and development environment [21, 27]. Next, we formalized the dynamic model. After looking at a number of specification languages, we identified the LOTOS process algebra as the target formal specification language. LOTOS has good support for representing states and events through processes and data transmitted on gates, different synchronization mechanisms, and integration with an algebraic data component (through the ACT ONE language). The support for integrating an algebraic component was important since a key part of our formalization (that is, integrating informal and formal notations) was formalizing the integration between the three informal models. The final piece was the formalization of the functional model, defined in terms of data flow diagrams (DFDs). Because the DFDs depicted services of the objects, we needed a language that captured the observable behavior of the services. We selected a predicate logic-based approach since that provided the appropriate abstraction for the services. We were able to use the Larch Interface Language (LIL) to represent this part of the formalization. We explored the LILs for C and C++, depending on the specific application. The LIL approach worked well because it had a well-defined integration with the algebraic component (LSL) that was used to formalize the object model, which in turn, was also integrated with the dynamic model through the process algebra component. In essence, we had developed a three-pronged approach to specification that combined algebraic (LSL and ACT ONE), process algebra (LOTOS), and predicate logic (LIL) specifications.

The third dimension of integration was in the area of tools. We were able to leverage the existing tools to assist in the development and refinement of the models and the corresponding specifications. As mentioned previously, Larch has tool support for syntax checkers, theorem provers, and graphical browsers. LOTOS has tools for simulation, syntax and semantics analysis, and numerous state exploration techniques. In our investigations, we have found that many of the tools supporting formal methods have limitations, but they each also have their strengths. Through our integration efforts, we found that by using the different tools in a complementary fashion, we were able to overcome many of the shortcomings typically associated with analyzing formal specifications. For example, simulation can be quite effective in validating behavior, but it is not necessarily good for finding the source of errors. In contrast, model checking is effective in returning a counter example if a constraint is not satisfied, but it can quickly run into the state explosion problem if it is asked to exhaustively explore the behavior of a system. In our tool integration effort [5, 26], we have developed strategies for combining these kinds of techniques in order to perform high-level behavior validation, detection of syntactic and semantic errors, identification of source of errors, and the refinement of models to add design information.

3. Integration

There are several different perspectives to consider when evaluating the benefits gained from integrating informal and formal techniques. First, integration has immediate technical benefits. Second, several benefits exist from an economical standpoint. Finally, from a user's perspective, the resulting systems should be of better quality.

By integrating techniques that each have merits on their own, the intent is that the combined use would give even greater benefits. Informal methods are typically graphical in nature and easy to use, but it can also be easy for the developer to construct erroneous models since there is no systematic way to rigorously check the diagrams. In contrast, formal techniques are well-defined and are amenable to automated analysis. Example analysis techniques that can be applied include simulation, syntax and semantics checking, and numerous constraint checking techniques, such as model checking, rewriting techniques, and theorem provers. Unfortunately, some formal methods may be difficult to use in that the formal specifications may not be easy to construct from scratch. And modifications to the specifications may not be easy to effect. The integration of the two types of techniques will largely overcome the disadvantages to each approach and highlight the advantages. Formal specification techniques can enhance the application of informal techniques, by providing the means for rigorously analyzing properties that they informally represent. Rigorous analysis can uncover errors that are difficult to capture in reviews of informal models, which would otherwise allow errors to propagate to the later stages of development thereby increasing the overall development costs. Numerous types of automated analysis techniques can now be applied to the diagrams via their respective formal specifications. The analysis tools for the formal Examples include intra- and inter-model consistency checking [22, 25, 34], specification verification and validation through the use of model checking and simulation techniques [22, 34], behavior simulation [35], and rapid prototype development [22, 24]. From the development point of view, the formal specifications enable developers to explore rigorous and automated design refinement techniques, including code generation [22] and test case generation [28]. Formal techniques can reduce the burden currently placed on testing.

From the economical point of view, several potential benefits exist. "Integrated" techniques provide an evolutionary path to the use of formal specification techniques. There are user communities for both the informal and formal techniques. There are support tools for both types of methods. The integration enables the overall user community to increase, and the migration from a completely informal approach to one that is supported by formal techniques is supported by the existing tools. From management's point of view, the development team is not abandoning a known technology, rather, they are enhancing its capabilities. In addition, the cost savings that can be obtained by being able to rigorously check requirements and designs before a system is implemented, tested, or deployed to the field will be significant, thus further motivating the integrative approach. The integration of informal and formal techniques also facilitates customer and developer interaction when dealing with requirements. The graphical models are easier for the customers to understand, and the simulation capabilities afforded by the formalization techniques enable developers to simulate the behavior of the requirements for validation purposes.

In terms of the Laprie Dependability tree (depicted in Figure 3), integrating informal and formal techniques enables us to address the attributes *safety, confidentiality, and integrity*. The means to address these attributes is through *fault prevention* and *fault tolerance*. The threats that are addressed by this approach are typically due to requirements and design *errors*.

4. General Integration Tasks

This paper has thus far focused on how informal and formal techniques can be integrated, as well as the benefits of their integration. For the purposes of the workshop, we can draw upon lessons learned from this type of integration when attempting to integrate analysis and development techniques from the three focus areas of the workshop: assurance, fault tolerance, and security.

4.1. Domain Analysis and Engineering

First, it is important to recognize that in order to make a significant impact with a specific type of development technique, particularly one involving automated techniques, it is useful to perform a thorough domain analysis. The domain analysis enables us to identify the key development needs and constraints for a particular application domain. For example, in the embedded systems domain, we would need to identify development techniques that had strong support for capturing state-based modeling. In contrast, an information-management system would require a development technique that has good support for representing complex data abstractions. During this assessment, it should be noted as to what types of verification and validation tasks will be needed. Is behavior simulation more important than being able to establish definitively the satisfaction of specific properties, such as constraint checks, consistency checks, safety, fairness, liveness, and absence of deadlock. What fault-tolerance properties need to be checked? Which of the dependability attributes need to be evaluated? What is the objective for development and maintenance (i.e., fault prevention, tolerance, forecasting, or removal)? What are the threats to be considered? (see Figure 3).

Based on this assessment, then we can proceed to make a formal methods evaluation. What types of formal methods will support the analysis needs? What tool support is available to support these types of analysis techniques?

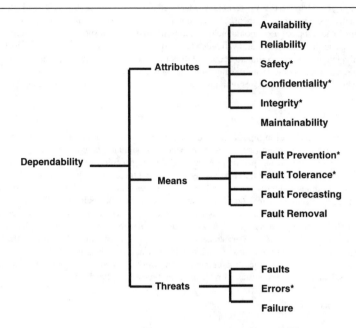

* Denotes those items relevant to the integration of informal and formal development techniques

Figure 3. Laprie's Dependability Tree

4.2. Common Framework

Before we can integrate analysis and development techniques from the three focus areas, we need to establish a universally recognized vocabulary and identify common areas of interest. In short, we need to develop a *common framework*. The Dependability tree can be used as a vehicle for determining universally understood vocabulary and identifying common goals. The common framework will facilitate communication between researchers from the different areas, as well as ensure that we are interacting with the customers in a consistent fashion.

While many things might be suitable for this common framework, three items are of particular note. First, we need to identify critical properties from each of the three fields that should be established for high assurance, fault-tolerant, and secure applications. Presumably, the exercise of identifying these critical properties will reveal the overlaps between properties from the three fields, as well as polymorphic terms. Again, the Laprie Dependability Tree can assist in distinguishing these properties. It is noted that not all applications will require all of these properties to be satisfied, but it provides a basis for verification and validation tasks for these types of systems. Second, we need to identify a systematic development process for building high assurance, fault-tolerant, and secure applications. In order to focus this effort, it might be useful to identify a specific class of applications (the next section discusses this issue further). This process should identify specific techniques that should be used for each stage of the development lifecycle. A driving force for this development process will be the collection of critical properties for these types of applications described above. These properties will help determine which techniques should be used and during which development stage(s). It is assumed that the techniques identified to establish these properties will cut across all three fields. Finally, the common framework should contain several repositories in addition to the critical properties collection. These repositories should include techniques and the corresponding tools to support the development process and the verification and validation tasks, specification patterns for critical properties in various specification languages, and complete documentation for case studies within the same domain area. The objective of the repositories is to promote reuse and integration of techniques and development artifacts for individual as well as integrative purposes with respect to assurance, fault-tolerance, and security.

4.3. Industrial-Strength Applications

Another key task in the integration process is to identify a specific application area as a target for the integration efforts. A specific problem (area) can guide what will populate the common framework. For example, researchers can identify what specific properties need to be specified and established for the area of electronic commerce, where it is clear that effort is needed from all three areas. Based on this assessment, appropriate analysis techniques and tools can be acquired and/or developed to be used within the framework. A specific problem gives researchers real problem parameters to instantiate their respective analysis and development techniques/tools. In addition, a real problem gives researchers realistic constraints and demands that need to be handled in order to ensure that the techniques are feasible and scalable. By focusing the integrative efforts on a specific problem, the researchers will have a tangible result to demonstrate the utility of their combined techniques. The common framework should serve as an evolving testbed for the integrative research activities. As results are obtained, the common framework can evolve to support refined and/or additional techniques, handle more properties, provide different types of feedback, and so on.

4.4. Integration Strategy

It is not practical to assume that researchers from all three communities will be able to instantaneously start working together and somehow make significant progress without some intermediate steps. For example, a pairwise approach to integration might be more feasible to determine if a common framework can be established between two areas. In many cases, efforts along these lines are already underway, such as formal methods and security and between formal methods and fault-tolerance. A common application domain can be used to focus these pairwise integration activities. The results will facilitate an overall integration effort among the researchers. The common framework that supports all three areas should be validated by using the same analysis and development techniques applied to a different problem domain. Therefore, if the initial common framework was developed according to the specifics of an electronic commerce domain, then attempting to apply the framework to a *Command and Control* system would force the researchers to handle potentially much more complex control logic issues, whereas applying the common framework to critical information systems, such as patient medical records, might require more complex data processing capabilities. The validation effort will guide the researchers to refine the integrated techniques.

5. Summary

In the past twenty-five years, there has been significant research conducted in the areas of formal methods, fault tolerance, and security. Unfortunately, the majority of the software development workforce do not use nor are they familiar with much of the work that has been done in these areas. While many application domains are not critical, that is they are not life-threatening, the exponentially increasing demand for software has forced new interest in these three areas, individually and collectively.

This paper has reviewed a research project that has integrated informal and formal development techniques in an effort to facilitate the use of formal techniques by a larger community. The results of this type of research can be integrated with research in all three areas to generally increase the use of techniques from these areas. The Laprie Dependability Tree can be used to focus the integrative research activities. Identifying common problem domains of interest can be a driving force for the integrative as well as the individual research directions.

The meeting has highlighted the need for integration, synthesis, and experimental research. Perhaps the Y2K issue has heightened our awareness of the potential impact of *ad hoc* approaches to software development. While there will continue to be a demand for "basic research", it is clear that in the areas of formal methods, security, and fault tolerance, there are exceedingly strong motivations to join efforts to address common problems and develop real solutions.

References

[1] J. Atlee and J. Gannon. State-based model checking of event-driven system requirements. In *Proceedings of the ACM SIGSOFT '91 Conference on Software for Critical Systems. Software Engineering Notes. Volume 16 Number 5*, 1991.
[2] V. Basili and B. Perricone. Software errors and complexity: an empirical investigation. *Communications of the ACM*, 21(1):42–52, January 1984.
[3] B. Boehm. Software engineering economics. *IEEE Transations on Software Engineering*, SE-10(1):4–21, January 1984.
[4] R. H. Bourdeau and B. H. C. Cheng. A formal semantics of object models. *IEEE Trans. on Software Engineering*, 21(10):799–821, October 1995.
[5] L. Campbell, B. H. Cheng, and E. Y. Wang. Enabling automated analysis through the formalization of object-oriented modeling diagrams. Technical Report MSU-CPS-99-13, Department of Computer Science and Engineering, Michigan State University, East Lansing, Michigan, March 99.
[6] B. H. C. Cheng. Automated Synthesis of Data Abstractions. In *Proc. of Irvine Software Symposium*, pages 161–176, June 1991.
[7] B. H. C. Cheng. Synthesis of Procedural Abstractions from Formal Specifications. In *Proc. of COMPSAC'91*, pages 149–154, September 1991.
[8] B. H. C. Cheng. Applying formal methods in automated software development. *Journal of Computer and Software Engineering*, 2(2):137–164, 1994.
[9] P. Coad and E. Yourdon. *Object-Oriented Analysis*. Yourdon Press, Prentice Hall, Englewood, New Jersey, 1990.
[10] D. Coleman, P. Arnold, S. Bodoff, C. Dollin, H. Gilchrist, F. Hayes, and P. Jeremaes. *Object-Oriented Development: The Fusion Method*. Object-Oriented Series. Prentice Hall, 1993.
[11] E. W. Dijkstra. *A Discipline of Programming*. Prentice Hall, Englewood Cliffs, New Jersey, 1976.
[12] S. Garland and J. Guttag. A guide to lp, the larch prover. Technical Report TR 82, DEC SRC, December 1991.
[13] D. Gries. *The Science of Programming*. Springer-Verlag, 1981.
[14] D. Harel. Statecharts: A visual formalism for complex systems. *Science of Computer Programming*, 8:231–274, 1987.
[15] M. P. Heimdahl and N. Leveson. Completeness and Consistency Analysis of State-Based Requirements. In *Proceedings of the 17th International Conference on Software Engineering*, Apr. 1995.
[16] C. L. Heitmeyer, B. L. Labaw, and D. Kiskis. Consistency checking of SCR-style requirements specifications. In *Proceedings of the International Symposium on Requirements Engineering*, March 1995.
[17] J. E. Hopcroft and J. D. Ullman. *Introduction to Automata Theory, Languages and Computation*. Addison-Wesley Publishing Company, Inc., 1979.
[18] J. Horning and J. Guttag. Larch shared language checker. Private communication.
[19] C. B. Jones. *Systematic Software Development Using VDM*. Prentice Hall International Series in Computer Science. Prentice Hall International (UK) Ltd., second edition, 1990.
[20] J. C. Kelly, J. S. Sherif, and J. Hops. An analysis of defect densities found during software inspections. *Journal of Systems Software*, 17:111–117, 1992.
[21] M. R. Laux, R. H. Bourdeau, and B. H. C. Cheng. An integrated development environment for formal specifications. In *Proc. of International Conference on Software Engineering and Knowledge Engineering*, pages 681–688, San Francisco, California, July 1993.
[22] LGI-IMAG and INRIA. CAESAR/ALDEBARAN. http://www.inrialpes.fr/vasy/cadp.html.
[23] R. R. Lutz. Targeting safety-related errors during software requirements analysis. In *SIGSOFT'93 Symposium on the Foundations of Software Engineering*, 1993.
[24] J. A. Mañas and T. de Miguel. From LOTOS to C. In K. Turner, editor, *Formal Description Techniques*, pages 79–84. Elsevier Science Publishers B.V., 1988.

[25] J. A. Mañas, T. de Miguel, T. Robles, J. Salvachúa, G. Huecas, and M. Veiga. TOPO: Quick reference: Front-end – version 3R1.

[26] W. E. McUmber and B. H. Cheng. UML-based analysis of embedded systems using a mapping to VHDL. Technical Report MSU-CPS-99-11, Department of Computer Science and Engineering, Michigan State University, East Lansing, Michigan, February 99.

[27] M. Morin and B. H. C. Cheng. Graphical Development Environment for Larch Shared and Interface Languages. Technical Report CPS-94-18, Michigan State University, Department of Computer Science, A714 Wells Hall, East Lansing, MI 48824-1027, April 1994.

[28] S. Pavon and M. Llamas. The testing functionalities of LOLA. In J. Quemada, J. A. Manas, and E. Vazquez, editors, *Formal Description Techniques*, volume III, pages 559–562. IFIP, Elsevier Science B.V. (North-Holland)., 1991.

[29] R. S. Pressman. *Software Engineering: A Practitioner's Approach*. McGraw Hill, third edition, 1992.

[30] J. Rumbaugh, M. Blaha, W. Premerlani, F. Eddy, and W. Lorensen. *Object-Oriented Modeling and Design*. Prentice Hall, Englewood Cliffs, New Jersey, 1991.

[31] J. Rumbaugh, I. Jacobson, and G. Booch. *The Unified Modeling Language Reference Manual*. Addison Wesley, 1999.

[32] J. Rushby. Formal methods and the certification of critical systems. Technical Report SRI-CSL-93-07, SRI International, Computer Science Laboratory, 333 Ravenswood Ave., Menlo Park, CA 94025-3493, November 1993. Available via anonymous ftp from ftp.csl.sri.com.

[33] D. R. Smith. KIDS: A Semi-automatic Program Development System. *IEEE Transactions on Software Engineering*, 16(9):1024–1043, September 1990.

[34] D. I. Telematica". TOPO. "topo@dit.upm.es".

[35] J. Q. Vives, S. P. Gómez, and D. L. López. LOLA: Quick reference version 3R6.

[36] E. Y. Wang and B. H. C. Cheng. Formalizing and integrating the functional model into object-oriented design. In *Proc. of International Conference on Software Engineering and Knowledge Engineering*, June 1998. Nominated for Best Paper.

[37] E. Y. Wang and B. H. C. Cheng. A rigorous object-oriented design process. In *Proc. of International Conference on Software Process*, Naperville, Illinos, June 1998.

[38] E. Y. Wang, H. A. Richter, and B. H. C. Cheng. Formalizing and integrating the dynamic model within OMT. In *Proc. of IEEE International Conference on Software Engineering (ICSE97)*, Boston, MA, May 1997.

[39] J. M. Wing. A Specifier's Introduction to Formal Methods. *IEEE Computer*, 23(9):8–24, September 1990.

[40] R. Wirfs-Brock, B. Wilkerson, and L. Wiener. *Designing Object-Oriented Software*. Prentice Hall, Englewood, New Jersey, 1990.

Error Recovery in Critical Infrastructure Systems

John C. Knight, Matthew C. Elder, Xing Du
Department of Computer Science
University of Virginia
Charlottesville, VA
{knight, elder, xd2a}@cs.virginia.edu

Abstract

Critical infrastructure applications provide services upon which society depends heavily; such applications require survivability in the face of faults that might cause a loss of service. These applications are themselves dependent on distributed information systems for all aspects of their operation and so survivability of the information systems is an important issue. Fault tolerance is a key mechanism by which survivability can be achieved in these information systems. Much of the literature on fault-tolerant distributed systems focuses on local error recovery by masking the effects of faults. We describe a direction for error recovery in the face of catastrophic faults where the effects of the faults cannot be masked using available resources. The goal is to provide continued service that is either an alternate or degraded service by reconfiguring the system rather than masking faults. We outline the requirements for a reconfigurable system architecture and present an error recovery system that enables systematic structuring of error recovery specifications and implementations.

1. Introduction

The provision of dependable service in infrastructure applications such as electric power generation and control, banking and financial systems, telecommunications, and transportation systems has become a major national concern [34], [35]. Society has become so dependent on such services that the loss of any of them would have serious consequences. Such services are often referred to as *critical infrastructure applications.*

As has occurred in many domains, sophisticated information systems have been introduced into critical infrastructure applications as the cost of all forms of computing hardware has dropped and the availability of sophisticated software has increased. This has led to dramatic efficiency improvements and service enhancements but, along with these benefits, a significant vulnerability has been introduced: the provision of service is now completely dependent in many cases on the correct operation of computerized information systems. Failure of an information system upon which a critical infrastructure application depends will often eliminate service quickly and completely. The dependability of the information systems, which we refer to as *critical information systems*, has therefore become a major concern.

Dependability has many facets—reliability, availability and safety, and so on [24]—and critical infrastructure applications have a variety of dependability requirements. In most cases, very high availability is important, but reliability and safety arise in such systems as transportation control, and security is becoming an increasingly significant dependability property in all application domains.

An important dependability requirement of critical infrastructure applications is that, under predefined adverse circumstances that preclude the provision of entirely normal service to the user, such systems must provide predefined forms of *alternate* service. The necessary service might be a degraded form of normal service, a different service, or some combination. Adverse circumstances might be widespread environmental damage, equipment failures, software failures, sophisticated malicious attacks, and so on. This particular dependability requirement is referred to as *survivability*. In the terminology of fault tolerance, survivability can be thought of as requiring very specific (and usually elaborate) error recovery after a fault.

This paper is about the mechanisms that are needed within the applications themselves to provide error recovery, i.e., state restoration and continued service, under circumstances where the application has been subjected to extreme damage. Application systems must be designed to permit effective state restoration and appropriate continued service, and we address the issues of application system design in this context. We are concerned with faults that affect either large parts of the system or the entire system and which cannot be masked. Thus, faults such as the failure of a single processor or a single communications link are not within the scope of this paper. Faults such as these can be tolerated by local redundancy and their effects can be totally masked at reasonable cost. Faults of interest include widespread physical damage in which substantial resources are lost, and coordinated security attacks in which multiple attacks occur in a short time period. We assume that error detection and damage assessment are taken care of by some other mechanism such as a control-system architecture [45].

The outline of the paper is as follows. In the next section we summarize briefly the functionality and characteristics of critical infrastructure applications and their associated information systems, and then present a detailed example of survivability. In section 4, we discuss the role of fault tolerance and the requirements for an approach to survivability. In section 5, we present some related work, and in section 6 we define directions for a solution approach. Finally, we present our conclusions.

2. Critical infrastructure applications

Some background material about critical infrastructure applications is helpful in understanding the technical approaches that might be developed to realize survivability. Detailed descriptions of four applications are available elsewhere [20]. In this section we summarize three applications very briefly and then outline a set of important characteristics that tend to be present in information systems supporting critical infrastructure applications. Finally in this section, we discuss characteristics of future critical infrastructure applications that impact approaches to survivability that might be developed.

2.1. Applications

The nation's banking and finance systems provide a very wide range of services—check clearing, ATM service, credit and debit card processing, securities and commodities markets, electronic funds transfers, foreign currency transfers, and so on. These services are implemented by complex, interconnected, networked information systems.

The most fundamental financial service is the payment system. The payment system is the mechanism by which value is transferred from one account to another. Transfers might be for relatively small amounts, as occur with personal checks, all the way up to very large amounts, typical of commercial transactions. For a variety of practical and legal reasons, individual banks do not communicate directly with each other to transfer funds. Rather, most funds are transferred in large blocks by either the Federal Reserve or by an Automated Clearing House (ACH).

The freight-rail transport system, another critical infrastructure application, moves large amounts of raw materials, manufactured good, fuels, and food. Although not responsible for moving everything in any one of these categories, loss of freight-rail transportation would be devastating. Management of the freight-rail system uses computers extensively for a variety of purposes. For example, every freight car in North America is tracked electronically as it moves and databases are maintained of car and locomotive locations. Tracking is achieved using track-side equipment that communicates in real time with computers maintaining the database.

An especially important application that is being used increasingly in the freight-rail system is just-in-time delivery. Train movements are scheduled so that, for example, raw materials arrive at a manufacturing plant just as they are required. This type of service necessitates analysis of demands and resources over a wide area, often nationally, if optimal choices are to be made.

The generation and distribution of electric power, the third critical infrastructure application we consider, is accomplished by a wide variety of generating, switching, and transmission equipment that is owned and operated by a number of different utility companies. However, all of this equipment is interconnected, and control is exercised over the equipment using a system that is rapidly becoming a single national network. The control mechanisms within a region are responsible for managing the equipment in that region and interconnection of area control mechanisms is responsible for arranging and managing power transfers between regions. The complexity of the control mechanisms in the power generation industry is being affected considerably by industry deregulation.

2.2. Application system characteristics

The architecture of the information systems upon which critical infrastructure applications rely are tailored very substantially to the services of the industries which they serve and influenced inevitably by cost-benefit trade-off's. For example, the systems are typically distributed over a very wide area with large numbers of nodes located at sites dictated by the application. Beyond this, however, there are a number of characteristics that these applications possess in whole or in part which are important in constraining the ways by which these applications approach error recovery. These characteristics are as follows:

- *Heterogeneous nodes.* Despite the large number of nodes in many of these systems, a small number of nodes are often far more critical to the functionality of the system than the remainder. This occurs because critical parts of the system's functionality are implemented on just one or a small number of nodes. Heterogeneity extends also to the hardware platforms, operating systems, application software, and even authoritative domains.

- *Stylized communication structures.* In a number of circumstances, critical infrastructure applications use dedicated, point-to-point links rather than fully-interconnected networks. Reasons for this approach include meeting application performance requirements, better security, and no requirement for full connectivity.

- *Composite functionality.* The service supplied to an end user is often attained by composing different functionality at different nodes. Thus entirely different programs running on different nodes provide different services, and complete service can only be obtained when several subsystems cooperate and operate in some predefined sequence. This is quite unlike more familiar applications such as mail servers routing mail through the Internet.

- *Performance requirements.* Some critical infrastructures applications, such as the financial payment system, have soft real-time constraints and throughput requirements (checks have to be cleared and there are lots of checks) while others, such as parts of many transportation systems and many energy control systems, have hard real-time constraints. In some systems, performance requirements change with time as load or functionality changes—over a period of hours in financial systems or over a period of days or months in transportation systems, for example.

- *Extensive databases.* Infrastructure applications are all about data. Many employ several very extensive databases with different databases being located at different nodes and with most databases handling very large numbers of transactions.

- *COTS and legacy components.* For all the usual reasons, critical infrastructure applications utilize COTS components including hardware, operating systems, network protocols, database systems, and applications. In addition, these systems contain legacy components—custom-built software that has evolved with the system over many years.

2.3. Future system characteristics

The characteristics listed in the previous section are important, and most are likely to remain so in systems of the future. But the rate of introduction of new technology into these systems and the introduction of entirely new types of application is rapid, and these suggest that error recovery techniques must take into account the likely characteristics of future systems also. We hypothesize that the following will be important architectural aspects of future infrastructure systems:

- *Very large number of nodes.* The number of nodes in infrastructure networks is likely to increase dramatically as enhancements are made in functionality, performance, and user access. The effect of this on error recovery is considerable. In particular, it suggests that error recovery will have to be regional in the sense that different parts of the network will require different recovery strategies. It also suggests that the implementation effort involved in error recovery will be substantial because there are likely to be many regions and there will be many different anticipated faults, each of which might require different treatment.

- *Extensive, low-level redundancy.* As the cost of hardware continues to drop, more redundancy will be built into low-level components of systems. Examples include mirrored disks and redundant server groups. This will simplify error recovery in the case of low-level faults; however, catastrophic errors will still require sophisticated recovery strategies.

- *Packet-switched networks.* For many reasons, the Internet is becoming the network technology of choice in the construction of new systems, in spite of its inherent drawbacks (e.g. poor security and performance guarantees). However, the transition to packet-switched networks, whether it be the current Internet or virtual-private networks implemented over some incarnation of the Internet, seems inevitable and impacts solution approaches for error recovery.

3. Survivability—an example

In this section, we present an example of survivability requirements to illustrate the extent, scope, and complexity of the error recovery that might well be needed in a typical critical infrastructure application. We use as an example application a *highly* simplified version of the national financial payment system. It is important to note that, inevitably, most of the details of the payment system are missing from this example and simplifications have been made since we seek only to illustrate certain points. The interested reader is referred to the text by Summers for comprehensive details of the payment system [46]. In addition, the faults and continued service requirements in this example are *entirely* hypothetical and designed for illustration only, but characteristic of strategies that might be employed for error recovery.

3.1. System architecture and application functionality

The information system that implements a major part of the payment system is very roughly a hierarchic, tree-like network as illustrated in Figure 1. At the top level is a central facility operated by the Federal Reserve. At the second level are the twelve regional Federal Reserve banks. At the third level of the tree are the approximately 9,500 commercial banks that are members of the Federal Reserve. Finally, at the lowest level of hierarchy are the remaining 16,500 or so banks and their branch banks [20].

Processing a retail payment (an individual check) in this system proceeds roughly as follows. At the lowest level, nodes simply accept checks, create an electronic description of the relevant information, and forward the details to the next level in the hierarchy. At the next level, payments to different banks are collected together in a batch and the details forwarded to the Federal Reserve system. Periodically (typically once a day) the Federal Reserve moves funds between accounts that it maintains for commercial banks and then funds are disbursed

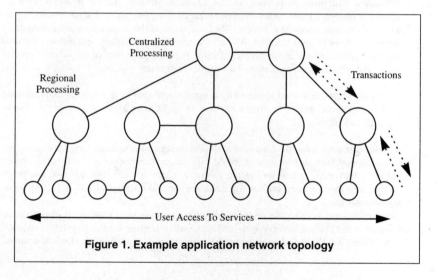

Figure 1. Example application network topology

down through the system to individual user accounts. Large commercial payments originate electronically and are handled individually as they are presented.

Extensive amounts of data are maintained throughout this system. User account information is maintained at central facilities by retail banks, and this information provides all the expected user services together with check authentication (as occurs when a check is scanned at a retail outlet). The Federal Reserve maintains accounts for all its member banks together with detailed logs and status information about payment activity. But, of course, this is just a small part of the data maintained by the banking and financial system. Vast amounts of data are also needed for all the other financial services, and the databases are used in combination and in different ways by different services.

3.2. Survivability requirements

A complete survivability specification must document precisely all of the faults that the system is required to handle and, for each, document the prescribed system response. Hypothetical examples of the possible faults and their high-level responses for our simplified version of the payments system are shown in Table 1. We include in the table faults ranging from the loss of a single leaf node to the loss of the a critical node and its backup facilities.

For purposes of illustration, we examine one particular fault in more detail to see what error recovery actions are needed. The fault we use for illustration is the loss of the top-level node of the financial payment system—the Federal Reserve system's main data center and its backup facilities. Using our highly simplified architecture of the payment system in this example, we assume that this node consists of a single processing entity with a single backup that maintains mirror image databases. The actual Federal Reserve system uses a much more sophisticated backup system. The survivability requirements for this fault are the following:

- *Fault:* Federal Reserve main processing center failure (common-mode software failure, propagation of corrupt data, terrorism).

- *On failure:* Complete suspension of all payment services. Entire financial network informed (member banks, other financial organizations, foreign banks, government agencies). Previously identified Federal Reserve regional bank designated as temporary replacement for Federal facilities. All services terminated at replacement facility, minimal payment service started at replacement facility (e.g., payment service for federal agencies only). All communication redirected for major client nodes.

- *On repair:* Payment system restarted by resuming applications in sequence and resuming service to member banks in sequence within an application. Minimal service on replacement facility terminated.

For this particular fault, we assume that all processing ceases immediately. This is actually the most benign fault that the system could experience at the top-level node. More serious faults that could occur include undetected hardware failure in which data was lost, a software fault that corrupted primary and backup databases, and an operational failure in which primary data was lost.

State restoration in this case involves establishing a consistent state at all of the clients connected to the Federal Reserve system. This requires determining the transaction requests that have been sent to the Federal Reserve but not processed. Since this is a standard database

Table 1. Survivability requirements summary

Fault	Response
Single local bank fails (local power failure, hardware failure, operator error).	*On failure:* Local bank ceases service. Regional center buffers transactions for local bank. *On repair:* Local bank informs regional center. Regional center transmits transaction backlog. Regional center resumes transaction transmission. Local branch resumes normal service.
Multiple local banks fail (wide-area power failure, wide-area environmental stress, common-mode software failure).	*On failure:* Local banks cease service. Regional center buffers transactions for local banks. Regional center starts minimal user services (e.g., electronic funds transfer for selected major customers only). *On repair:* Local banks inform regional center as they are repaired. Regional center transmits transaction backlog. Regional center resumes transaction transmission. Local branch resumes normal service. Regional center terminates minimal user services.
Security penetrations of multiple local banks associated with a single commercial bank (coordinated security attack).	*On failure:* Each local bank ceases service and disconnects itself from the network when its local intrusion alarm is raised. Federal Reserve suspends operations with commercial member bank under attack and buffers all transactions for that bank. *On repair:* Reset all nodes owned by commercial bank under attack. All nodes change cryptographic keys and switch to aggressive intrusion detection. System-wide restart of crucial services only.
Regional center primary site fails (power failure, hardware failure, software failure, operational error, environmental stress).	*On failure:* Primary site ceases service. Backup site starts service. All connected nodes informed. All communications—up to Federal system and down to branches—switched from primary to backup. Appropriate service selection made—full or reduced. Appropriate switch selection made—instantaneous or delayed. *On repair:* Primary site informs all connected nodes that it is repaired. Primary site databases synchronized. Communications switched. Primary site resumes services in prescribed priority order. Backup site ceases service.
Regional center primary *and* backup sites fail (wide-area power failure, common-mode software failure, wide-area environmental stress, terrorism).	*On failure:* Primary and backup sites cease service. All connected nodes informed. Previously identified local bank processing center designated as temporary replacement for regional facilities. All services terminated at replacement facility, minimal regional service started at replacement facility (e.g., account services for commercial and government clients only). *On repair:* Regional service restarted by resuming applications in sequence and resuming service to local banks in sequence within an application. Minimal service on replacement facility terminated.

issue, we do not consider it further. We note, however, that notification or detection of failure by the clients is an essential element of error recovery.

The provision of continued service is more complex in this fault scenario. Given the loss of the most critical node in the network with a tree topology, the network is now effectively partitioned. One part of error recovery will involve re-establishing connectivity between the partitioned subtrees, each of which has a Federal Reserve regional bank at its top node. There are a number of alternatives for re-establishing connectivity:

- Promote one regional bank to be the new root node in the tree and have all other regional banks establish links to it. (This requires 11 new links to be established.)

- Establish links between each pair of regional banks, resulting in a fully-interconnected 12-node network. (This requires 66 new links to be established.)

- Establish links to provide some other topology; for example, connect the 12 regional banks with a ring topology. (This requires 12 new links to be established.)

In practice, it is unlikely that any of the above three alternatives would be used. A combination using different strategies in different locations is the most likely approach and it is very possible that even in this case parts of the network would remain unconnected.

Once whatever connectivity that is possible is reestablished, a major reorganization through the network would be required. First, the new root of the tree will have to suspend most but probably all of its normal service activities. Second this node will have to prepare the copies of the databases that are needed for payment processing and that it would have to have maintained during normal processing if it were to function as an emergency backup. Third, the entire set of clients will have to be informed of the change and of the level of service that will be provided and when this will occur. These clients will have to take their own actions including eliminating many services, reducing others, and perhaps starting certain emergency services. Fourth, the new root node will have to initiate payment applications up to the limit of the processing and communications capacity that was available. The available capacity will be greatly reduced and the services that the system could provide once operational would be far less that would normally be the case. Which customers get what service would have to be have been defined ahead of time as part of the survivability specification.

Much more complex but probably more useful recovery scenarios are possible for critical services if a restricted form of service is acceptable. For example, one of the services of the Federal Reserve is maintenance of member bank accounts. Maintenance of member bank accounts could be taken over by the temporary replacement node but, because of reduced facilities, services would be severely reduced. This function could be distributed following a catastrophic failure, however. We consider two possible solution strategies:

- Each member bank maintains only its own account details, and only sends a batch message to be processed if it has the funds to cover the deposit. (This approach distributes responsibility for maintaining positive balances.)

- Each regional bank maintains an account balance for every other regional bank with which it exchanges batch messages. (This approach requires more resources, but allows more value to be transferred throughout the system.)

The details of the fault scenario we have described in this example are possible from the computer science perspective as are many others. What the banking community requires in practice depends upon the many details and priorities that exist within that domain and will probably be far more elaborate that our example. However, our example does illustrate many of the issues that have to be considered in application error recovery and shows how complex this process is.

An important aspect of survivability that is omitted form this example is the need to cope with multiple sequential faults. It will be the case in many circumstances that a situation gets worse over time. For example, a terrorist attack on the physical equipment of a critical information system might proceed in a series of stages. The attack might be detected initially during an early stage (although it is highly unlikely that the detection process would be able to diagnose a cause in this case) and the system would then take appropriate action. Subsequent failures of physical equipment would have to be dealt with by a system that had already been reconfigured to deal with the initial attack. This complicates the provision of error recovery immensely.

4. Survivability and fault tolerance

4.1. The role of fault tolerance

In general, survivability is a requirement or a set of related requirements that a system must meet. As illustrated by the example above, the requirements can be quite complex and will often involve many different aspects of the application. For different faults that a system might experience, the requirements that have to be met might be quite different from each other and require entirely different actions by the application. In particular, for critical infrastructure applications, it will often be the case that the effects of a fault leave the system with greatly reduced resources (processing services, communications capacity, etc.) and substantial changes in the service provided to the user will be necessary.

Fault tolerance is one of the mechanisms by which dependability (and thus survivability) can be obtained. It is not the only mechanism of course since fault elimination and fault removal are often alternate (and complementary) possibilities. In the case of critical infrastructure applications, however, the manifestation of faults during operation is inevitable. Such systems cannot be protected against all environmental damage, terrorist acts, operational mistakes, software defects, and so on. Thus, adding the ability to tolerate certain types of fault is the only practical approach to achieving survivability.

Tolerating a fault does not necessarily mean masking its effects, however. The essential meaning of survivability is the ability of a system to deal with more "serious" faults by providing a prescribed service that is not the same as the normal service. The catastrophic faults to which a system of interest must respond are those that are not masked, i.e. by design there is insufficient redundancy for the system to be able to handle the faults transparently. If it were intended that the system mask such faults, as will be the case for many faults, then the system would do so. Catastrophic faults that are not masked in any given system are not necessarily unanticipated. Rather, a conscious decision is made in favor of an approach to error recovery other than masking because the cost of handling faults transparently is redundancy. And redundancy is expensive. Some redundancy is necessary even if a fault is not to be masked, and, in addition, redundancy is necessary for the detection of errors. However, replicating all the elements of a critical information system so that all faults of interest can be masked is prohibitively expensive.

Since we are concerned with faults whose effects will not be masked, fault tolerance in general requires actions by the application. The particular actions required in any given system are application-specific but they will require such functionality as stopping some services, starting others, and modifying yet others. In order to make such changes, the application must be prepared to make the changes and so must be designed with this in mind.

For purposes of analysis, we view an application executing on a distributed system as a concurrent program with one or more processes running on each node and with processes communicating via a protocol that operates over network links. Although there is no shared memory in the conventional sense, it is very likely that there are shared files. This view is useful because it permits existing work on fault tolerance in concurrent systems to act as a starting point from which to develop application error recovery mechanisms in the sense that we desire.

4.2. Requirements for a solution

The general requirements that have to be met by any realistic approach to application error recovery derive from the characteristics of the applications and the need to tolerate serious faults that cannot be masked. More precisely, we identify the following solution requirements:

- *Very large networks running sophisticated applications must be supported.* The scale of critical infrastructure applications necessitates a solution approach that scales to networks with thousands of nodes. Similarly, the size of the application software presents significant performance challenges that must be met.

- *Resuming normal processing following the repair of fault must be supported.* The problem of dealing with the effects of a fault is really only half of the problem. The systems of interest typically have very high availability requirements and will be repaired while in operation. Thus, resuming prescribed levels of service after repair must be part of any viable solution.

- *There must be minimal application re-write required.* For many reasons—economic, political, technical, and otherwise—it is nearly impossible to re-write the software within critical information systems from scratch. Critical information systems will most likely have to evolve to provide improved survivability; however, the extensive use of COTS and legacy software currently in these systems complicates revision of the software. Revision to the applications must be kept to a minimum, but the application will have to make provision for support of new error recovery services.

- *Error recovery must be performed securely.* Security attacks against these systems are a major threat. It must be the case that any new error recovery services that are provided do not introduce an additional security vulnerability that can be exploited to perpetrate further damage to the system.

- *Link failure and partitioning are errors that must be handled.* The stylized connection structure of most critical infrastructure applications dictates that, by default, every node will not be able to communicate with every other node. This introduces the possibility that a link failure will partition the network. Because the service provided is composed of functionality provided by multiple application nodes, error recovery must include strategies for circumventing link failure and network partitions.

- *There are highly structured requirements for continued service.* The requirements for continued service will not be homogenous—in fact they will be far from it. Different nodes and different node classes will be required to implement different services. Similarly, nodes in different geographic regions might be called upon to act differently after a fault. Complicating the problem even further is the virtual certainty that different services on different nodes will have to be coordinated and that the coordination might have a hierarchic structure given the topology of the system.

In seeking an approach to meeting these requirements, we begin by reviewing previous work in a variety of areas and then we proceed to discuss a direction for solution.

5. Related work

Developments in several technical fields can be exploited to help deal with the problem of error recovery in distributed applications. In this section we review related work in the areas of system-level approaches to fault tolerance, fault tolerance in wide-area networking applications, reconfigurable distributed systems, and system specification and architectural description languages.

5.1. System-level approaches to fault tolerance

Jalote presents an excellent framework for fault tolerance in distributed systems [19]. Jalote structures the various services and approaches to fault tolerance into levels of abstraction. The layers, from highest to lowest, of a fault-tolerant distributed system according to Jalote are shown in Figure 2. Each level of abstraction provides services for tolerating faults, and in most cases there are many mechanisms and approaches for implementing the given abstraction. At the lowest level of abstraction above the distributed system itself are the building blocks of fault tolerance, including fail-stop processors, stable storage, reliable message delivery, and synchronized clocks. One level above that is another important building block—reliable and atomic broadcast; different protocols provide different guarantees with respect to reliability, ordering, and causality of broadcast communication. The levels above that provide the services upon which systems can be built to tolerate certain types of fault, including abstractions for atomic actions and processes and data resilient to low-level failures. Finally, the highest level of abstraction enables tolerance of design faults in the software itself.

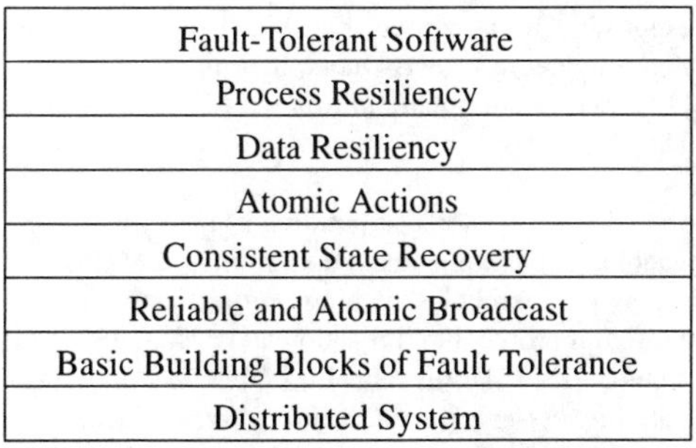

Fault-Tolerant Software
Process Resiliency
Data Resiliency
Atomic Actions
Consistent State Recovery
Reliable and Atomic Broadcast
Basic Building Blocks of Fault Tolerance
Distributed System

Figure 2. Levels of a fault-tolerant distributed system [19]

Given this framework for fault tolerance in distributed systems, many system-level approaches exist that provide various subsets of abstractions and services. In this subsection we survey some of the existing work on fault-tolerant system architectures.

5.1.1. Cristian/Advanced Automation System: Cristian provided a survey of the issues involved in providing fault-tolerant distributed systems [11]. He presented two requirements for a fault-tolerant system: 1) mask failures when possible, and 2) ensure clearly specified failure semantics when masking is not possible. The majority of his work, however, dealt with the masking of failures.

An instantiation of Cristian's fault tolerance concepts was used in the replacement Air Traffic Control (ATC) system, called the Advanced Automation System (AAS). The AAS utilized Cristian's fault-tolerant architecture [14]. Cristian described the primary requirement of the air traffic control system as ultra-high availability and stated that the approach taken is to design a system that can automatically mask multiple concurrent component failures.

The air traffic control system described by Cristian handled relatively low-level failures: redundancy of components was utilized and managed in order to mask these faults. Cristian structured the fault-tolerant architecture using a "depends-on" hierarchy, and modelled the system in terms of servers, services, and a "uses" relation. Redundancy was used to mask both hardware and software failures at the highest-level of abstraction, the application level. Redundancy was managed by application software server groups [14].

5.1.2. Birman/ISIS, Horus, and Ensemble: A work similar to that of Cristian is the "process-group-based computing model" presented by Birman. Birman introduced a toolkit called ISIS that contains system support for process group membership, communication, and synchronization. ISIS balanced trade-off's in closely synchronized distributed execution (which offers easy understanding) and asynchronous execution (which achieves better performance through pipelined communication) by providing the virtual synchrony approach to group communication. ISIS facilitated group-based programming by providing a software infrastructure to support process group abstractions. Both Birman and Cristian's work addressed a "process-group-based computing model," though Cristian's AAS also provided strong real-time guarantees made possible by an environment with strict timing properties [8].

Work on ISIS proceeded in subsequent years resulting in another group communications system, Horus. The primary benefit of Horus over ISIS is a flexible communications architecture that can be varied at runtime to match the changing requirements of the application and environment. Horus achieves this flexibility using a layered protocol architecture in which each module is responsible for a particular service [47]. Horus also works with a system called Electra, which provided a CORBA-compliant interface to the process group abstraction in Horus [26]. Another system that built on top of Electra and Horus together, Piranha, provided high availability by supporting application monitoring and management facilities [27].

Horus was succeeded by a new tool for building adaptive distributed programs, Ensemble. Ensemble further enabled application adaptation through a stackable protocol architecture as well as system support for protocol switching. Performance improvements were also provided in Ensemble through protocol optimization and code transformations [48].

An interesting note on ISIS, Horus, and Ensemble was that all three acknowledged the security threats to the process group architecture and each incorporated a security architecture into its system [38], [39], [40].

5.1.3. Other system-level approaches: Another example of fault tolerance that focuses on communication abstractions is the work of Schlichting. The result of this work is a system called Coyote that supports configurable communication protocol stacks. The goals are similar to that of Horus and Ensemble, but Coyote generalizes the composition of microprotocol modules allowing non-hierarchical composition (Horus and Ensemble only support hierarchical composition). In addition, Horus and Ensemble are focusing primarily on group communication services while Coyote supports a variety of high-level network protocols [7].

Many of the systems mentioned above focus on communication infrastructure and protocols for providing fault tolerance; another approach focuses on transactions in distributed systems as the primary primitive for providing fault tolerance. One of the early systems supporting transactions was Argus, developed at MIT. Argus was a programming language and support system that defined transactions on software modules, ensuring persistence and recoverability [9].

Another transaction-based system, Arjuna, was developed at the University of Newcastle upon Tyne. Arjuna is an object-oriented programming system that provides atomic actions on objects using C++ classes [42]. The atomic actions ensure that all operations support the properties of serializability, failure atomicity, and permanence of effect.

5.2. Fault tolerance in wide-area network applications

Fault tolerance is typically applied to relatively small-scale systems, dealing with single processor failures and very limited redundancy. Critical information systems are many orders of magnitude larger than the distributed systems that most of the previous work has addressed. There are, however, a few research efforts addressing fault tolerance in large-scale, wide-area network systems.

In the WAFT project, Marzullo and Alvisi are concerned with the construction of fault-tolerant applications in wide-area networks. Experimental work has been done on the Nile system, a distributed computing solution for a high-energy physics project. The primary goal of the WAFT project is to adapt replication strategies for large-scale distributed applications with dynamic (unpredictable) communication properties and a requirement to withstand security attacks. Nile was implemented on top of CORBA in C++ and Java. The thrust of the work thus far is that active replication is too expensive and often unnecessary for these wide-area network applications; Marzullo and Alvisi are looking to provide support for passive replication in a toolkit [3].

The Eternal system, built by Melliar-Smith and Moser, is middleware that operates in a CORBA environment, below a CORBA ORB but on top of their Totem group communication system. The primary goal is to provide transparent fault tolerance to users [32].

Babaoglu and Schiper are addressing problems with scaling of conventional group technology. Their approach for providing fault tolerance in large-scale distributed systems consists of distinguishing between different roles or levels for group membership and providing different service guarantees to each level [6].

5.3. Reconfigurable distributed systems

Given the body of literature on fault tolerance and the different services being provided at each abstraction layer, many types of faults can be addressed. However, the most serious fault—the catastrophic, non-maskable fault—is not addressed in any of the previous work. The previous approaches rely on having sufficient redundancy to cope with the fault and mask it; there are always going to be classes of faults for which this is not possible. For these faults, reconfiguration of the existing services on the remaining platform is required.

Considerable work has been done on reconfigurable distributed systems. Some of the work deals with reconfiguration for the purposes of evolution, as in the CONIC system, and, while this work is relevant, it is not directly applicable because it is concerned with reconfiguration that derives from the need to upgrade rather than cope with major faults. Less work has been done on reconfiguration for the purposes of fault tolerance. Both types of research are explored in this section.

5.3.1. Reconfiguration supporting system evolution: The initial context of the work by Kramer and Magee was dynamic configuration for distributed systems, incrementally integrating and upgrading components for system evolution. CONIC, a language and distributed support system, was developed to support dynamic configuration. The language enabled specification of system configuration as well as change specifications, then the support system provided configuration tools to build the system and manage the configuration [22].

More recently, they have modelled a distributed system in terms of processes and connections, each process abstracted down to a state machine and passing messages to other processes (nodes) using the connections. One relevant finding of this work is that components must migrate to a "quiescent state" before reconfiguration to ensure consistency through the reconfiguration; basically, a quiescent state entailed not being involved in any transactions. The focus remains on the incremental changes to a distributed system configuration for evolutionary purposes [23].

The successor to CONIC, Darwin, is a configuration language that separates program structure from algorithmic behavior [31]. Darwin utilizes a component- or object-based approach to system structure in which components encapsulate behavior behind a well-defined interface. Darwin is a declarative binding language that enables distributed programs to be constructed from hierarchically-structured specifications of component instances and their interconnections [28].

5.3.2. Reconfiguration supporting fault tolerance: Purtilo developed the Polylith Software Bus, a software interconnection system that provides a module interconnection language and interfacing facilities (software toolbus). Basically, Polylith encapsulates all of the interfacing details for an application, where all software components communicate with each other through the interfaces provided by the Polylith software bus [36].

Hofmeister extended Purtilo's work by building additional primitives into Polylith for support of reconfigurable applications. Hofmeister studied the types of reconfigurations that are possible within applications and the requirements for supporting reconfiguration. Hofmeister leveraged heavily off of Polylith's interfacing and message-passing facilities in order to ensure state consistency during reconfiguration [18].

Welch and Purtilo have extended Hofmeister's work in a particular application domain, Distributed Virtual Environments. They utilize Polylith and its reconfiguration extensions in a toolkit that helps to guide the programmer in deciding on proper reconfigurations and implementations for these simulation applications [49].

5.4. System specification and architectural description languages

Finally, many issues related to system and software architecture arise in the description and analysis of complex distributed systems. It is helpful, therefore, to be able to describe these architectures in a concise and comprehensive manner. A specification technology that suggests itself for systems of such magnitude is architectural description languages (ADLs). ADLs describe a particular piece of a system, the architecture in terms of components and connectors. A focus of architectural description languages is often that the specification of the architecture provide a mechanism to facilitate automatic construction of the distributed system [16].

Magee and Kramer's work on Darwin is an example of an architectural description language intended to facilitate construction of distributed systems. The Darwin language has a precise semantics that enables the construction of distributed systems from their specification in Darwin. The work has evolved from specifying and executing dynamic changes in a distributed system to specification of a distributed system and generation of its implementation; though Darwin still provides facilities for specification of dynamic change, elaboration of a Darwin specification is an important goal as well [30].

There are many other architectural description languages, each with its own focus and goals. Allen and Garland proposed the Wright architectural specification language in order to support direct specification and analysis of architectural description. A key idea behind Wright is that interaction relationships between components of a software system should be directly specified, in the case of Wright as protocols describing the interaction [2].

Shaw et al. proposed an informal model for an architectural description language, then developed an initial system for architectural description, UniCon. Their work is based upon recognizing common patterns in software architectures, such as pipe and filter, implicit invocation, etc., and then providing abstraction mechanisms for those element types [41].

Luckham et al. developed a specification system for prototyping architectures of distributed systems using an event-based, concurrent, object-oriented language, Rapide. Rapide allows the simulation and behavioral analysis of software system architectures during the development process [25].

Finally, Moriconi and Qian explored the process of transforming an abstract software architecture into an instance architecture correctly and incrementally using refinements [33].

6. A solution direction

Despite the many results that have been achieved in survivability and related fields, existing technology does not satisfy the requirements for a solution that were identified in Section 4.2. In this section, we describe a solution direction for error recovery (state restoration and continued service) in critical information systems following catastrophic, non-masked failures. The solution direction is conceptual and is based on previous work in the areas of fault tolerance and reconfigurable distributed systems. Many detailed issues are identified in the development of this solution direction.

Figure 3 shows the general layered structure that we anticipate in a single node. Note that our solution direction does not address *local* faults. By local, we mean faults that affect a single hardware or software component. We assume that all faults that are local are dealt with by some mechanism that masks their effects. In Figure 3 this functionality would be provided by mechanisms associated with the local recovery layer. Thus synchronized, replicated hardware components are assumed so that losses of single processors, disk drives, communications links, and so on are masked by hardware redundancy. If necessary, more sophisticated techniques such as virtual synchrony can be used to ensure that the application is unaffected by local failures.

The faults with which we are concerned, faults that are not masked, are dealt with by the global recovery layer shown in Figure 3. The high-level concept that we suggest is the use of formal specification to define the survivability requirements together with synthesis of the

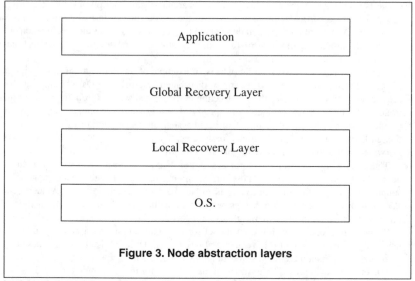

Figure 3. Node abstraction layers

implementation of the application. The synthesized system would use the global recovery layer to achieve error recovery.

We begin by explaining this concept and then review the details including the system software architecture used in each node. Finally, we discuss some of the implementation details.

6.1. Specification and synthesis

The size of current and expected critical information systems, the variety and sophistication of the services they provide, and the complexity of the survivability requirements means that a solution approach that depends upon traditional development techniques is infeasible in all but the simplest cases. The likelihood is that future systems will involve tens of thousands of nodes, have to tolerate dozens, perhaps hundreds, of different types of fault, and have to support applications that provide very elaborate user services. Programming such a system using conventional methods is quite impractical, and so our solution direction is based on the use of a formal specification to describe the required application reconfiguration and the use of synthesis to generate the implementation from the formal specification. The approach is illustrated in Figure 4.

There are many advantages to working with specifications rather than implementations. First and foremost is the ability to specify solutions at a high-level, thereby abstracting away to some extent the details of working with so many nodes, of so many different types, that provide so many different services. An implementation-based solution would require too much work, dealing with such a wide variety of nodes, applications, errors, and recovery strategies at a lower level. In addition, specifications provide the ability to reason about and analyze solutions at a higher level. An implementation synthesized from a specification also allows recovery strategies to be changed quickly; different error recovery schemes can be rapidly prototyped and explored using a specification-based approach.

Precise specification of the error recovery in a critical information system is a complex undertaking. It involves three major sub-specifications: (1) the topology of the system and a

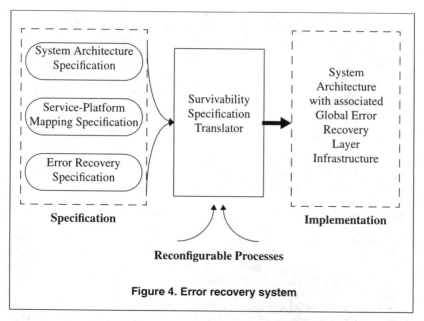

Figure 4. Error recovery system

detailed description of the architecture and platform; (2) an abstraction of the services each node supplies to the system and the mapping of services to platform for cases involving full functionality and degraded or alternate service; and (3) a specification of the necessary state changes from any acceptable system reconfiguration to any other in terms of topology, functionality, and geometry (assignment of services to nodes). More precisely, the sub-specifications that together make up the input to the translator are the following:

- *System Architecture Specification (SAS)*. The system architecture specification describes the nodes and links, including detailed parametric information for key characteristics. For example, nodes are named and described additionally with node type, hardware details, operating system, software versions, and so on. Links are specified with connection type and bandwidth capabilities, for example.

- *Service-Platform Mapping Specification (SPMS)*. The service-platform mapping specification relates the names of programs to the node names described in the SAS. The program descriptions in the SPMS include the services that each program provides, including alternate and degraded service modes.

- *Error Recovery Specification (ERS)*. The overall structure of the specification is that of a finite-state machine that characterizes the requisite responses to each fault. Arcs are labelled with faults and show the state transitions for each fault from every relevant state. The actions associated with any given transition are extensive because each action is essentially a high-level program that implements the error recovery component of the full system survivability specification. The full system survivability specification names the different states (system environments) that the system can be in, including the errors that will be detected and handled. The ERS takes this list of system states and describes the actions—i.e., reconfigurations—that must be performed when the system transitions from one environment to another. The ERS uses the SAS and the SPMS to describe the different system configurations and alternate service modes under each system state.

We make no specific comments about the syntax that might be used for these notations. However, existing work on architectural description languages provides an excellent starting point for the development of syntax and precise semantics.

6.2. Reconfigurable processes

We define a specialized type of application process, the *reconfigurable process*, that is used as the building block for critical information systems. The key specialization is that a reconfigurable process supports certain *critical services* that are needed for error recovery in addition to implementing some aspect of the required system functionality. A critical information system is then a collection of reconfigurable processes that cooperate in the normal way to implement normal application functionality. However, they can be manipulated using their critical-service interfaces to prepare for error recovery and to effect that recovery.

The importance of the addition of critical services is that they are the basic services needed for reconfiguration and they are available with every process. Thus the survivability specification need not be concerned with the idiosyncrasies of individual node functionality. As an example of critical service, consider the obvious implementation requirement that some processes in a system undergoing error recovery will need to be started and others stopped. A critical service that processes must provide is the ability to be started and another is the ability to be stopped. Neither of these actions is trivial, in fact, and neither can be left to the basic services of the operating system.

A second more detailed example of a critical service arises in the provision of backward error recovery. In the event that a system designer wishes to exploit a backward-error recovery mechanism, he or she will want to be sure that all the processes involved are capable of establishing recovery points and that groups of processes are capable of discarding them in synchrony. Since this is such a basic facility in the context of error recovery, a set of critical services is required to permit the manipulation of recovery points.

The following is a preliminary list of the critical services that a reconfigurable process has to support:

- Start, suspend, resume, terminate, delay.

- Change process priority.

- Report prescribed status information.

- Establish recovery point, discard recovery point.

- Effect local forward recovery by manipulation of local state information (e.g., reset the state).

- Switch to an alternate application function as specified by a parameter.

- Database management functions such as synchronizing copies, creating copies, withdrawing transactions, and restoring a default state.

The critical services are conceptually simple in many cases but this simplicity is deceptive. Many application processes will include very extensive functionality and this functionality does not necessarily accommodate services such as process suspension. Far worse are situations that involve processes which manipulate databases. Such processes will have to be very carefully developed if the creation of a checkpoint is to be efficient.

6.3. Node architecture

Each node in a critical information system that supports comprehensive error recovery using the approach outlined here will have a fixed (but not a restrictive) architecture. The basic application will be constructed in a standard manner as a collection of processes each of which is enhanced to support critical services. Under benign circumstances, these processes execute in a normal manner and provide normal functionality. Their critical services will be used periodically in a proactive manner to make provision for some form of recovery such as the establishment of recovery points or the forced synchronization of a database with backup copies.

The most obvious architectural requirement that has to be met at each node is that the node architecture support the provision of the various forms of degraded service associated with each fault. The software that implements degraded service is provided by application or domain experts, and the details (functional, performance, design, etc.) of this software are not part of the approach being outlined here. In practice, the way in which the software that provides degraded service is organized is not an issue either. The various degraded modes could be implemented as cases within a single process or as separate processes, as the designer chooses.

The interface between the node and the error detection mechanism (the control system) is a communications path from the control system to an *actuator* resident on the node. The actu-

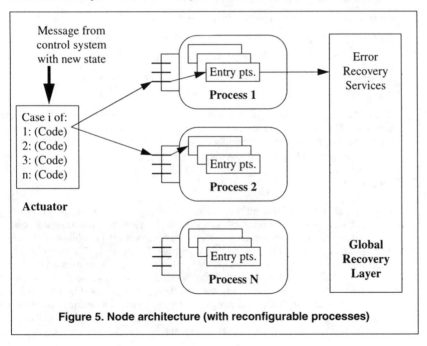

Figure 5. Node architecture (with reconfigurable processes)

ator is a process that accepts notifications from the control system about erroneous states and undertakes the actions needed on that node to cope with the errors. Thus, the actuator implements the changes dictated by the survivability specification, and it does this by making the necessary changes to the node's software using the critical services of the various reconfigurable processes. The actuator implementation is synthesized by the survivability specification translator.

6.4. Critical service implementation

The critical services provided by a reconfigurable process are implemented by the process itself in the sense that the service is accessed by a remote procedure call (or similar) and a mechanism internal to the process implements the service. The exact way in which the implementation is done will be system specific but an obvious layered architecture that supports this implementation suggests itself (see Figure 3).

The global recovery layer provides the interface that is used in the implementation of critical services within reconfigurable processes. The following is a preliminary list of the functions that the global recovery layer has to support:

- Process synchronization.

- Inter-process communication.

- Multicast to a set of processes.

- Establishment of a checkpoint for a process.

- Establishment of a set of coordinated checkpoints for a group of processes.

- Restoration of the state of a process from a checkpoint.

- Restoration of the states of a group of processes from a set of checkpoints.

- Reset of a process' state in support of forward error recovery.

- Synchronizing two or more processes to establish lock-step operation.

- Redirection of communication.

The global recovery layer would provide these services in a largely application-independent manner. Thus, a common global recovery layer implementation could be used by multiple applications with initial configuration achieved by generation parameters such as a process name table and target system topology.

7. Conclusion

In this paper, we have explored the problem of error recovery in critical infrastructure applications, from needs to solutions. We have described the problem context (system characteristics and survivability requirements) and solution framework (fault tolerance) in order to better understand the constraints on and requirements of a solution. Finally, we suggest a solution direction involving system specification and generation in an error recovery system.

This work is being conducted in the context of general survivability research at the University of Virginia. As mentioned previously, the error detection and damage assessment phases of fault tolerance are handled by a control-system architecture—hierarchical, adaptive, and overlayed upon the critical information system [45]. In addition, we have developed a modelling and simulation framework to enable experimentation on example critical information systems [44]. A model of the financial payments system has been constructed using this experimentation system, and experiments and evaluation on both error detection and error recovery strategies are being conducted using this system.

8. Acknowledgments

It is a pleasure to thank Kevin Sullivan for numerous discussions about the ideas expressed in this paper. This effort was sponsored by the Defense Advanced Research Projects Agency and Rome Laboratory, Air Force Materiel Command, USAF, under agreement number F30602-96-1-0314. The U.S. Government is authorized to reproduce and distribute reprints for governmental purposes notwithstanding any copyright annotation thereon. The views and conclusions contained herein are those of the authors and should not be interpreted as necessarily representing the official policies or endorsements, either expressed or implied, of the Defense Advanced Research Projects Agency, Rome Laboratory or the U.S. Government. This work was also done under the support of a National Science Foundation Research Fellowship. Any opinions, findings, conclusions, or recommendations expressed in this publication are those of the authors and do not necessarily reflect the views of the National Science Foundation.

9. References

[1]   Agnew, B., C. Hofmeister, and J. Purtilo. "Planning for Change: A Reconfiguration Language for Distributed Systems," Proceedings of the 2nd International Workshop on Configurable Distributed Systems, IEEE Computer Society Press, Los Alamitos, CA, March 1992, pp. 15-22.

[2]   Allen, R. and D. Garlan. "Beyond Definition/Use: Architectural Interconnection," ACM SIGPLAN Notices, Vol. 28 No. 9, August 1994, pp. 35-45.

[3]   Alvisi, L. and K. Marzullo. "WAFT: Support for Fault-Tolerance in Wide-Area Object Oriented Systems," Proceedings of the 2nd Information Survivability Workshop, IEEE Computer Society Press, Los Alamitos, CA, October 1998, pp. 5-10.

[4]   Anderson, T. and J. Knight. "A Framework for Software Fault Tolerance in Real-Time Systems," IEEE Transactions on Software Engineering, Vol. SE-9 No. 3, May 1983, pp. 355-364.

[5]   Anderson, T. and P. Lee. Fault Tolerance: Principles and Practice. Prentice Hall, Englewood Cliffs, NJ, 1981.

[6]   Babaoglu, O. and A. Schiper. "On Group Communication in Large-Scale Distributed Systems," ACM Operating Systems Review, Vol. 29 No. 1, January 1995, pp. 62-67.

[7]   Bhatti, N., M. Hiltunen, R. Schlichting, and W. Chiu. "Coyote: A System for Constructing Fine-Grain Configurable Communication Services," ACM Transactions on Computer Systems, Vol. 16 No. 4, November 1998, pp. 321-366.

[8]   Birman, K. "The Process Group Approach to Reliable Distributed Computing," Communications of the ACM, Vol. 36 No. 12, December 1993, pp. 37-53 and 103.

[9]   Birman, K. Building Secure and Reliable Network Applications. Manning, Greenwich, CT, 1996.

[10] Cowan, C., L. Delcambre, A. Le Meur, L. Liu, D. Maier, D. McNamee, M. Miller, C. Pu, P. Wagle, and J. Walpole. "Adaptation Space: Surviving Non-Maskable Failures," Technical Report 98-013, Department of Computer Science and Engineering, Oregon Graduate Institute of Science and Technology, May 1998.

[11] Cristian, F. "Understanding Fault-Tolerant Distributed Systems," Communications of the ACM, Vol. 34 No. 2, February 1991, pp. 56-78.

[12] Cristian, F. and S. Mishra. "Automatic Service Availability Management in Asynchronous Distributed Systems," Proceedings of the 2nd International Workshop on Configurable Distributed Systems, IEEE Computer Society Press, Los Alamitos, CA, March 1992, pp. 58-68.

[13] Cristian, F. "Automatic Reconfiguration in the Presence of Failures," Software Engineering Journal, Vol. 8 No. 2, March 1993, pp. 53-60.

[14] Cristian, F., B. Dancey, and J. Dehn. "Fault-Tolerance in Air Traffic Control Systems," ACM Transactions on Computer Systems, Vol. 14 No. 3, August 1996, pp. 265-286.

[15] Ellison, B., D. Fisher, R. Linger, H. Lipson, T. Longstaff, and N. Mead. "Survivable Network Systems: An Emerging Discipline," Technical Report CMU/SEI-97-TR-013, Software Engineering Institute, Carnegie Mellon University, November 1997.

[16] Garlan, D. and D. Perry. "Introduction to the Special Issue on Software Architecture," IEEE Transactions on Software Engineering, Vol. 21 No. 4, April 1995, pp. 269-274.

[17] Hofmeister, C., E. White, and J. Purtilo. "Surgeon: A Packager for Dynamically Reconfigurable Distributed Applications," Software Engineering Journal, Vol. 8 No. 2, March 1993, pp. 95-101.

[18] Hofmeister, C. "Dynamic Reconfiguration of Distributed Applications," Ph.D. Dissertation, Technical Report CS-TR-3210, Department of Computer Science, University of Maryland, January 1994.

[19] Jalote, P. Fault Tolerance in Distributed Systems. Prentice Hall, Englewood Cliffs, NJ, 1994.

[20] Knight, J., M. Elder, J. Flinn, and P. Marx. "Summaries of Three Critical Infrastructure Systems," Technical Report CS-97-27, Department of Computer Science, University of Virginia, November 1997.

[21] Knight, J. and J. Urquhart. "On the Implementation and Use of Ada on Fault-Tolerant Distributed Systems," IEEE Transactions on Software Engineering, Vol. SE-13 No. 5, May 1987, pp. 553-563.

[22] Kramer, J. and J. Magee. "Dynamic Configuration for Distributed Systems," IEEE Transactions on Software Engineering, Vol. SE-11 No. 4, April 1985, pp. 424-436.

[23] Kramer, J. and J. Magee. "The Evolving Philosophers Problem: Dynamic Change Management," IEEE Transactions on Software Engineering, Vol. 16 No. 11, November 1990, pp. 1293-1306.

[24] Laprie, J. "Dependable Computing and Fault Tolerance: Concepts and Terminology," Digest of Papers FTCS-15: 15th International Symposium on Fault-Tolerant Computing, June 1985, pp. 2-11.

[25] Luckham, D., J. Kenney, L. Augustin, J. Vera, D. Bryan, and W. Mann. "Specification and Analysis of System Architecture Using Rapide," IEEE Transactions on Software Engineering, Vol. 21 No. 4, April 1995, pp. 336-355.

[26] Maffeis, S. "Electra - Making Distributed Programs Object-Oriented," Technical Report 93-17, Department of Computer Science, University of Zurich, April 1993.

[27] Maffeis, S. "Piranha: A CORBA Tool For High Availability," IEEE Computer, Vol. 30 No. 4, April 1997, pp. 59-66.

[28] Magee, J., N. Dulay, and J. Kramer. "Structuring Parallel and Distributed Programs," Software Engineering Journal, Vol. 8 No. 2, March 1993, pp. 73-82.

[29] Magee, J., N. Dulay, and J. Kramer. "A Constructive Development Environment for Parallel and Distributed Programs," Distributed Systems Engineering Journal, Vol. 1 No. 5, September 1994, pp. 304-312.

[30] Magee, J., N. Dulay, S. Eisenbach, and J. Kramer. "Specifying Distributed Software Architectures," Lecture Notes in Computer Science, Vol. 989, September 1995, pp. 137-153.

[31] Magee, J. and J. Kramer. "Darwin: An Architectural Description Language," http://www-dse.doc.ic.ac.uk/research/darwin/darwin.html, 1998.

[32] Melliar-Smith, P. and L. Moser. "Surviving Network Partitioning," IEEE Computer, Vol. 31 No. 3, March 1998, pp. 62-68.

[33] Moriconi, M. and X. Qian. "Correctness and Composition of Software Architectures," ACM SIGSOFT Software Engineering Notes, Vol. 19 No. 5, December 1994, pp. 164-174.

[34] Office of the Undersecretary of Defense for Acquisition and Technology. "Report of the Defense Science Board Task Force on Information Warfare - Defense (IW-D)," November 1996.

[35] President's Commission on Critical Infrastructure Protection. "Critical Foundations: Protecting America's Infrastructures The Report of the President's Commission on Critical Infrastructure Protection," United States Government Printing Office (GPO), No. 040-000-00699-1, October 1997.

[36] Purtilo, J. "The POLYLITH Software Bus," ACM Transactions on Programming Languages and Systems, Vol. 16 No. 1, January 1994, pp. 151-174.

[37] Purtilo, J. and P. Jalote. "An Environment for Developing Fault-Tolerant Software," IEEE Transactions on Software Engineering, Vol. 17 No. 2, February 1991, pp. 153-159.

[38] Reiter, M., K. Birman, and L. Gong. "Integrating Security in a Group Oriented Distributed System," Proceedings of the 1992 IEEE Symposium on Research in Security and Privacy, IEEE Computer Society Press,

Los Alamitos, CA, May 1992, pp. 18-32.

[39] Reiter, M., K. Birman, and R. van Renesse. "A Security Architecture for Fault-Tolerant Systems," ACM Transactions on Computer Systems, Vol. 12 No. 4, November 1994, pp. 340-371.

[40] Rodeh, O., K. Birman, M. Hayden, Z. Xiao, and D. Dolev. "Ensemble Security," Technical Report TR98-1703, Department of Computer Science, Cornell University, September 1998.

[41] Shaw, M., R. DeLine, D. Klein, T. Ross, D. Young, and G. Zelesnik. "Abstractions for Software Architecture and Tools to Support Them," IEEE Transactions on Software Engineering, Vol. 21 No. 4, April 1995, pp. 314-335.

[42] Shrivastava, S., G. Dixon, G. Parrington. "An Overview of the Arjuna Distributed Programming System," IEEE Software, Vol. 8 No. 1, January 1991, pp. 66-73.

[43] Shrivastava, S. and D. McCue. "Structuring Fault-Tolerant Object Systems for Modularity in a Distributed Environment," IEEE Transactions on Parallel and Distributed Systems, Vol. 5 No. 4, April 1994, pp. 421-432.

[44] Sullivan, K., J. Knight, J. McHugh, X. Du, and S. Geist. "A Framework for Experimental Systems Research in Distributed Survivability Architectures," Technical Report CS-98-38, Department of Computer Science, University of Virginia, December 1998.

[45] Sullivan, K., J. Knight, X. Du, and S. Geist. "Information Survivability Control Systems," Proceedings of the 21st International Conference on Software Engineering, IEEE Computer Society Press, Los Alamitos, CA, May 1999, pp. 184-192.

[46] Summers, B. The Payment System: Design, Management, and Supervision. International Monetary Fund, Washington, DC, 1994.

[47] van Renesse, R., K. Birman, and S. Maffeis. "Horus: A Flexible Group Communications System," Communications of the ACM, Vol. 39 No. 4, April 1996, pp. 76-83.

[48] van Renesse, R., K. Birman, M. Hayden, A. Vaysburd, and D. Karr. "Building Adaptive Systems Using Ensemble," Technical Report TR97-1638, Department of Computer Science, Cornell University, July 1997.

[49] Welch, D. "Building Self-Reconfiguring Distributed Systems using Compensating Reconfiguration," Proceedings of the 4th International Conference on Configurable Distributed Systems, IEEE Computer Society Press, Los Alamitos, CA, May 1998.

Security and Fault-Tolerance in Distributed Systems: An Actor-Based Approach

Gul A. Agha and Reza Ziaei
Open Systems Laboratory
University of Illinois at Urbana-Champaign
1304 W. Springfield Ave,
Urbana, IL 61801 – USA
{agha|ziaei}@cs.uiuc.edu
http://www-osl.cs.uiuc.edu/

Abstract

The inherent complexity of real-world distributed applications makes developing and maintaining software for these systems difficult and error-prone. We describe an actor-based meta-level model to address the complexity of distributed applications. Specifically, meta-level framework allow code implementing different design concerns to be factored into separate modules – thus enabling the separate development and modification of code for different non-functional requirements such as security and fault-tolerance. This paper reviews current research based on the model and outlines some research directions.

1   Introduction

Real-world distributed applications consist of many asynchronously operating components communicating over networks. They are open to interaction with their environment. Besides satisfying sophisticated functional requirements, such systems are subject to rigorous non-functional requirements such as coordination, timing, fault-tolerance and security. The large number of requirements and their evolutionary nature adds an extra dimension to the complexity of real-world system design. For instance, an avionic control system can be seen as an open distributed system involving a large number of controlling components that interact asynchronously. The specification of such systems usually consists of thousands of requirements that may be modified dynamically to adapt to changes in the environment, control policies, or mission plans.

We believe the problem of maintaining software can be simplified by enabling a modular implementation of distinct design concerns, i.e., the code implementing the functionality of an application should be separated from the code implementing non-functional requirements. A large number of mechanisms have been devised to meet different non-functional requirements, and different mechanisms are suited for different classes of applications. Since the non-functional requirements that we are interested in capturing are ones that affect to the interaction of distributed components, we call such mechanisms *interaction protocols*.

A composable, reusable, and transparent implementation of interaction protocols greatly simplifies software development and maintenance. Because traditional architectures do not allow separate customizable modules for synchronization, scheduling, back-up and error recovery, etc., it is impossible to develop such modular implementations for non-functional requirements.

The goal of this paper is to review the state of the art in Actor research, and to outline research directions. Individual results reported here have been reported in previous publications by the Illinois Open Systems Lab (e.g., [3, 5, 20, 18]). Rather than provide complete technical details here, we refer the reader to these publications.

The outline of this paper is as follows. The next describes the Actor model of concurrency. The model provides a representation for computation in open distributed systems and methods for reasoning about applications in such systems. We then introduce a meta-level framework which allows interaction protocols and application software to be implemented separately and composed. Finally, we discuss how security and dependability protocols may be specified and analyzed using this model.

2 Actors

Actors [3] provide a general and flexible model of concurrent and distributed computation. As atomic units of computation, actors may be used to build typical architectural elements including procedural, functional, and object-oriented components. Moreover, actor interactions may be used to model standard distributed coordination mechanisms such as remote procedure call (RPC), transactions, and other forms of synchronization [4, 21, 9, 23]. Modern languages are readily extended with the actor primitives (*cf.* [13]).

Conceptually, each actor has a unique name and an associated behavior. The behavior encapsulates the actor's state and procedures to manipulate the state. Actors communicate by sending messages to one another. Actors compute by serially processing messages sent to them. The serial processing of messages represents a thread of control for the actor. When an actor is idle, it waits for the next message sent to it (see Figure 1).

While processing a message, an actor may perform three types of basic actions that potentially affect computation; namely:

- *send* messages asynchronously to other actors;
- *create* actors with specified behaviors; and
- become *ready* to receive the next message.

Communication between actors is point-to-point and assumed to be weakly fair: executing a *send* eventually causes the message to be delivered to the recipient, provided the recipient is not permanently blocked (e.g., doing an internal computation that results in an infinite loop). The sender need not be blocked waiting for messages that have been sent to

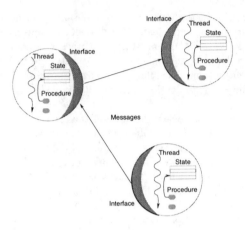

Figure 1. Actors encapsulate state and procedures to manipulate state. Each actor has a thread of control and multiple actors can run concurrently.

be delivered. Different messages arrive in an arbitrary order. The *create* primitive creates a new actor with a specified behavior. Initially, only the creating actor knows the name of a newly created actor. Actor names are communicable values, thus other actors can find out the names of newly created actors and the configuration of actors' interconnections may change dynamically. The *ready* primitive is used to indicate that the signaling actor is ready to process the next message in its mail queue. Upon invoking *ready*, the calling actor either begins processing the next available message, or waits until a new message arrives in its mail queue.

Actors are a formal model for concurrent objects: an actor is an object with a private local state, a set of *methods*, a unique name, and a thread of control. Message passing in actors can be viewed as the asynchronous invocation of methods, and standard method invocation can be seen as passing continuations in a message. Serialization of message delivery by an actor provides an object with the semantics of a monitor (without condition variables). Note that the operations *send* and *create* are explicit requests, while *ready* is implicit – method completion frees the monitor and permits processing of the next message.

An Actor Language and its Semantics

One can extend a sequential language with actor constructs. For example, the call-by-value λ-calculus is extended in [2]. Specifically, extension adds the following operations to the language:

$send(a, v)$ creates a new message with content v whose receiver is the actor with name a.

`newactor(b)` creates a new actor with initial behavior b and returns its address.

`ready(b)` captures local state change: the behavior of the actor executing the `ready` expression becomes b and the actor is then free to accept another message.

Instantaneous snapshots of actor systems are called *configurations*. An actor configuration is a collection of actors together with undelivered messages. Actor computation is defined by a transition relation on configurations. The notion of open systems is captured by allowing configurations to be composed into new configurations. Composition is meaningful only when configurations have matching interfaces. An interface comprises a set of *receptionists* that can receive messages from actors outside a configuration, and a set of actors *external* to a configuration that can receive messages from the actors within. Interfaces are dynamic and they change as messages pass into or out of a configuration. Formally, an actor configuration is defined as follows:

Definition (Actor Configurations):   An *actor configuration* with actor map, α, multiset of messages, M, receptionists, ρ, and external actors, χ, is written

$$\langle \alpha \mid M \rangle_\chi^\rho$$

where ρ, χ are finite sets of actor names, α maps a finite set of actor names to the corresponding actor behavior, M is a finite multiset of undelivered messages, and if $A = \mathrm{Dom}(\alpha)$, that is A is the domain of actor names, then:

(0) $\rho \subseteq A$ and $A \cap \chi = \emptyset$,
(1)   if $a \in A$, then $\mathrm{FV}(\alpha(a)) \subseteq A \cup \chi$, where $\mathrm{FV}(\alpha(a))$ represents the free variables in $\alpha(a)$, the behavior of actor a, and if $\langle a \Leftarrow v_1 \rangle$ is a message with content v_1 to actor name a, then $\mathrm{FV}(v_i) \subseteq A \cup \chi$ for $i < 2$.

For an actor with name a, we indicate its states as $[e]_a$.

Now we can extend the local transitions defined for a sequential language ($\overset{\lambda}{\mapsto}$), by providing transitions for the actor program as shown in Figure 2. Assume that R is the reduction context in which the expression currently being evaluated occurs. Note that in the call-by-value λ-calculus expressions can be uniquely decomposed into a reduction context and a reduction expression (redex). Thus the behavior of an actor in response to a message is deterministic. The nondeterminism in actor systems results from the indeterminacy in the arrival order of messages.

Based on a variation of the transition system described above, a rigorous theory of actor systems is developed in [2]. Specifically, in that work several notions of equivalence over actor expressions and configurations are defined. The model assumes fairness, namely that any message will be delivered unless its recipient fails. Fairness is an important requirement for reasoning about eventuality properties. It is particularly relevant in supporting modular reasoning. One important consequence of fairness is that each actor makes progress independent of how busy the other actors are. Therefore, if we compose one configuration with another that has an actor with a nonterminating computation, computation in the first configuration may nevertheless proceed as before.

$$e \xmapsto{\lambda}_{\mathrm{Dom}(\alpha) \cup \{a\}} e' \Rightarrow \langle \alpha, [e]_a \mid M \rangle^\rho_\chi \mapsto \langle \alpha, [e']_a \mid M \rangle^\rho_\chi$$

$$\langle \alpha, [R[\mathtt{newactor(e)}]]_\mathtt{a} \mid M \rangle^\rho_\chi \mapsto \langle \alpha, [R[a]]_a, [e]_{a'} \mid M \rangle^\rho_\chi \qquad a' \text{ fresh}$$

$$\langle \alpha, [R[\mathtt{send}(a, v_1)]]_a \mid M \rangle^\rho_\chi \mapsto \langle \alpha, [R[\mathtt{nil}]]_a \mid M, msg \rangle^\rho_\chi \qquad msg = \langle a \Leftarrow v_1 \rangle$$

$$\langle \alpha, [R[\mathtt{ready}(v)]]_\mathtt{a} \mid \langle a \Leftarrow cv \rangle, M \rangle^\rho_\chi \mapsto \langle \alpha, [\mathtt{app}(v, cv)]_a \mid M \rangle^\rho_\chi$$

$$\langle \alpha \mid M, msg \rangle^\rho_\chi \mapsto \langle \alpha \mid M \rangle^{\rho'}_\chi \qquad \qquad \text{if } msg = \langle a \Leftarrow cv \rangle, a \in \chi,$$
$$\text{and } \rho' = \rho \cup (\mathrm{FV}(cv) \cap \mathrm{Dom}(\alpha))$$

$$\langle \alpha \mid M \rangle^\rho_\chi \mapsto \langle \alpha \mid M, msg \rangle^\rho_{\chi \cup (\mathrm{FV}(cv) - \mathrm{Dom}(\alpha))}$$
$$\text{if } msg = \langle a \Leftarrow cv \rangle, a \in \rho \text{ and } \mathrm{FV}(cv) \cap \mathrm{Dom}(\alpha) \subseteq \rho$$

Figure 2. Actor transitions.

Equivalence is a fundamental property that is often used in reasoning about programs. Specifically, equivalences between actor expressions and actor configurations are significant. The notion of equivalence in our theory is a kind of observational equivalence that is defined by adding an observable distinguished *event* to the set of transitions. This technique is a variant of operational equivalence as defined in [15]. Two actor expressions may be plugged into a context to see if the event occurs in one or the other case. Two expressions are considered equivalent if they have the same observations over all possible contexts.

Equivalence laws and proof techniques to simplify reasoning about actor systems have been developed. In particular, the proof techniques allow us to use canonical multi-step transitions as well as to reduce the number of contexts that need to be considered in studying the equivalence of systems. The algebraic properties of equivalence laws and the compositionality of configurations allows algebraic proof techniques to be used as well. A more abstract model of actors has been developed in [22].

A concrete way to think of actors is that they represent an abstraction over concurrent architectures. An actor runtime system provides the interface to services such as global addressing, memory management, fair scheduling, and communication. It turns out that these services can be efficiently implemented, thus raising the level of abstraction while reducing the size and complexity of code on concurrent architectures [11]. Alternately, such services can be implemented by developing libraries in traditional programming languages.

3 Meta-Level Architectures and Programming Abstractions

A number of *meta-level models* have been devised to manage the complexity of large systems. Such models support a separation of functional design concerns from non-functional ones (e.g. see [24]). In these models, a meta-architecture allows components to be placed into *base* and *meta* layers. *Base-level* components capture the functional aspects of an application, while other aspects of the system such as synchronization, security, fault-tolerance, and coordination of base-level objects are performed by *meta-level* components. New meta-levels can be recursively imposed on each meta-level and therefore the same flexibility in separating concerns can be provided for each level.

Meta-level architectures have been used to support a number of application areas [5, 21, 8]. For example, Astley and Agha define for instance new abstractions called *components*, *connectors*, and *actor groups* [6] (see also [5]). In this model, an actor group represents an encapsulation boundary, which protects internal actors from external interactions: actors within a group may only exchange messages with other actors in the same group. Composition operators are used to build connections between groups. These composition operators are also used to install meta-level customizations on group actors.

Programming abstractions can be built in terms of a meta-level architecture and such abstractions allow a more declarative implementation of different kinds of non-functional requirements in open distributed systems. For example, Frolund and Agha introduce meta-level abstractions to coordinate the interaction among base-actors [10, 8]. In this work, a programming construct called *synchronizers* is defined to coordinate the interactions of a group of actors. A variant of synchronizers has been used to represent real-time constraints [16, 12]. Other meta-level abstractions developed at the University of Illinois Open Systems Laboratory provide abstractions to represent protocols that can be dynamically installed [21, 5]. In particular, a number of fault-tolerance protocols have been expressed and implemented in this way.

Adaptability is an important property of dependable systems and can be obtained through the use of meta-level frameworks. Adaptively dependable systems function for long durations despite changing execution environments. An effective mechanism to achieve adaptability is dynamic installation of protocols. Dynamic protocol installation can be used in combination with exception handling to build robust applications with respect to faults and unpredicted changes. Sturman and Astley use meta-level frameworks to implement dynamic protocol installation [21, 5].

In the following section we illustrate an actor-based meta-framework and its application in designing dependability protocols.

A Meta-Architectural framework for Actors

The event meta-architecture, developed in [6, 5], allows the modification of the basic semantics of actors to enable transparent addition of new services such as dependability services. To do this we extend the basic actor model by a meta layer, modeled as actor computations, and a customized protocol which links the base application and meta layers. In this subsection we explain basic concepts and mechanisms of the extended model.

Inter-Level Interaction

To support the addition of transparent meta-level services, we need mechanisms to notify meta-level components whenever relevant actions take place at the base-level. These mechanisms are based on several of primitives. The first primitive, which is the main constituent of semantics of concurrent systems, is the notion of *event*. An event represents some state change in the system. Events, together with a partial-order causal relation, define the semantics of an actor computation. In an actor system, there are three important events : *message send*, *actor creation*, and *request for next message* (performed by the ready() primitive). In other smeantic models, other events can be defined.

The model of computation used for the meta-level determines the nature of the protocol for notifying meta-level components whenever base-level events occur. In our framework, meta-level computation is performed by actors. A natural solution to the problem of informing meta-actors entails sending them messages with descriptions of base-level events. A *signal* is the means through which base-level events create meta-messages. For each type of event, we define a signal and the format and contents of associated meta-messages. Whenever a base-level event occurs, the corresponding signal will generate a meta-message. An important design decision is to determine which meta-actor should receive the generated message. Figure 3 lists the typical signals and notifications defined in the Astley's framework.

ACTOR TRANSITIONS		
EVENT		BEHAVIOR
SIGNALS	transmit(*msg*)	Triggered when a base-actor executes a send(*m*) operation. Base actor blocks until a **continue** is received. The argument *msg* is a message structure which encapsulates the destination, method to invoke, and arguments of the message (that is, *m*). The default system behavior is to send the message and send a **continue** notification to the signaling actor.
	ready()	Triggered when a base-actor requests the next available message via a ready() operation. The default system behavior is to get the next available message and deliver it to the actor by generating a **deliver** notification.
	create(*beh*)	Triggered when a base-actor executes a create(*beh*) operation. Base-actor blocks until a **newActor** is received. The argument *beh* is the behavior of the new actor to be created. The default system behavior is to create the new actor and deliver its address to the base-actor via a **newActor** notification.
NOTIFICATIONS	continue()	Resumes a base-actor blocked on a send(*m*) operation.
	deliver(*msg*)	Delivers a message to a base-actor. The argument *msg* is a message structure indicating the method and arguments to invoke on the resumed actor.
	newActor(*a*)	Returns the address of a newly created actor to a base-actor blocked on a create(*beh*) operation. The argument *a* is the address of the newly created actor.

Figure 3. Each signal has a default behavior corresponding to the actor semantics of the associated operation. (From [5])

The events we are concerned with here are all atomic; in that their executions never overlap in time. Atomicity is an important property in this case – it prevents interference between semantics of different events. To guarantee atomicity in our framework, we block base-level computation whenever a signal is generated. When a meta-level actor finishes its computation, it notifies the blocked base-level actor to resume its computation. Such notifications release base-level computation and transfer information that is needed by the resuming event (see Figure 4).

In several models there is one meta-actor for every base-actor (e.g. [5, 24]). However, other models are possible. For example, Yonezawa's group has used a model with shared meta-object [25]. Composition of protocols is achieved by stacking events and notifications, that is, a meta-actor is customized by a meta-meta-actor.

Example: Transparent Encryption

So far we have seen that in our framework we can add a meta-actor for every base-actor. The meta-actor has one method for each type of signal. Here we illustrate the signal-notify

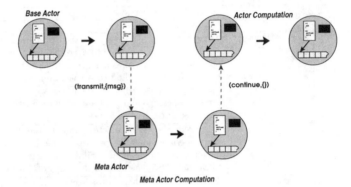

Figure 4. Inter-Level Interaction: A *meta-actor* **customizes a** *base-actor* **by intercepting signals. The meta-actor generates a notification after each signal has been processed and frees the blocked base-actor.**

framework by a simple example that shows how an encryption scheme can be transparently added to actor communications.

```
actor Encrypt (actor receiver) {
    // Encrypt outgoing messages if
    // they are targeted to the receiver
    method transmit(Msg msg) {
        actor target = msg.dest;
        if (target == receiver)
            target ← encrypt(msg);
        else
            target ← msg;
        continue();
    }
}
```

```
actor Decrypt() {
    // Decrypt messages targeted
    // for base actor (if necessary)
    method ready() {
        msg = Scheduler.NextMsg(
            baseactor);
        if (encrypted(msg))
            deliver(decrypt(msg));
        else
            deliver(msg);
    }
}
```

Figure 5. Meta-Level Implementation of Encryption: **The** Encrypt **meta-actor intercepts** transmit **signals and encrypts outgoing messages. The** Decrypt **policy actor intercepts messages targeted for the receiver (via the** ready **method) and, if necessary, decrypts an incoming message before delivering it (From [5].**

Figure 5 defines two meta-actors written in high level code . These actors add an encryption service to base-level computation. One meta-actor, Encrypt, listens to messages sent by the corresponding base-actor to a certain destination. It has only one method, transmit(), which is invoked via the signal mechanism whenever the base-actor sends a message. transmit() then verifies the destination of the message and if it matches the intended receiver, it encrypts the message using some scheme. Otherwise it simply delivers the original message.

The second meta-actor, Decrypt, listens to ready() messages caused by ready instructions executed by base actors. In this example, we suppose the invocation is performed after the scheduler chooses a message to be delivered. That message is passed to Decrypt as an argument of ready(). The meta-actor then the message if necessary and delivers the result to the receiving base-actor.

3.0.1 Example: Transparent Implementation of Primary-Backup Protocol

Using the signal-notify framework, a simple replication scheme based on the *primary-backup* protocol can be implemented. Figure 6 shows a Replicator and a Backup actor. Replicator perceives signals from a base-actor, which must be replicated. For every message delivered to the base-actor, Replicator sends a stamped copy to Backup, which saves it. In case of failure, Backup will contain a history of state snapshots that can be used for recovery.

4 Verification of Security Protocols

A significant problem in the design of secure distributed systems is authentication of communicating principals and distribution of session keys. Recently, several models and frameworks have been proposed to study and analyze authentication protocols and to verify their safety under various types of attacks. The bases of these frameworks vary from logics, such as belief logics[7] and inductive methods [14], to semantic ones, such as CSP [17] and CCS [1].

The Actor model provides a semantic approach to specifying and reasoning about security protocols which has some potential advantages. In this approach, attackers and possible threats are expressed in terms of actor configurations containing malicious attackers modeled as actors. These configurations are composed with a configuration containing actors that implement a protocol, and the effects of the interaction that results from this composition are analyzed in order to verify the security of the protocol.

An advantage of using the Actor model is that it can naturally express asynchrony and concurrency – this allows specification and analysis of overlapping executions of protocol instances something that has not yet been addressed in other modeling frameworks. Moreover, because a protocol is modeled as an open configuration, one can, in principle, model and analyze general schemes of attacks as arbitrary configurations that can be composed with the protocol.

The motivating idea is to verify that an application using a security protocol expresses the same behavior in a threatless environment as in all possible environments in which

```
actor Replicator(actor backup) {                    actor Backup() {

    int processed = 0;                                  int count;
    int count = 0;                                      State last;
    boolean waiting = false;                            PriorityQueue unprocessed;
    Queue mailQ;
                                                        // Receive new unprocessed message
    // Copy incoming messages to backup                 method rcvMsg(Msg m, int seq) {
    method rcv(Msg m) {                                     unprocessed.enqueue(m, seq);
        // Send a stamped message to the backup     }
        backup ← rcvMsg(m, count++);
                                                        // Receive new state
        // Queue until our base actor is ready          method rcvState(State s, int seq) {
        if (waiting) {                                      last = s;
            waiting = false;
            deliver(m);                                     Remove all message in "unprocessed"
        } else                                              with sequence number less than seq
            mailQ.enqueue(m);                       }
    }                                               }

    // Forward state to backup and
    // deliver next message
    method ready(State s) {
        backup ← rcvState(s, processed++);

        if (!mailQ.empty())
            deliver(mailQ.dequeue());
        else
            waiting=true;
    }
}
```

Figure 6. Meta-Level Implementation of Replication: **An instance of** Replicator **is installed on the actor to be replicated. An instance of** Backup **receives state snapshots from the** Replicator **so that it can assume the role of the replicated actor if a failure occurs (From [5]).**

an arbitrary attacker might threaten the security of the application. In this section, we briefly describe the work of Skalka and Smith [18], who have analyzed security properties of the NSPK protocol under specific types of attack by formalizing them using Specdiag, a graphical specification language for actors [19]. It should be observed that research is currently in progress to find proofs of security by making weaker assumption about the nature of attackers.

Skalka and Smith have specified the NSPK authentication protocol in Specdiag. Different classes of attackers are modeled as actors or configurations of actors. The reasoning uses a notion of observational equivalence defined in terms of interaction paths [22].

The NSPK protocol as analyzed in Skalka and Smith's paper is defined as follows:

$$A \rightarrow B : p_b(n_a.A)$$
$$B \rightarrow A : p_a(n_a.n_b.B)$$
$$A \rightarrow B : p_b(n_b)$$

where $X \rightarrow Y : m$ means that X sends message m to Y, p_a and p_b are public keys for A and B respectively, and $x.y$ is used for concatenation of message contents x and y. $p_x(m)$ refers to the encoded message using X's public key. Only X can decode the message using its private key. n_a and n_b refer to *nonces* generated by A and B respectively (nonces can be thought of as freshly generated identifiers). For theoretical analysis, it is generally assumed that nonces cannot be guessed.

The protocol starts when A sends a nonce and its identity to B. B replies with corresponding information about itself, plus A's nonce. A can verify B's identity and be certain the received message was in reply to its own message and not a replay of a past communication. By sending B's nonce back to B, A similarly assures B of the validity of A's identity.

A (the *initiator* of the protocol) and B (the *responder*) are modeled as actors that interact via asynchronous messages (see Figure 7and Figure 8). We must also model an environment in which malicious attackers may try to impose threats on the protocol by intercepting messages, replaying messages, or disguising themselves as one of the principals involved in the protocol.

The medium through which the initiator and the responder communicate is explicitly modeled as an actor called *router* (see Figure 9). The router can be replaced by *enemy* actor(s) that simulate various attackers and, as a result, one can analyze their effect on the protocol by verifying the interaction paths of *initiator* and *responder*. The diagrams for "adversary" actors are not shown here, but Skalka and Smith argue that they are not needed for the verification process because all that is needed is the sort of messages these adversaries send defines the attack.

Skalka and Smith use a proof technique to overcome this difficulty. The idea is to identify the main characteristics of the enemy configuration and devise a simpler diagram that divides the original diagram into more intuitive parts. The motivating idea here is that proofs may become easier using intuitive visual representation. However, this step is by no means automated – it requires rigorous understanding of the nature of attackers' behavior.

The next step of the proof is to show the equivalence of the obtained diagram to the original one. Skalka and Smith give a semantic proof of this equivalence by using the interaction paths semantics of Talcott [22].

Because Actors model open distributed systems, sequentiality and closed-world assumptions can be relaxed. For example, one can model the possibility of concurrent sessions. Future research to explore the implications of this is on-going.

Initiator(a,r,s,x) =

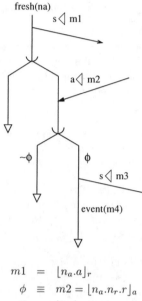

$$
\begin{aligned}
m1 &= \lfloor n_a.a \rfloor_r \\
\phi &\equiv m2 = \lfloor n_a.n_r.r \rfloor_a \\
m3 &= \lfloor n_r \rfloor_r \\
m4 &= succ(a, r, n_a, n_r)
\end{aligned}
$$

Figure 7. *Initiator* **with name a (From [18]). The initiator sends an encrypted copy of its nonce to the other principal. If the reply contains intiator's nonce, a reply will be sent to confirm the recpetion of the other principal's nonce. The initiator generates an event announcing values that indicate a valid termination of this principal's behavior. Only pahts that generate a correct event are considered to guarantee security of the protocol. (All messages are encrypted with the public key of the receiver.)**

5   Discussion

A primary advantage of a meta-level approach to software design is its provision for dynamic and transparent addition and modification of non-functional services to the system. Nevertheless, when adding meta-level objects, one must be careful not to interfere with

Responder(b,a,x) =

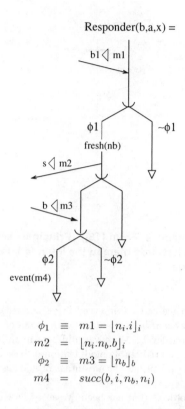

$$\phi_1 \equiv m1 = \lfloor n_i.i \rfloor_i$$
$$m2 = \lfloor n_i.n_b.b \rfloor_i$$
$$\phi_2 \equiv m3 = \lfloor n_b \rfloor_b$$
$$m4 = succ(b, i, n_b, n_i)$$

Figure 8. *Responder* **with name b (From [18]). The responder receives the initiator's nonce and decrypts it using its private key.** ϕ_1 **indicates the paths taken if the message is correctly decrypted. The responder will then generate a nonce and send it back to the initiator. After receiving the initiator's final response, it generates a success event if the last response is from the initiator and belong to the current session.**

intended domain-specific behavior of the base-level components, or at least be able to control interferences if intended.

Much research in this area remains to be done. Some early work has been carried out by Venkatasubramanian and Talcott [24] who develop a two-level meta-level model of open distributed system. The TLAM model(Two Level Actor Machine) provides a formal semantics for such systems and therefore a basis for specifying and reasoning about properties of and interactions between components.

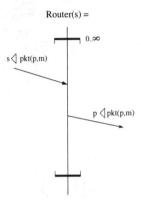

Figure 9. *Router* **with name s (From [18]). Principals send their messages to the router, which then forwards them to the intended destinations. The router repeats this cycle forever.**

Several kinds of interference can be observed in an actor-based meta-level framework. Potentially, interferene may occur between actors with a common acquaintance, or even between actors lying at different levels. Moreover, different meta-level actors may implement different services and cause unpredictable modification of base-actor interactions. Making non-interference properties explicit has the advantage of making specifications modular and composable.

The work on security protocols that has been presented here can be extended in another direction, namely, showing how the protocol may be embedded in a meta-level component and its behavior composed with arbitrary applications with security requirements. Moreover, newer generation of distributed systems are commonly implemented using protocol stacks. This can be modelled by the meta-level approach. By contrast, traditional analysis techniques do not provide methods to drill down into the implementation layers of the underlying network and operating system. Modelling such interaction in a compositional way will allow reasoning about protocol interactions. This research will lead to a formulatation of proof rules that simplify reasoning about security protocols in an open, concurrent systems which has fault-tolerant protocols embedded in it. At the same time, the meta-architecture will provide a modular implementation of protocols and applications – going a long way towards addressing the difficulty of software maintenance.

Acknowledgements

We'd like to thank past and present members of the Open Systems Laboratory whose research continues to provide an inspiration to our current work. In addition, we would like to thank Carlos Varela and James Waldby for comments on this paper. The research described in this paper has been made possible in part by NSA contract MDA904-98-C-A081 and the Air Force Office of Science Research under F49620-97-1-0382.

References

[1] Martin Abadi and Andrew D. Gordon. A calculus for cryptographic protocols: The spi calculus. *Information and Computation*, 148(1):1–70, January 1999.

[2] G. Agha, I. A. Mason, S. F. Smith, and C. L. Talcott. A foundation for actor computation. *Journal of Functional Programming*, 7:1–72, 1993.

[3] Gul Agha. *Actors: A Model of Concurrent Computation*. MIT Press, 1986.

[4] Gul Agha, Svend Frølund, Wooyoung Kim, Rajendra Panwar, Anna Patterson, and Daniel Sturman. Abstraction and modularity mechanisms for concurrent computing. *IEEE Parallel and Distributed Technology*, May 1993.

[5] Mark Astley. *Customization and Composition of Distributed Objects: Policy Management in Distributed Software Architectures*. PhD thesis, University of Illinois at Urbana-Champaign, May 1999.

[6] Mark Astley and Gul Agha. Customization and composition of distributed objects: Middleware abstractions for policy management. *Sixth International Symposium on the Foundations of Software Engineering ACM SIGSOFT*, 23(6):1–9, November 1998.

[7] Michael Burrows, Martin Abadi, and Roger Needham. A logic of authentication. *ACM Transactions on Computer Systems*, 8:18–36, February 1990.

[8] Svend Frølund. *Constraint-Based Synchronization of Distributed Activities*. PhD thesis, Department of Computer Science, University of Illinois at Urbana Champaign, 1994.

[9] Svend Frølund. *Coordinating Distributed Objects: An Actor-Based Approach to Synchronization*. MIT Press, 1996.

[10] Svend Frølund and Gul Agha. A language framework for multi-object coordination. In *Proceedings of ECOOP 1993*. Springer Verlag, 1993. LNCS 707.

[11] W. Kim and G. Agha. Efficient Support of Location Transparency in Concurrent Object-Oriented Programming Languages. In *Supercomputing '95*. IEEE, 1995.

[12] B. Nielsen and sc G. Agha. Towards reusable real-time objects. In *Annals of Software Engineering: Special Volume on Real-Time Software Engineering*. to be published.

[13] Open Systems Lab. The Actor Foundry: A Java-based Actor Programming Environment. Available for download at http://www-osl.cs.uiuc.edu/foundry.

[14] L. C. Paulson. The inductive approach to verifying cryptographic protocols. *J. Computer Security*, 6:85–128, 1998.

[15] G. Plotkin. Call-by-name, call-by-value and the lambda calculus. *Theoretical Computer Science*, 1:125–159, 1975.

[16] Shangping Ren. *An Actor-Based Framework for Real-Time Coordination*. PhD thesis, Department Computer Science. University of Illinois at Urbana-Champaign, 1997.

[17] Steve Schneider. Modelling Security Properties with CSP. Technical report, Royal Holloway Technical Report CSD-TR-96-04, 1996.

[18] C. Skalka and S. Smith. Verifying security protocols with specification diagrams. Submitted for publication.

[19] Scott Smith. On specification diagrams for actor systems. In C. Talcott, editor, *Proceedings of the Second Workshop on Higher-Order Techniques in Semantics*, Electronic Notes in Theoretical Computer Science. Elsevier, 1998. (to appear).

[20] Daniel C. Sturman. Fault-adaptation for systems in unpredictable environments. Master's thesis, University of Illinois at Urbana-Champaign, January 1994.

[21] Daniel C. Sturman. *Modular Specification of Interaction Policies in Distributed Computing*. PhD thesis, University of Illinois at Urbana-Champaign, May 1996.

[22] C. L. Talcott. Interaction semantics for components of distributed systems. In *FMOODS'96*, 1996.

[23] C. Varela and G. Agha. A Hierarchical Model for Coordination of Concurrent Activities. In P. Ciancarini and A. Wolf, editors, *Third International Conference on Coordination Languages and Models (COORDINATION '99)*, number 1594 in LNCS, pages 166–182. Springer-Verlag, April 1999. http://osl.cs.uiuc.edu/Papers/Coordination99.ps.

[24] N. Venkatasubramanian and C. L. Talcott. Reasoning about Meta-Level Activities in Open Distributed Systems. In *Principles of Distributed Computing*, 1995.

[25] A. Yonezawa, editor. *ABCL An Object-Oriented Concurrent System*, chapter Reflection in an Object-Oriented Concurrent Language, pages 45–70. MIT Press, Cambridge, Mass., 1990.

Why Should Architectural Principles be Enforced?

Naftaly H. Minsky*
minsky@cs.rutgers.edu
Department of Computer Science
Rutgers University
New Brunswick, NJ, 08903 USA

Abstract

There is an emerging consensus that an explicit architectural model *would be invaluable for large evolving software systems, providing them with a framework within which such a system can be reasoned about and maintained. But the great promise of architectural models has not been fulfilled so far, due to a gap between the model and the system it purports to describe. It is our contention that this gap is best bridged if* the model is not just stated, but is enforced.

This gives rise to a concept enforced architectural model—*or, a* law— *which is explored in this paper. We argue that this model has two major beneficial consequences: First, by bridging the above mentioned gap between an architectural model and the actual system, an enforced architectural model provides a truly reliable framework within which a system can be reasoned about and maintained. Second, our model provides software developers with a carefully circumscribed flexibility in molding the law of a project, during its evolutionary lifetime—while maintaining certain architectural principles as* invariant of evolution.

Keywords: architectural model, law-governed software, evolution, invariants of evolution, fire-walls, protection.

Work supported in part by NSF grants No. CCR-9308773

1 Introduction

There is an emerging consensus that an explicit *architectural model* should be invaluable for large evolving software systems [5]. This should be particularly true for the part of the model that specifies the principles and guidelines that are to govern the structure of the system, and its evolution over time—such as the requirement that the system be *layered*[1]. The hope is that broad principles of this kind would provide a framework within which the system can be reasoned about and maintained.

But the great promise of architectural models has not been fulfilled so far. The main reason for this has been aptly described by Murphy, Notkin and Sullivan [18], in the following manner:

> "Although these [architectural] models are commonly used, reasoning about the system in terms of such models can be dangerous because the models are almost always inaccurate with respect to the system's source."

In other words, there is a gap between the model and the system it purports to describe, which makes it an unreliable basis for reasoning about the system.

The currently prevailing approach for bridging this gap has been described by Sefica, Sane and Cambell [22], as follows:

> "the use of codified design principles [i.e., an architectural model] must be supplemented by checks to ensure that the actual implantation adheres to its design constraints and guidelines."

This approach led to the development of various tools whose purpose is to verify that a given system satisfies a given architectural model [3, 18, 22].

But the mere existence of verification tools is not sufficient for ensuring the compliance with a principle, particularly not for rapidly evolving systems. This is due to the lack of assurance that the appropriate tools would actually be employed, after every update of the system, and that any discrepancies thus detected would be immediately corrected.

It is our thesis that the gap between the architectural model and the implemented system can be bridged effectively if the model is not just stated, but is enforced. Moreover, we maintain that the resulting *enforced architectural model*—which we call a *law*—has some profound beneficial implications for software engineering. Besides providing a truly reliable basis for reasoning about the system governed by it, the law provides the ability to regulate the evolution of the architectural model itself, and the ability to ensure that certain properties of an evolving system would be *invariant of its evolution*.

Our concept of enforced architectural model, is based squarely on the author's concept of law-governed architecture (LGA), which so far has been implemented in two different manners (by means of Darwin-E software development environment [13], and by means of the Moses toolkit [15].) and which has been applied experimentally to a wide range of applications. This paper, then, is mostly of a polemic— arguing the need for and the benefit of enforced architectural models—with some discussion of new technical results.

We start, in Section 2 with a definition of our concept of enforced architectural model, emphasizing its application to evolving systems. We continue, in Section 3, with an informal case study: defining an enforced architectural model for of an evolving software embedded in an intensive-care unit, In Section 4 we present a concrete implementation of this case study under the the LGA-based Darwin-E environment [13]. In Section 5 we describe some related work, and we conclude in Section 6.

---

[1] The well known concept of layered system (used here only as a familiar example) is the partition of all modules in the system into ordered groups called "layers", along with the constraint that there should be no *up-calls* in the system—i.e., no calls from a lower layer to a higher one—and no down-call across more than one layer.

2 On the Nature of Enforced Architectural Models

As we attempt here to model *evolving system*, it is important to first clarify the type of evolution we have in mind. We are not dealing here with the common phenomenon of Darwinian-like evolution of software, where certain systems, such as text-editors, evolves through the independent creation of many variations of existing editors, and through "natural selection" between these variations in the market place. We limit the discussion in this paper to software embedded in some long-term enterprise—such as a manufacturing plant, or a financial establishment—which *evolves in its operational context*. In other words, we are dealing here with a time-sequence of systems $\{S_i\}$, operating more or less in the same context[2], where each S_i is a variant of its predecessor.

It stands to reason that the enterprise served by such a time-sequence of systems has some policy concerning the evolution of this sequence, and the structure of each of its instances—such as that each instance $\{S_i\}$ should be layered. What we propose here is to make such a policy explicit, and to *enforce it*, thus creating what we call an *e-system*[3] (for "evolving system"), denoting it by $\overline{S}$. This is made possible by what we call *law-governed architecture*[4] (LGA) [11], under which an e-system is defined as follows:

Definition 1 *An e-system $\overline{S}$ is a triple $\langle S, \mathcal{L}, \mathcal{E} \rangle$, where*

1. *S is the* system, *at a given moment in time. (That is, at time t, S is one of the stages S_t of $\overline{S}$.)*

2. *$\mathcal{L}$, called the* law *of $\overline{S}$, is an explicit collection of rules about the structure of the system S, about its process of evolution, and about the evolution of the law itself.*

3. *$\mathcal{E}$ is the environment in which $\overline{S}$ "lives," and which enforces the law. (The structure of one such environment is discussed in Section 2.3; another one is mentioned in that section briefly.)*

Since the law of an e-system $\overline{S}$ is enforced, one can be confident that any architectural principle expressed in it is actually satisfied by the system governed by it—there is no gap between the architectural model expressed by the law and the system itself.

In the rest of this section we elaborate on our concept of LGA as follows: we start with a brief discussion of the self regulatory nature of the law under LGA, and of the concept of *initial law* of an e-system; this is followed with our concept of *evolution invariant*; we then discuss two current implementations of this concept; and we conclude this section with some comments about the expressive power of laws, under both implementations.

2.1 The Evolution of the Law of an E-System

It is self evident that the law of an evolving system should not, in general, be immutable—this would be far too restrictive for the evolution of the system. On the other hand, the law is too critical an element to be allowed to change arbitrarily. Therefore, LGA provides for a self-regulated evolution of the law of an e-system, as prescribed by its initial law $\mathcal{L}_0$. This gives the *initial law* a very critical role—somewhat akin to the role played by the constitution of a country in determining its legal structure. As we shall demonstrate with the case study in this paper, $\mathcal{L}_0$ can provide software developers with a carefully circumscribed flexibility in molding the law of an e-system during its evolutionary lifetime, while maintaining certain architectural principles invariant.

---

[2]We say "more or less," because the operational context of such along-lived sequence of systems is itself likely to change, even if relatively slowly.

[3]The term "e-system" is used here, in part, to recall a somewhat related concept called an "e-type program" introduced by Lehman [8].

[4]The term "architecture" is used here in a somewhat different sense than in a phrase "architectural principle"—which is what is being established under LGA.

2.2   The Concept of Evolution-Invariant

If a certain property of an e-system $\overline{S}$ is entailed by its law $\mathcal{L}$, then this property is obviously an invariant of the evolution of the system, *as long as it is entails by the law*. So, for example, if the law requires the system S to be layered, it is guaranteed to be actually layered unless and until the law itself is changed not to require layering any longer.

The ability to have such *evolution invariants* could have profoundly beneficial effect on software development. But one can have an even stronger concept of invariant. It is possible to design the initial law of an e-system in such a way that it will always entail a certain property—as we shall see in our case study. This gives rise to a concept of *strong invariant*, which is a property (or a principle) of an evolving system that can never be changed—not even by the programmers of that system or by its managers.[5]

Such uncompromising concept of invariant may seem unnecessary, undesirable and even bizarre. Why not rely on the programmers or on their manager to decide which principle to employ, at every stage of system evolution? Why tie up the manager's hands before the construction of the system even began?

Our answer to these questions is that the manager of an e-systems that serves some critical societal role should not be the highest authority concerning the system he is building—and neither should be the one who pays for the system to be built. This is analogous to constructing a bridge, a public building or a financial system—which must be subject to certain principles and standards imposed by the society. A public building, for example, must have firewalls of certain kind, regardless of its shape or precise function, and a financial system must provide for some *internal controls* that support auditability, regardless of its design. The concept of strong invariant provides useful and necessary means for ensuring that certain high level societal principles will always be satisfied. (For a demonstration of how this can be done for the principle of internal control in financial systems the reader is referred to [10].

2.3   On the Implementation of LGA

So far we have built two different implementation of LGA: Darwin-E [13], and Moses [15]. They deal with different kinds of systems, support different types of laws, use different enforcement techniques, and have different advantages and limitations. They are basically complementary, and are intended to be eventually combined into one comprehensive environment.

Darwin-E is an experimental software development environment that plays the role of $\mathcal{E}$ in the definition above. Darwin-E supports the development and evolution of centralized (non-distributed) object-oriented systems (currently only systems written in Eiffel).

Moses, on the other hand, deals with heterogeneous distributed systems. It regulates the interaction between the components of a system, assuming nothing about the nature of these components themselves, which can be written in arbitrary languages.

Darwin-E enforces the law mostly statically, while Moses enforces its law dynamically, by intercepting the messages exchanged between the components of a system. The expressive power of both systems will be discussed in the next section, here we continue with some details about the structure of Darwin-E, which is the context of our case study in this paper.

Under our Darwin-E implementation, the state of a given e-system $\overline{S}$ developed within environment $\mathcal{E}$, is represented by a persistent object-base $\mathcal{B}_{\overline{S}}$. This is a collection of objects of various kinds, including: program *modules*, such as classes; *rules*, which are the component parts of the law; *metaRules*, which are instrumental in the creation of new rules; and *builders*, which serve as loci of activity for the people who participate in the process of software development. These objects have various properties, or attributes, associated with them, defined by terms such as `property_name(value)`. Suppose, for example, that $\overline{S}$ is designed to be partitioned into a set

---

[5]This, of course, is true only as long as the system is being developed under the environment $\mathcal{E}$ that enforces the law of the system in question.

of *divisions*, with some permanent—i.e., evolution-invariant—"firewalls" between them. Such divisions can be defined by associating an attribute division(d) with every module we wish place in division called d. We will see later how these attributes are used in the formulation of the law that establishes firewalls between various divisions.

One operates on a given e-system $\overline{S}$ only through environment $\mathcal{E}$, by sending it instructions to perform various operations, such as to add, remove or update an object in $\mathcal{B}_{\overline{S}}$.[6] Every such instruction is evaluated with respect to the law $\mathcal{L}$ of $\overline{S}$, and is treated accordingly. Consider, for example, an instruction to add a module m into division d of S. It could have one of the following consequences: (a) module m would be accepted, if it is found to be consistent with $\mathcal{L}$; (b) m would be rejected, if it is found to violate $\mathcal{L}$—say, if it is determined that m might, at run time, attempt to do something that is not permitted to any code in division d; and (c) m might be admitted with some changes, if so mandated by the law—for example, conditionals might be inserted into the code, to perform run-time checks in conformance with the law. In any case, $\mathcal{E}$ ensures that the system maintained in the object-base $\mathcal{B}_{\overline{S}}$ does not violate the law of $\overline{S}$. In practice, this enforcement of the law is carried out mostly statically, when a new code is inserted into the system, with some amount of run-tome checking due to case (c) above. (The law of the case study introduced in the following section is enforced entirely statically.)

2.4 On the Expressive Power of the Law

For an architectural principle to be defined into the law of an e-system it must be enforceable, and the enforcement must be reasonably efficient. This is, of course, a severe limitation on the expressive power of the law. Yet, the range of useful principles that can be established as a law under LGA is quite broad. Some indication of this range is given by the type of principles we already implemented under Darwin-E and Moses. These include, under Darwin-E, access-control regimes of the kind exemplified by our case study in this paper; more dynamic access-control of the kind used in operating systems [14]; auditability, which is particularly critical for financial systems [10]; establishing various programming styles [20]; and making sure that certain programming patterns are not misused [19]. Under Moses we have implemented a wide range of distributed coordination mechanisms [15]; dynamic reconfiguration mechanisms for distributed systems [17]; and very sophisticated security and access control policies [16].

3 Intensive-Care System: an Informal Case study

Consider the software system embedded in an *intensive care unit*[7]. Suppose that this system has been designed to be partitioned into the following three disjoint *divisions* (see Figure 3), each of which may contain any number of modules: the *kernel-division* $\mathcal{D}_k$, intended to interact directly with the patient, and to serve as the interface between the patient and the rest of the system; the *therapy*-division $\mathcal{D}_t$, intended to model and supervise the therapy of the patient; and the *observation-division* $\mathcal{D}_o$, intended to provide the users and operators of this system with the ability to observe its state while the system is running, without affecting it in any way.

Under conventional software development this design would function as general guidelines for programmers to observe when they build the system. But, as already pointed out, one cannot completely rely on the actual system to conform strictly to the constraints implied by this design; and it is clear that violations of these constraints—such as direct access to the patient from the observation division—could be literary fatal.

If, on the other hand, this intensive-care software is developed as an e-system $\overline{S}$, then this this general design, with some important elaborations to be introduced later, can be made into the law of the system, and thus be maintained as an invariant of its evolution.

---

[6]Note that the actual programming of a module does not have to be done under $\mathcal{E}$, and it is not under Darwin-E, in particular. It is the insertion of a module into a e-system that needs to be mediated by $\mathcal{E}$.

[7]This is an elaboration of an example given in [13].

In this section we describe the initial law $\mathcal{L}_0$ of $\overline{S}$ as a set of informally stated "principles," which will be formalized in Section 4 using the language for writing laws built into the Darwin-E environment. Altogether, we have six principles in $\mathcal{L}_0$, which are grouped into three sub-sections.

3.1 Constructing Permanent Firewalls between Divisions

The first three principles of $\mathcal{L}_0$ provides the various divisions of S with specific powers with respect to the patient and with respect to each other, in effect constructing firewalls between the three division.

Principle 1 *The kernel-division $\mathcal{D}_k$ has* **exclusive** *access to the actuators that control the flow of various fluids and gases into the veins of the patient, and to the gauges that monitor the patient's status.*

This principle localizes the direct interaction with the patient in $\mathcal{D}_k$, providing us with the ability build into $\mathcal{D}_k$ a model of the patient that is completely independent of the rest of the system, and invariant of the evolution of anything but $\mathcal{D}_k$ itself. This makes our systems much more reliable, easier to reason about, and much easier to evolve. Unfortunately, neither conventional programming languages nor software development environments provide any means for confining the ability to make system-calls—required to operate on any external devise, like the actuators connected to a patient—to a specific division of an evolving system.

To see the importance of this invariant it is instructive to consider the analogous invariant that exists in many operating systems, whose kernel has exclusive power to carry out *privileged operation*. This critical property of operating system is made invariant by the hardware of the host machine, which cannot be employed for analogous use in the software above the OS-kernel.

Our next principle confines division $\mathcal{D}_o$ to a purely observational role:

Principle 2 *The observation-division, $\mathcal{D}_o$, cannot affect the state or behavior of either $\mathcal{D}_k$ or $\mathcal{D}_t$.*

Specifically, this principle permits code in $\mathcal{D}_o$ to make only *side-effect-free* (SEF) calls to methods defined in the other two divisions of S; i.e., it can only make calls to methods guaranteed not to leave any side-effects on the rest of the system.

The main merit of this principle is that it significantly reduces the harm that can be caused by careless programming of $\mathcal{D}_o$, making this division much less safety-critical than the rest of the system[8]. As a consequence, updates of $\mathcal{D}_o$ do not have to be subjected to the same rigorous process of verification and testing as one is likely to employ for the rest of the system.

Principle 3 *The access that therapy-division $\mathcal{D}_t$ has to the kernel is limited to the methods that are explicitly declared as exported by the kernel-division.*

The point of this principle is to provide a way for the kernel to keep some of its methods for internal use only. (The manner in which methods can be declared internal to a division, or exported from it, is discussed in [12].) The enforcement of this principle is again essential because it protects the kernel, guaranteeing that a non exported method will *never* be called by *any* code in the therapy-division. (Unlike the previous two principles, this one can be established as an invariant under some conventional languages, such as Java, in particular.)

3.2 Establishing a Malleable Access-Control Policy

To demonstrate some of the implications of the self-regulated evolution of laws under LGA, we illustrate here two general evolutionary patterns for the law of an e-system, which we call *refinements*, and *relaxations*.

---

[8]It should be pointed out that limiting the observation-division to only side-effect-free calls does not render it *completely* harmless, because it might hog some resources (such as CPU time) eventually crashing the system. But this principle would make changes in the observation-division far less risky.

Refinements of the Law: Some aspects of a system must generally be left unregulated by the initial law, but may need to be regulated later on, when more of the system is designed or constructed, or when the system is put to actual use. The framework providing for such future regulation can be established in $\mathcal{L}_0$. For instance, let the following principle be included in the initial law of of our example system $\overline{S}$:

Principle 4 *Every intra-division calls is permitted—unless it is explicitly forbidden by a special kind of rule that only the manager of the division in question can add to the law, or remove from it.*

In other words, the initial law imposes no constraints over intra-division calls. But it does provide for such constraints to be imposed in the future, by adding to the law rules of a certain structure, specified in $\mathcal{L}_0$ (see Section 4 for details). Moreover, only the manager of a given division is authorized by this principle to thus regulate the calls within his division.

Relaxation of the Law: A principle may be formulated into $\mathcal{L}_0$, with explicit provisions for making a carefully circumscribed exceptions to it in the future. For example, let the following principle be included in the initial law of $\overline{S}$:

Principle 5 *The kernel $\mathcal{D}_k$ has no access to the rest of the system—unless such an access is explicitly approved by a special kind of rule that only the manager of team of kernel programmers $\mathcal{D}_k$ can add to the law, or remove from it.*

The motivation for this principle is as follows: Denying the kernel any access to the rest of the system has the advantage of making the kernel completely self contained, and thus much easier to reason about. But a rigid denial of such access may be considered impractical and counter productive. Consequently, Principle 5 is a default prohibition of any access from $\mathcal{D}_k$ to the rest of the system, which can be overridden by the manager of $\mathcal{D}_k$ by adding to the law "permission rules" of a certain structure, specified in $\mathcal{L}_0$ (see Section 4 for details).

3.3 Making the Initial Law Immutable

The initial law of an e-system can specify which kind of rules can never be recanted, and are, thus, an immutable part of the law. A simple example of such immutability is provided by the following principle of our initial law:

Principle 6 *All the principles of the initial law of this e-system are immutable.*

This means, in particular, that Principles 1 through 3 are *strong invariants* of the evolution of this system, in the sense of 2.2, because they are guaranteed never to be repealed. Also, due to Principle 6 the law of this e-system can evolve *only* in the manner specified by Principles 4 and 5.

This principle is analogous to saying that the constitution of a country is immutable. This does not mean that the body of laws of this country is immutable, but that the only way for the law to change is as prescribed in the immutable constitution. Of course, this last principle does not have to be included in the initial law of an e-system, one can as easily model the analogue of a mutable constitution, in analogy to the constitution of the USA.

4 Implementation of the Intensive-Care System Under Darwin-E

We introduce in this section the formal definition of the law of the e-system $\overline{S}$ embedded in an intensive-care unit, which has been discussed informally in Section 3. We do this under the Darwin-E environment, assuming that the system is to be written in the Eiffel language. We start with a very brief description of the structure of laws under Darwin-E, referring the reader to [13, 10] for more details. We then present the complete initial law of $\overline{S}$, and we conclude with a brief discussion of the long-term behavior of the law of $\overline{S}$.

4.1 The Structure of Laws Under Darwin-E

Broadly speaking, the law of an e-system $\overline{S}$ under Darwin-E consists of two collections, called sub-laws, of Prolog-like rules:

1. The *system sub-law*, that governs the structure and behavior of any system instance S of $\overline{S}$.

2. The *evolution sub-law*, that governs the process of development and evolution of $\overline{S}$, and of of the law itself.

The System Sub-Law This part of the law of $\overline{S}$ regulates various types of interactions between the component parts of the system S being developed. An example of such a *regulated interaction* is the relation `inherit(c1,c2)`, which means that class[9] c1 inherits directly from class c2 in S. Another regulated interaction is the relation `call(f1,c1,f2,c2)` which means that routine f1 featured by class c1 contains a call to feature f2 of class c2. These, and other regulated interactions, are discussed in detail in [13].

The disposition of a given interaction t is determined by evaluating the "goal" can_t with respect to the the system-part of law $\mathcal{L}$, which is expected to contain some rules that deal with this interaction. For example, the following rule

```
can_inherit(C1,C2) :-division(D)@C1,division(D)@C2.
```

deals with the `inherit` interaction, permitting classes in the same division to inherit from each other.

Evolution Sub-law The evolution sub-law regulates the operations carried out on the object-base of $\overline{S}$, generally by its programmers. The disposition of a message sent by programmer p to an on object o, invoking method m is determined by evaluating the "goal" canDo(p,m,o) with respect to the the evolution-part of law $\mathcal{L}$, which is expected to contain appropriate rules. For example, the following rule

```
canDo(P,M,O) :- division(D)@P,division(D)@O.
```

authorizes all messages whose sender and target belong to the same division, thus providing programmers with complete access to all objects in their own division.

Finally, we point out that Darwin-E provides means for the changing of the law itself, which are themselves controllable by the law. In particular there is a special type of objects called *metaRules*, each of which serves as a template for a certain kind of rules. Given one such metaRule mr, one can create a specific rule of its kind by sending a message `createRule` to it. Such messages, like all others in Darwin-E, are regulated by the law. We shall see an example of such a regulation later.

4.2 The Initial Law of the Intensive-Care System

Each of the rules in this law is prefixed by a label, used for our discussion only, and is followed with a comment (in italic), which, together with the accompanying discussion, should make the rules understandable even by a reader not familiar with the details of our formalism, or with the Prolog language which it resembles. The law is presented in two section, the first contains the system sub-law, and the second contains the evolution sub-law.

The Initial System Sub-law This part of $\mathcal{L}_0$, contains the rules displayed in Figure 1, and explained in some detail below.

---

[9] Note that contrary to the convention of Eiffel we use lower case symbols to name classes, because upper-case symbols have a technical meaning in our rules, analogous to that of *variables* in Prolog.

$\mathcal{R}$1. `can_useC(C1,_) :- division(kernel)@C1.`

C-code can be used only by the kernel, which thus has has exclusive power to operate on the patient by making system calls.

$\mathcal{R}$2. `can_inherit(C1,C2) :- division(D)@C1, division(D)@C2.`

Only classes in the same division are allowed to inherit from each other.

$\mathcal{R}$3. `can_call(F1,C1,F2,C2) :-`
`        division(D)@C1,division(D)@C2`
`        not prohibition(D,F1,C1,F2,C2).`

All intra-division calls are permitted, provided that there is no prohibition rule that blocks them.

$\mathcal{R}$4. `can_call(F1,C1,F2,C2) :-`
`        division(application)@C1,division(kernel)@C2,`
`        exported(F2)@C2.`

Calls from the application to the kernel are permitted, provided that the called method, F2, is defined as an "exported" method.

$\mathcal{R}$5. `can_call(F1,C1,F2,C2) :-`
`        division(kernel)@C1,division(application)@C2,`
`        permission(F1,C1,F2,C2).`

Calls from the kernel to the application are permitted only if there is a special permission *rule that authorizes it.*

$\mathcal{R}$6. `can_call(F1,C1,F2,C2) :-`
`        division(observation)@C1,`
`        (division(application)@C2|(division(kernel)@C2,`
`        sef(F2)@C2.`

Side-effect-free (SEF) calls from the monitor to the other two divisions are permitted.

Figure 1. Rules in $\mathcal{L}_0$ that Regulate the structure of $\mathcal{S}$

- Rule $\mathcal{R}1$ allows Kernel-classes only to have methods written in bare C-code, which (in a Unix environment) can be used to make system-calls to operate on the patient. Since Eiffel itself provides no means for making system-calls, this rule provides the kernel with the exclusive power to operate directly on the patient, as required by Principle 1.

- Rule $\mathcal{R}2$ regulated the *inheritance* relation between classes, allowing only classes in the same division to inherit from each other. This leaves *calls* as the only possible means for interaction between the two different divisions of S. *Calls* are regulated by rules $\mathcal{R}3$ through $\mathcal{R}6$, as explained below.

- Rule $\mathcal{R}3$ authorizes all intra-division calls, *unless* they are forbidden by some `prohibition` rule. Such rules have the form

  ```
  prohibition(D,F1,C1,F2,C2) :- c(F1,C1,F2,C2).
  ```

  and they serve here to prohibit the set (defined by condition c(...)) of call-interactions call(F1,C1,F2,C2) within division D.

  Note that there are no such rules in the initial law $\mathcal{L}_0$, but as we shall see later, rules of this kind, for a given division, can be created by the manager of this division, at his discretion. This is in accordance with Principle 4, which calls for the manager of each division to be able impose additional constraints on calls within his division. Using such rules the manager may, in particular, specify in details which module can call which other module, or he may establish some general principle, such as layered organization, within his division, or he may choose to create no prohibitions at all.

  It should also be pointed out that the `prohibition` rules discussed above have no built-in semantics in the Darwin-E environment. Their semantics in this particular e-system is defined by Rule $\mathcal{R}3$ of its initial law.

- Rule $\mathcal{R}4$ authorizes the application-division to call *exported methods* of the kernel, in accordance with Principle 3. An exported method `f` in class `c` is defined by an attribute `exported(f)` associated with the object representing class `c`.

- Rule $\mathcal{R}5$ authorizes calls from the kernel to the application-division, *provided* they are approved by some `permission` rule. Note that like in the case of the `prohibition` rules discussed above, there are no `permission` rules in the initial law $\mathcal{L}_0$, but, as we shall see, such rules can be created while the system evolves, by the manager of kernel, in accordance with Principle 5.

- Finally, Rule $\mathcal{R}6$ authorizes the observation-division to make, what we call, side-effect-free (SEF) calls to methods in the other two divisions. These are calls to routines that are guaranteed *not* to make any permanent change to the system. This concept of side-effect-free routines is established by a small set of primitive rules permanently associated with every e-system under Darwin-E environment, in a manner described in [10].

The Initial Evolution Sub-law Let us turn now to the control provided by $\mathcal{L}_0$ over the process of evolution of $\overline{S}$, including the manner in which the law itself is allowed to be changed. This control is provided by the set of rules listed in Figure 2, which are explained below:

- Rule $\mathcal{R}7$ provides for the creations of new objects (of various kinds) into the object base $\mathcal{B}$ of the e-system, forcing the newly created object to reside in the division of its creator. In other words, by this rule, programmers can create new objects only in their own division.

- Rule $\mathcal{R}8$ allows programmers to operate almost freely on objects in their own division, sending them any message except those defined by Rule $\mathcal{R}9$ as "special." These special messages include `new` which is handled by Rule $\mathcal{R}7$; messages that create and destroy rules, which are handled by Rules $\mathcal{R}10$ and $\mathcal{R}11$; and messages that can change the division of an object, which are not permitted by this law, for obvious reasons.

- Rules $\mathcal{R}10$ and $\mathcal{R}11$ regulates the evolution of the law itself. Rule $\mathcal{R}10$ authorizes managers to create new rules, by sending a `createRule` message to some *metaRule* object at his own division. The newly created rules are automatically placed in the manager's division. The

$\mathcal{R}$7. `canDo(P,new(X,_),O) :- division(D)@P, $do(set(division(D))@X).`

All new objects (like program-modules) created by programmers would reside in the division of their creator.

$\mathcal{R}$8. `canDo(P,M,O) :-`
`        division(D)@P,division(D)@O,`
`        not special(M).`

Programmers can operate almost freely on objects in their own division, sending them any message except those defined by Rule $\mathcal{R}$9 as "special."

$\mathcal{R}$9. `special(M) :- M= createRule(_,_)| M= createMetaRuke(_,_,_)|`
`        M= new(_,_)| M= set(division(_))| M= recant(division(_)) )`

This auxiliary rule defines some messages to be "special," and thus not subject to Rule $\mathcal{R}$8. This include messages that create rules and metaRules, and operations that change the division to which an object belongs.

$\mathcal{R}$10. `canDo(P,createRule(R,_),O) :-`
`        role(manager)@P,division(D)@P,`
`        type(metaRule)@O,division(D)@O,`
`        $do(set(division(D))@R).`

An manager can create new rules, using metaRule objects that belong to his division; the newly created rule would be automatically included in the manager's division.

$\mathcal{R}$11. `canDo(P,removeRule,O) :-`
`        role(manager)@P,division(D)@P,division(D)@O.`

A manager can remove rules defined as belonging to his own division

Figure 2. Rules in $\mathcal{L}_0$ that Regulate the Process of Evolution

actual effect of Rules $\mathcal{R}10$ in e-system $\overline{S}$ is determined by the set of metaRules provided in the initial state of this e-system, because $\mathcal{L}_0$ does not provide for the creation of any other metaRules. We assume that the initial state of $\overline{S}$ contains a metaRule that can be used for the creation of `permission` rules, and which belongs to the kernel-division, and metaRule in each of our three divisions, which can be used to create `prohibition` rules for this division. Space limitation precluded any discussion of the structure of these metaRules, but see [9] for a general discussion of metaRules and for rule-formation.

- Finally, Rule $\mathcal{R}11$ allows the manager of each division to remove rules defined as belonging to his own division. These are the `permission` and the `prohibition` rules created according to Rules $\mathcal{R}10$ above. (Note that this rule *does not* permit the removal of any rules defined in the initial law itself.

4.3 The Long Term Behavior of the Law of $\overline{S}$

Concluding our discussion of the law $\mathcal{L}$ of $\overline{S}$ we note here that this law is destined to always consist of the following three collection of rules:

1. The eleven rules of the initial law, which cannot be changed or removed.

2. Any number of rules of the form

   ```
   prohibition(D,F1,C1,F2,C2) :- c(F1,C1,F2,C2).
   ```

   that impose restrictions on inter-division calls, in each of the three division of S, and which can be created and removed by the managers of the respective divisions.

3. Any number of rules of the form

   ```
   permission(F1,C1,F2,C2) :- c(F1,C1,F2,C2).
   ```

   which authorize calls from the kernel to $\mathcal{D}_t$, and which can be created and removed by the manager of the kernel.

5 Related Work

This work is related to two distinct research directions: on *Software Architecture* (SA), and on *process-centered environment*

We share with the emerging research on SA the conviction that a complex evolving system needs an explicit *architectural model*, which provides a framework within which the system can be reasoned about and maintained [21, 4, 23]. The main difference between this body of work and ours is that under SA an architectural model is a high level *specification*, which is not guaranteed to be satisfied by the actual system; reasoning about a system on the basis of such a model is unreliable and dangerous. Our architectural model, on the other hand, is, in very real sense "the law of the system," and is guaranteed to be satisfied by it. Of course, we do pay a price in terms of expressive power: not everything that can be stated in one of the conventional ADL's can be stated as a law under LGA.

The process of software evolution is the subject of an extensive body of research on what is called *process-centered environments* such as Arcadia [6], Marvel [7], Polis [2], and Adele-Tempo [1]. There are similarities between our law—as a means for regulating the process of software development—and the concept of "process programming" in Arcadia, or the set of rules of Marvel Polis or Adele. But the rules of Marvel, and the process programs of Arcadia, do not deal with the structure of the evolving system itself, and, thus, cannot establish architectural principles regarding that systems—nor are they trying to do so.

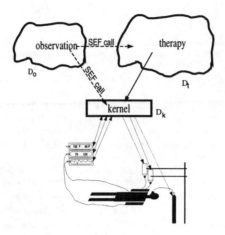

legend: SEF means side-effect-free

Figure 3. An Intensive Care System

6 Conclusion

The thesis of this paper is that for an architectural model to yield its full benefits it needs to be enforced. We have described a specific concept of *enforced architectural model*—or, a *law*—that has the following beneficial consequences: (a) it can provide a truly reliable and stable framework within which a system can be reasoned about and maintained; and (b) It provides software developers with a carefully circumscribed flexibility in molding the law of a project, during its evolutionary lifetime—while maintaining certain architectural principles as invariant of evolution. The concept of evolutionary invariance, in particular, can be invaluable for safety-critical systems, and, more generally, for systems that play some sensitive societal role.

This paper is based on the general concept of law-governed architecture (LGA) which has been implemented in two different but complementary manners: in Darwin-E for centralized object-oriented systems, and in Moses for heterogeneous distributed systems.

References

[1] N. Belkhtair, J. Estublier, and W. Melo. Adele-tempo: An environment for process modeling and enaction. In A. Finkelstein, J. Kramer, and B. Nuseibeh, editors, *Software Process Modeling and Technology*. John Wiley and Sons, 1994.

[2] Paolo Ciancarini. Enacting rule-based software processes with polis. Technical report, University of Pisa, october 1991.

[3] C. K. Duby, S. Meyers, and S. P. Reiss. CCEL: A metalanguage for C++. In *USENIX C++ Conference*, August 1992.

[4] D. Garlan. Research direction in software architecture. *ACM Computing Surveys*, 27(2):257–261, 1995.

[5] D. Garlan and D. Perry. Introduction to the special issue on software architecture. *IEEE Transactions on Software Engineering*, April 1995.

[6] D. Heimbinger. Prescription versus proscription in process-centered environments. In *Proceedings of the 6th International Software Process Workshop, Hakkaido Japan*, October 1990. To appear.

[7] G. Kaiser. Intelligent assistance for software development and maintenance. *IEEE Software*, May 1988.

[8] M.M. Lehman. *Program Evolution*, pages 3–24. IFIP, 1985. Teichroew and David Eds.

[9] N.H. Minsky. Law-governed systems. *The IEE Software Engineering Journal*, September 1991.

[10] N.H. Minsky. Independent on-line monitoring of evolving systems. In *Proceedings of the 18th International Conference on Software Engineering (ICSE)*, pages 134–143, March 1996.

[11] N.H. Minsky. Law-governed regularities in object systems; part 1: An abstract model. *Theory and Practice of Object Systems (TAPOS)*, 2(1), 1996.

[12] N.H. Minsky. Taking software architecture seriously. Technical report, Rutgers University, April 1996. (available through `http://www.cs.rutgers.edu/~minsky/index.html`).

[13] N.H. Minsky. Law-governed regularities in object systems; part 2: A concrete implementation. *Theory and Practice of Object Systems (TAPOS)*, 3(2), 1997.

[14] N.H. Minsky and P. Pal. Providing multiple views for objects by means of surrogates. Technical report, Rutgers University, LCSR, November 1995. (available through `http://www.cs.rutgers.edu/~minsky/`).

[15] N.H. Minsky and V. Ungureanu. Regulated coordination in open distributed systems. In David Garlan and Daniel Le Metayer, editors, *Proc. of Coordination'97: Second International Conference on Coordination Models and Languages; LNCS 1282*, pages 81–98, September 1997.

[16] N.H. Minsky and V. Ungureanu. Unified support for heterogeneous security policies in distributed systems. In *7th USENIX Security Symposium*, January 1998.

[17] N.H. Minsky, V. Ungureanu, W. Wang, and J. Zhang. Building reconfiguration primitives into the law of a system. In *Proc. of the Third International Conference on Configurable Distributed Systems (ICCDS'96)*, March 1996. (available through `http://www.cs.rutgers.edu/~minsky/`).

[18] G.C. Murphy, D. Notkin, and K. Sullivan. Software reflection models: Bridging the gap between source and high level models. In *Proceedings of the Third ACM Symposium on the Foundation of Software Engineering*, 1995.

[19] P. Pal. Law-governed support for realizing design patterns. In *Proceedings of the 17th Conference on Technology of Object-Oriented Languages and Systems(TOOLS-17)*, pages 25–34, August 1995.

[20] P. Pal and N.H. Minsky. Imposing the law of demeter and its variations. In *Proceedings of the 18th Conference on Technology of Object-Oriented Languages and Systems(TOOLS-18)*, August 1996.

[21] D.E. Perry and A.L. Wolf. Foundations for the study of software architecture. *Software Engineering Notes*, 17(4):40–52, October 1992.

[22] M. Sefica, A Sane, and R.H. Campbell. Monitoring complience of a software system with its high-level design model. In *Proceedings of the 18th International Conference on Software Engineering (ICSE)*, March 1996.

[23] M. Shaw. Architectural issues in software reuse: It's not just the functionality, it's the packaging. In *Proceedings of IEEE Symp. on Software Reuse*, 1995.

Toward a Scalable Method for Quantifying Aspects of Fault Tolerance, Software Assurance, and Computer Security

Philip Koopman
Department of Electrical and Computer Engineering
& Institute for Complex Engineered Systems
Carnegie Mellon University, Pittsburgh, PA
koopman@cmu.edu

Abstract

Quantitative assessment tools are urgently needed in the areas of fault tolerance, software assurance, and computer security. Assessment methods typically employed in various combinations are fault injection, formal verification, and testing. However, these methods are expensive because they are labor-intensive, with costs scaling at least linearly with the number of software modules tested. Additionally, they are subject to human lapses and oversights because they require two different representations for each system, and then base results on a direct or an indirect representation comparison.

The Ballista project has found that robustness testing forms a niche in which scalable quantitative assessment can be achieved at low cost. This scalability stems from two techniques: associating state-setting information with test cases based on data types, and using one generic, but narrow, behavioral specification for all modules. Given that this approach has succeeded in comparing the robustness of various operating systems, it is natural to ask if it can be made more generally applicable.

It appears that Ballista-like testing can be used in the fault tolerance area to measure the generic robustness of a variety of API implementations, and in particular to identify reproducible ways to crash and hang software. In software assurance, it can be used as a quality check on exception handling, and in particular as a means to augment black box testing. Applying it to computer security appears more problematic, but might be possible if there is a way to orthogonally decompose various aspects of security-relevant system state into analogs of Ballista data types.

While Ballista-like testing is no substitute for traditional methods, it can serve to provide a useful quality assurance check that augments existing practice at relatively low cost. Alternately, it can serve to quantify the extent of potential problems, enabling better informed decisions by both developers and customers.

> When you can measure what you are speaking about, and express it in numbers, you know something about it; but when you can not measure it, when you can not express it in numbers, your knowledge is of a meager and unsatisfactory kind: it may be the beginning of knowledge, but you have scarcely, in your thought, advanced to the stage of science.
>
> — Lord Kelvin

1. Introduction

One of the more difficult aspects of working in the areas of fault tolerance, software assurance, and computer security is quantifying results. Quantification is absolutely essential attain a mature capability for creating systems of any kind. And yet, despite significant research efforts, the attainment of quantification is proving elusive in the area of software-intensive systems. While there is no doubt that progress has been made in the area of general software development methodology, the focus has been on the primary attributes of productivity and software correctness. Less attention has been paid to what are often considered secondary attributes, such as fault tolerance, software safety, and security. These three areas seem to share a common problem in that it is difficult to attain quantification, largely because of the interaction of four problems.

First, the properties of software-intensive systems that need to be measured are typically very dependent on the details of the system specification or usage. Examples include functional defect rates, whether a system is "safe," and whether a system is "secure." This means that any measurement tool must be provided with a wealth of information about the system, and in general this requires access to a substantial portion of the system specification. Complicating the situation is that the specification, or indeed even the detailed implementation, may be unavailable for software components purchased off-the-shelf. Obtaining such information costs time and money. To illustrate how difficult this makes things, compare the difficulty of determining whether a computer system is secure to determining its speed at executing a prepackaged benchmark suite.

Second, the desired measurement outcome is often desired to be perfection (attaining a zero defect rate, completely safe,' or never fails). Even though such perfection is generally unattainable in practice, it means that tests are focussed on finding deviations from a specification of some sort. This is in sharp contrast to more traditional computer system metrics such as computation speed or achieved network bandwidth. It also raises issues if, as is often (always?) the case, the specification itself is imperfect.

Third, it is common for the same tests that are used to measure the system to be used directly to fix any shortcomings found. For example, a project measuring bug reports per week of testing would naturally feed all bug reports to the maintenance group for correction. Thus, it is common for the measurement process itself to be coupled to changes in the system being measured. While it is clear that traditional speed measurements result in systems being optimized to perform better, the situation is different here in that there is no fundamental quantity to be measured (such as a particular workload to complete). Rather, deviations from perfection are being both measured and corrected by the same process.

Fourth, and perhaps most important from a practical implementation point of view, is that the process of measuring "bad things" such as bugs is often seen as a destructive act, as opposed to measuring "good things" such as performance. The outcome of a metric value of less than perfection can be seen as a label implying defective goods, whereas the outcome of a positive metric such as speed is merely a measurement of an inherent property.

Despite these problems, it is imperative that we find ways to quantify properties of systems that we wish to understand and to improve over time. (Of course there is always the risk of inventing numbers just for the sake of having numbers, so it is also important to find metrics that are at least correlated to actual desirable properties.) Thus, it would be desirable to have a measurement tool or methodology that does not require much detailed information about the system it is measuring, does not attempt to measure quantities that deviate very slightly from perfection, uses novel tests for each measurement or otherwise disentangles measurement from defect correction, and is somehow seen as a constructive measurement rather than a destructive activity.

The work discussed herein does not satisfy all the criteria for providing high-quality numbers that will stand the test of time. Thus, we still seek the true numbers that Lord Kelvin exhorts us to use. However, on the principle that progress in measurement is a generally worthy goal, our approach might be considered a step in the right direction. In particular, this work demonstrates that it is possible in some cases to automate testing a large amount of software without simply turning a large testing effort into a similarly large exercise in providing detailed information to the automated testing system.

1.1. General existing techniques for software measurement

It is, of course, currently possible to measure many properties of software. The most mature of these approaches were born of the so-called software crisis that has somehow managed to last, at this point, several decades. These metrics attempt to measure productivity and thus evaluate ways to improve that productivity. They include the venerable source lines of code (SLOC), the widely used cyclomatic complexity metrics [27], and other more advanced metrics (*e.g.,* as discussed in [16]). While these metrics variously use measurements of the software itself, the software is not being evaluated for inherent utility. Instead, software is measured to determine complexity, which is then used to estimate development and maintenance costs (and, perhaps indirectly, to generate an estimated defect rate).

More recently, a wide variety of metrics and measurement methodologies have been proposed for the software reliability area. These metrics tend to use varying combinations of software complexity, development-phase defect discovery, testing-phase defect discovery, and in-service defect discovery to make predictions about residual defect rates for new and existing software systems (a broad discussion of such approaches can be found in [16] and [26]).

While software reliability metrics are definitely a productive step in the right direction, their use is not without problems. Testing-based approaches amount to requiring a software test suite development effort proportional to developing the original software in the first place, and thus are expensive. While in most cases testing of normal functionality is seen as necessary, there is a problem in that exception handling code and other portions of the system can overshadow the basic functionality in terms of testing complexity [5]. This means that in all but the most extreme safety-critical cases, limited time, budget, and manpower often result in testing effort being concentrated on "normal" functionality, giving short shrift to dependability aspects. In other words, reliability testing can fall victim to the problems of cost and not being seen as a primary value-added business activity beyond a certain point.

An alternate approach, that is often combined with a testing-based approach, is one based on monitoring defect discovery rates. If one assumes that defects are discovered at low marginal cost (*e.g.,* through an extensive beta testing program or a mandated functional correctness testing program), then such monitoring becomes a reasonably low cost exercise. However, this approach does suffer from the potential problem of delaying measurement feedback until downstream in the development cycle, when problems are potentially more expensive to fix. Additionally, defect rate monitoring has the problem that (presumably) the important defects are fixed, altering the system under test over time.

1.2. Robustness testing as an example of potentially general approach

This paper describes the attainment of a relatively generic, low cost, scalable, portable testing and measurement methodology for robustness. In particular, the methodology measures the robustness of an Application Programming Interface (API) with respect to exceptional parameter values. The current results have implications for fault tolerance, software assurance, and computer security, and the methodology might be extended further.

Robustness was selected for measurement because system crashes are a way of life in any real-world system, no matter how carefully designed. Software is increasingly becoming the source of system failures, and the majority of software failures in practice seem to be due to problems with robustness [10]. Thirty years ago, the Apollo 11 mission experienced three computer crashes and reboots during descent to lunar landing, caused by exceptional radar configuration settings that resulted in the system running out of memory buffers [19]. Decades later, the maiden flight of the Ariane 5 heavy lifting rocket was lost due to events arising from a floating point-to-integer conversion exception [24]. Today, exceptional conditions routinely cause system failures in telecommunication systems, desktop computers, and elsewhere. Given that such problems have persisted in mission-critical space computers for decades, it is not difficult to predict they will still be with us several decades hence in everyday computing. However, the problem then will be that everyday computing will have completed its change from luxury to necessity, making such failures potentially devastating instead of merely inconvenient or expensive.

Thus, the Ballista project was created to measure the robustness of systems. Because operating system (OS) software underlies most large systems, the first application area that was chosen was to produce quantified results for robustness testing of full-scale, off-the-shelf operating systems. Automated testing was performed on fifteen POSIX [18] operating system versions from ten different vendors across a variety of hardware platforms. More than one million tests were executed in all, covering up to 233 distinct functions and system calls for each OS. Many of the tests resulted in robustness failures, ranging in severity from complete system crashes to false indication of successful operation in unspecified circumstances.

In brief, the Ballista testing methodology involves automatically generating sets of exceptional parameter values to be used in calling software modules. The results of these calls are examined to determine whether the module detected and notified the calling program of an error, and whether the task or even system suffered a crash or hang. There are two key approaches that make this approach inexpensive and scalable: the use of an object-oriented testing approach based on data types rather than functionality, and the fact that testing is performed for a relatively simple property of robustness rather than for the more complex property of correctness.

In the following sections we shall discuss previous work in this area, the Ballista testing methodology, and potential applications of that methodology to the areas of fault tolerance, software assurance, and computer security. While part of the story is simply the application of existing Ballista results and methodologies to these areas, the rest of the discussion will be more speculative, and hypothesize ways in which the approach might be generalized and extended.

2. Previous work

While the Ballista robustness testing method described in this paper is a form of software testing, its heritage traces back not only to the software testing community, but also to the fault tolerance community as a form of software-based fault injection. In software testing terms, Ballista performs tests for responses to exceptional input conditions (sometimes called "dirty" tests, which involve exceptional situations, as opposed to "clean" tests of correct functionality in normal situations). The test ideas used are based on "black box," or functional testing techniques [Bezier95] in which only functionality is of concern, not the actual structure of the source code. However, Ballista in its current form is not concerned with validating functionality for ordinary operating conditions, but rather determining whether or not a software module is robust.

In common usage, the term robustness might refer to the time between operating system crashes under some usage profile. However, the authoritative definition of *robustness* that will be used in the current discussion is "the degree to which a system or component can function correctly in the presence of invalid inputs or stressful environmental conditions" [17]. This expands the notion of robustness to be more than catastrophic system crashes, and encompasses situations in which small, recoverable failures might also occur. Ballista work concentrates on the portion of robustness dealing with invalid inputs. While robustness under stressful environmental conditions is indeed an important issue, a desire to attain highly repeatable results has led the Ballista project to consider only robustness issues dealing with a single invocation of a software module from a single execution thread (however, as will be discussed, this is far less limiting an approach than one might think).

2.1. Crashme

An early and well known method for automatically testing operating systems for robustness was the development of the Crashme program [7]. Crashme operates by writing randomized data values to memory, then spawning large numbers of tasks that attempted to execute those random bytes as programs. While many tasks terminate almost immediately due to illegal instruction exceptions, on occasion a single task or a confluence of multiple tasks can cause an operating system to fail. The effectiveness of the Crashme approach relies upon serendipity (in other words, if run long enough it may eventually find some way to crash the system).

The crashme approach has the distinct advantage that it is relatively easy to implement, and can be ported readily to a wide variety of systems. It also has the compelling virtue that it actually does find ways to crash operating systems. However, as a technique it is not readily applied to other application areas, and does not produce repeatable, deterministic results that are desirable for concise bug reports. Finally, it is not really designed to quantify and compare systems so much as discover problems in a particular system.

2.2. Fault injection

Other work in the fault injection area has also tested aspects of robustness. The Fiat system [3] uses probes placed by the programmer to alter the binary process image in memory during execution. The Ferrari system [20] is similar in intent to FIAT, but uses software traps in a manner similar to debugger break-points to permit emulation of specific system-level hardware faults (*e.g.*, data address lines, condition codes). The FTAPE system [37] injects faults into a system being exercised with a random workload generator by using a platform-specific device driver to inject the faults. While all of these systems have produced interesting results, none was intended to quantify robustness on the scale of an entire OS API.

The Fuzz project at the University of Wisconsin has used random noise (or "fuzz") injection to discover robustness problems in operating systems. That work documented the source of several problems [29], and then discovered that the problems were still present in operating systems several years later [30]. The Fuzz approach tested specific OS elements and interfaces (compared to the completely random approach of Crashme), although it still relied on random data injection.

The Ballista testing approach builds upon a legacy of work in the fault injection area performed by Siewiorek and his students at Carnegie Mellon University. This work has long sought a combination of repeatability, high-level implementation, and portability (quantification was not an explicit goal, but can be accomplished given that the other goals have been met).

A first effort at Carnegie Mellon was the creation of a descendent of crashme called CMU-crashme. Instead of executing random data, CMU-crashme restricted randomness to parameter values for concurrently executed system calls. This had the effect of concentrating testing on the OS interface, and eliminating a large number of tests that simply resulted in illegal instruction exceptions. It still, however, relied on serendipity to discover problems and was not repeatable.

The next generation of work was called robustness benchmarking, in which carefully selected data values were sent to selected function calls, with one call executed at a time. The effort was labor-intensive in that it required developing a test suite, but attained repeatability. And, perhaps surprisingly, even with a single-call model it found ways to crash operating systems from user mode, including a space-qualified fault tolerant aerospace computer [14]. Eventually, several operating systems were tested with a handful of calls, demonstrating portability, and revealing that robustness failures were prevalent across various systems [22].

Once repeatability had been achieved, the obvious next step was to genericize the tests and attain scalability for larger APIs. Thus, work was done to extend the robustness benchmarks by genericizing different operations within a function and attempting to associate them with different test data types [31]. For example, many functions serve to create a data object, whether it be a file, an allocated block of memory, or a data structure. Similarly, other functions modify, delete, and copy such objects. Thus, one could think of genericizing the function of a particular module into one of a preset category, and then direct testing based on a combination of generic function and data type. While this approach did work, attempts to scale it to full-size systems were unsuccessful because the effort required to specify generic functionality scaled linearly with the number of functions being tested. The approach remains promising, but is not without further issues to be resolved.

After attempting to genericize functions, a fresh approach to the problem was taken by eliminating the involvement of functionality altogether, and creating test cases based on data type information alone. This approach was the source of the Ballista testing methodology [23], which attained repeatability, portability, and scalability, and is described in more detail in later sections. As an additional benefit, the ability to perform over a million tests on more than a dozen operating systems provided enough test data to create a strategy for quantification of robustness.

2.3. Software testing

Given a desire to provide crashme-like testing in a more deterministic, repeatable setting, one can turn to software testing to borrow concepts. Software testing for the purpose of determining reliability is often carried out by exercising a software system under representative workload conditions and measuring failure rates. In addition, emphasis is often placed on code coverage as a way of assessing whether a module has been thoroughly tested. Unfortunately, traditional software reliability testing may not uncover robustness problems that occur because of unexpected input values generated by bugs in other modules, or because of an encounter with atypical operating conditions.

Structural, or white-box, testing techniques are useful for attaining high test coverage of programs. But, they typically focus on the control flow of a program rather than handling of exceptional data values. For example, structural testing ascertains whether code designed to detect invalid data is executed by a test suite, but may not detect whether a check for invalid data is missing from the program altogether. Additionally, structural testing typically requires access to source code, which may be unavailable when using COTS software components.

A complementary approach is black-box testing, also called behavioral testing [5]. Black-box testing techniques are designed to demonstrate correct response to various input values regardless of the software implementation, and seem more appropriate for robustness testing. Two types of black-box testing are particularly useful as starting points for robustness testing: domain testing and syntax testing. Domain testing locates and probes points around extrema and discontinuities in the input domain. Syntax testing constructs character strings that are designed to test the robustness of string lexing and parsing systems. Both types of testing are among the approaches used in Ballista.

Automatically generating software tests requires three things: a Module under Test (*MuT*), a machine-understandable specification of correct behavior, and an automatic way to compare results of executing the MuT with the specification. Unfortunately, obtaining or creating a behavioral specification for a COTS or legacy software component is often impractical due to unavailability or cost.

Fortunately, robustness testing need not use a detailed behavioral specification. Instead, the almost trivial specification of "doesn't crash, doesn't hang" suffices. Determining whether a MuT meets this specification is straightforward -- the operating system can be queried to see if a test program terminates abnormally, and a watchdog timer can be used to detect hangs. Thus, robustness testing can be performed on modules (that don't intentionally crash or hang) in the absence of individual behavioral specifications.

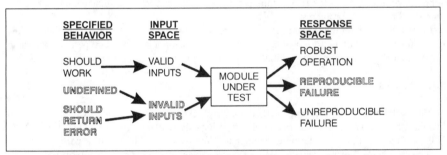

Figure 1. Ballista has a goal of identifying reproducible failures for invalid inputs to a module under test.

Any existing specification for a MuT might define inputs as falling into three categories: valid inputs, inputs which are specified to be handled as exceptions, and inputs for which the behavior is unspecified (Figure 1). Ballista testing, because it is not concerned with the specified behavior, collapses the unspecified and specified exceptional inputs into a single invalid input space. The robustness of the responses of the MuT can be characterized as robust (neither crashes nor hangs, but is not necessarily correct from a detailed behavioral view), having a reproducible failure (a crash or hang that is consistently reproduced), and an unreproducible failure (a robustness failure that is not readily reproducible). The objective of Ballista is to identify reproducible failures.

2.4. Instrumentation approaches

There are several commercial products that help in developing robust code, such as Purify [34] and Boundschecker[32], which instrument software to detect exceptional situations. They work by detecting exceptions that arise during development testing or usage of the software. However, they are not able to find robustness failures that might occur in situations which are not tested (and, even with what would normally be called 100% test coverage, it is unlikely in practice that every exceptional condition which will be encountered in the field is included in the software test suite). The Ballista approach differs from, and complements, these approaches by actively seeking out robustness failures; rather than being an instrumentation tool, it actually generates tests for exception handling ability and feeds them directly into software modules. Thus, Ballista is likely to find robustness failures that would otherwise be missed during normal software testing, even with available instrumentation tools.

3. The Ballista scalable robustness testing framework

A software component, for our purposes, is any piece of software that can be invoked as a procedure, function, or method with a non-null set of input parameters. While that is not a universal definition of all software interfaces, it is sufficiently broad to be of interest. In the Ballista approach, robustness testing of such a software component (a Module under Test, or *MuT*) consists of establishing an initial system state, executing a single call to the MuT, determining whether a robustness problem occurred, and then restoring system state to pre-test conditions in preparation for the next test. Although executing combinations of calls to one or more MuTs during a test can be useful in some situations, we have found that even this simple approach of testing a single call at a time provides a rich set of tests, and uncovers a significant number of robustness problems.

Ballista draws upon ideas from the areas of both software testing and fault injection. A key idea is the use of an object-oriented approach, driven by parameter list data type information, to achieve scalability and automated initialization of system state for each test case.

3.1. Ballista approach

The Ballista robustness testing methodology is based on combinational tests of valid and invalid parameter values for system calls and functions. In each *test case*, a single software MuT is called a single time to determine whether it is robust when called with a particular set of parameter values. These parameter values, or *test values*, are drawn from a pool of normal and exceptional values based on the data type of each argument passed to the MuT. A test case therefore consists of the name of the MuT and a tuple of test values that are passed as parameters (*i.e.*, a test case could be described as a tuple: *{MuT_name, test_value1, test_value2, ...}* corresponding to a procedure call of the form: *MuT_name(test_value1, test_value2, ...)*). Thus, the general approach to Ballista testing is to test the robustness of a single call to a MuT for a single tuple of test values, and then repeat this process for multiple test cases that each have different combinations of valid and invalid test values. A detailed discussion follows.

In Ballista, tests are based on the values of parameters and not on the behavioral details of the MuT. The set of test cases used to test a MuT is completely determined by the data types of the parameter list of the MuT and does not depend on a behavioral specification.

Figure 2 shows the Ballista approach to generating test cases for a MuT. Before conducting testing, a set of test values must be written for each data type used in the MuT. For example, if one or more modules to be tested require an integer data type as an input parameter, test values must be created for testing integers. Values to test integers might include 0, 1, and MAXINT (maximum integer value). Additionally, if a pointer data type is used within the MuT, values of NULL and -1, among others, might be used. A module cannot be tested until test values are created for each of its parameter data types. Automatic testing generates module test cases by drawing from pools of defined test values.

Each set of test values (one set per data type) is implemented as a testing object having a pair of constructor and destructor functions for each defined test value. Instantiation of a testing

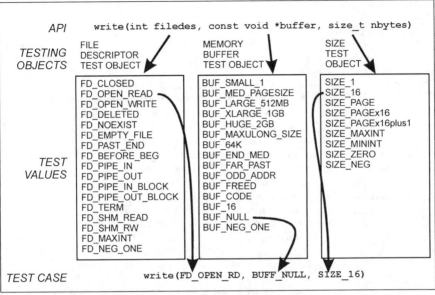

Figure 2. Each test case is composed of a function name with a tuple of test values. The test values are drawn from testing objects based on the data types of the API call being tested.

object (which includes selecting a test value from the list of available values) executes the appropriate constructor function that builds any required testing infrastructure (often called "scaffolding"). For example, an integer test constructor would simply return a particular integer value. But, a file descriptor test constructor might create a file, place information in it, set appropriate access permissions, then open the file requesting read permission. An example of a test constructor to create a file open for read is shown in Figure 2.

When a test case has completed execution, the corresponding destructors for the test values perform appropriate actions to free, remove, or otherwise undo whatever system state may remain in place after the MuT has executed. For example, a destructor for an integer value does nothing. On the other hand, a destructor for a file descriptor might ensure that a file created by the constructor is deleted.

Inheritance of test values is also possible, although not shown explicitly in Figure 2. In particular, test values for native machine data types (*e.g.*, integer, character, and pointer) are predefined as base test values. Other data types inherit these test values and add additional test values that are more specific to their particular interpretation. Additionally, data structures inherit the test values of their constituent element data types.

A natural result of defining test cases by objects based on data type instead of by behavior is that large numbers of test cases can be generated for functions that have multiple parameters in their input lists. Combinations of parameter test values are tested exhaustively by nested iteration without regard to the functionality of the MuT. In Figure 2, the name of any module taking the parameter types (fd, buf, len) could be tested simply by changing the write to some other function name. All test scaffolding creation is both independent of the behavior of the function being tested, and completely encapsulated in the testing objects.

3.2. Test harness

As a matter of efficiency, a single program for each MuT is compiled which is capable of generating all required test cases. A main program spawns a task which executes a single test case, with the main program using a watchdog timer to detect hangs and monitoring the task status to detect abnormal task terminations. The main program iterates through combinations of test values to execute all desired test cases. While one might think that executing tests in this manner would lead to failures caused by interactions among sequential tests, in practice essentially all failures observed in OS testing have been found to be reproducible in isolation. This independence of tests is attained because the constructor/destructor approach sets and restores a fresh copy of relevant system state for each test. (The independence may not hold in all situations, and especially in systems lacking hardware memory protection. However, understanding that issue in more detail is a subject of future research.)

While automatic generation of a large variety of test values is described in the next section, particular values used for the results reported in this section are hand-picked. An average of ten test values were selected by hand for each test object based on experience gained both in general programming and from previous generations of fault injection experiments. For most MuTs, an exhaustive testing approach is used in which all combinations of test values are used to create test cases. For a half-dozen of the POSIX calls tested, the number of parameters is large enough to yield too many test cases for reasonable exhaustive coverage; in these cases a pseudo-random sampling of 5000 test cases is used (based on a comparison to a run with exhaustive searching on one OS, the sampling gives results accurate to within 1 percentage point at a small fraction of the execution time).

It is important to note that this testing methodology does not generate test cases based on a description of MuT functionality, but rather on the data types of the MuT's arguments. This means that, for example, the set of test cases used to test write() would be identical to the test cases used to test read() because they take identical data types. This testing approach means that customized test scaffolding code does not need to be written for each MuT -- instead the amount of testing software written is proportional to the number of data types. As a result, the Ballista testing method was found to be highly scalable with respect to the amount of effort required per function, needing only 20 data types to test 233 POSIX function calls. An average data type has 10 test cases, each of 10 lines of C code, meaning that the entire test suite required only 2000 lines of C code for test cases (in addition, of course, to the general testing harness code used for all test cases).

An important benefit derived from the Ballista testing implementation is the ability to automatically generate the source code for any single test case the suite is capable of running. In many cases only a dozen lines or fewer of executable code in size, these short programs contain the constructors for each parameter, the actual function call, and destructors. These single test cases can be used to reproduce robustness failures in isolation for use by developers for verifying problems, by users as "bug reports," or to verify test results in isolation.

3.3. Categorizing test results

After each test case is executed, the Ballista test harness categorizes the test results according to the CRASH severity scale: [23]
• **Catastrophic** failures occur when the entire OS becomes corrupted or the machine crashes or reboots. In other words, this is a complete system crash. These failures are identified manually because of difficulties encountered with loss of newly written, committed, file data across system crashes on several operating systems.

- **Restart** failures occur when a function call to an OS function never returns, resulting in a task that has "hung" and must be terminated using a command such as "kill -9". These failures are identified by a watchdog timer which times out after several seconds of waiting for a test case to complete.
- **Abort** failures tend to be the most prevalent, and result in abnormal termination (a "core dump") of a task caused by a signal generated within an OS function. Abort failures are identified by monitoring the status of the child process executing the test case.
- **Silent** failures occur when an OS returns no indication of error on an exceptional operation which clearly cannot be performed (for example, writing to a read-only file). These failures are not directly measured, but can be inferred as discussed in Section 6.4.
- **Hindering** failures occur when an incorrect error code is returned from a MuT, which could make it more difficult to execute appropriate error recovery. Hindering failures have been observed as fairly common (forming a substantial fraction of cases which returned error codes) in previous work [22], but are not further discussed in this paper due to lack of a way to perform automated identification of these robustness failures.

There are two additional possible outcomes of executing a test case. It is possible that a test case returns with an error code that is appropriate for invalid parameters forming the test case. This is a case in which the test case passes -- in other words, generating an error code is the correct response. Additionally, in some tests the MuT legitimately returns no error code and successfully completes the desired operation. This happens when the parameters in the test case happen to be all valid, or when it is unreasonable to expect the OS to detect an exceptional situation (such as pointing to an address past the end of a buffer, but no so far past as to trigger a memory protection exception by touching an unallocated virtual memory page).

One of the tradeoffs made to attain scalability in Ballista testing is that the test harness has no way to tell which test cases are valid or invalid for any particular MuT. Thus, some tests returning no error code are Silent failures, while others are actually a set of valid parameter values which should legitimately return with no error indication. This has the effect of "watering down" the test cases with non-exceptional tests, making the raw failure rates underestimates. We estimate that 12% of tests are of this non-exceptional type for OS tests; but even the raw failure rates are significant enough to make the point that Ballista testing is effective in finding robustness failures.

4. Results

In all 1,082,541 data points were collected. Operating systems which supported all of the 233 selected POSIX functions and system calls each had 92,658 total test cases, but those supporting a subset of the functionality tested had fewer test cases. The final number was dependent on which functions were supported and the number of combinations of tests for each supported function.

4.1. Measured failure rates

The compilers and libraries used to generate the test suite were those provided by the OS vendor. In the case of FreeBSD, NetBSD, Linux, and LynxOS, GNU C version 2.7.2.3 was used to build the test suite.

There were five different functions that could be made to cause entire operating system crashes on some OS (either automatic reboots or system hangs). Restart failures were relatively scarce, but present in all but two operating systems. Abort failures were common, indicating that in all operating systems it is relatively straightforward to elicit a core dump from an instruction within a function or system call. (Abort failures do not have to do with subsequent use of an exceptional value returned from a system call -- they happen in response to an instruction within the vendor-provided software itself.) A check was made to ensure that Abort failures were not due to corruption of stack values and subsequent corruption/misdirection of calling program operation.

MuTs that underwent a catastrophic failure could not be completely tested, and resulted in no data on that MuT other than the presence of a catastrophic failure. Since the testing suite is automated, a system crash leaves it in an unrecoverable state with respect to the function in question. Further testing a function which suffered a catastrophic test would require either manual execution of individual cases, or adding tricky waiting and synchronization code into the test benchmark. Manual execution was performed for the Irix 6.2 catastrophic failure in munmap, and allowed the identification of this single line of user code which can crash the entire OS, requiring a manual reboot:

```
munmap(malloc((1<<30+1)),MAXINT);
```

4.2. Normalized failure rates

While it is tempting to simply use the raw number of tests that fail as a comparative metric, this approach is problematic. Most OS implementations do not support the full set of POSIX real-time extensions, so the raw number of failures cannot be used for comparisons. In addition, the number of tests executed per MuT is determined by the number and types of the arguments. So, a single MuT with a large number of test cases could significantly affect both the number of failures and the ratio of failures to tests executed. Similarly, an OS function with few test cases would have minimal effect on raw failure rates even if it demonstrated a large percentage of failures. Thus, some sort of normalized failure rate metric is called for, and is reported in the last column of Table 1.

Table 1: Measured failure rates for fifteen POSIX operating systems.

System	POSIX Calls Tested	Calls with Catastrophic Failures	Number of Tests	Abort Failures	Restart Failures	Normalized Abort + Restart Rate
AIX 4.1	186	0	64009	11559	13	9.99%
FreeBSD 2.2.5	175	0	57755	14794	83	20.28
HPUX 9.05	186	0	63913	11208	13	11.39
HPUX 10.20	185	1	54996	10717	7	13.05
IRIX 5.3	189	0	57967	10642	6	14.45
IRIX 6.2	225	1	91470	15086	0	12.62
Linux 2.0.18	190	0	64513	11986	9	12.54
Lynx 2.4.0	222	1	76462	14612	0	11.89
NetBSD 1.3	182	0	60627	14904	49	16.39
Digital Unix 3.2	232	1	92628	18074	17	15.63
Digital Unix 4.0	233	0	92658	18316	17	15.07
QNX 4.22	203	2	73488	20068	505	20.99
QNX 4.24	206	0	74893	22265	655	22.69
SunOS 4.13	189	0	64503	14227	7	15.84
SunOS 5.5	233	0	92658	15376	28	14.55

We define the normalized failure rate for a particular operating system to be:

$$F = \sum_{i=1}^{N} w_i \frac{f_i}{t_i} \quad \text{with a range of values from 0 to 1 inclusive, where:}$$

N = number of functions tested

w_i is a weighting of importance or relative execution frequency of that function where

$$\sum w_i = 1$$

f_i is the number of tests which produced robustness failure for function i

t_i is the number of tests executed for function i

This definition produces a sort of exposure metric, in which the failure rate within each function is weighted and averaged across all functions tested for a particular OS. This metric has the advantage of removing the effects of differing number of tests per function, and also permits comparing OS implementations with differing numbers of functions implemented according to a single normalized metric. For the results given in Table 1 and the remainder of this paper, an equal weighting is used (*i.e.*, $w_i = 1/N$) to produce a generically applicable result. However, if an OS were being tested with regard to a specific application, weightings should be developed to reflect the dynamic frequency of calling each function to give a more accurate exposure metric.

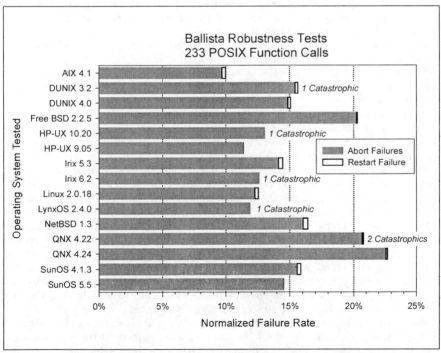

Figure 3. Normalized robustness failure rates for fifteen POSIX operating systems.

Figure 3 shows the normalized failures rates as calculated for each operating system (this is the same data as the rightmost column in Table 1). Overall failure rates for both Abort and Restart failures range from the low of 9.99% (AIX) to a high of 22.69% (QNX 4.22). The mean failure rate is 15.158% with a standard deviation of 3.678 percentage points. As mentioned previously, these are raw failure rates that include non-exceptional test cases which dilute the failure rates, and do not include Silent failures.

5. Generalizing Ballista & applying to other interfaces

The initial approach to Ballista and its predecessors was focussed on testing an increasingly larger set of operating system calls. It is, of course, natural to be skeptical that the approach can scale to increased thoroughness and other applications. To date, implementations have been completed to the proof-of-concept point in a simulation API and a mechanism has been created for performing finer-grained testing.

5.1. Experience with distributed simulation API

Testing operating system calls requires the ability to test traditional subroutine-call-plus-parameter-list interfaces with single calls and a minimum of system state. However, other APIs may have significantly different requirements. To probe the extensibility of Ballista, an entirely different API is being tested, based on a distributed simulation system.

The High Level Architecture (HLA) Run Time Interface (RTI) is an API used for a distributed simulation system by the U.S. Department of Defense [11]. This system is written in C++ in an entirely object-oriented style, and has significantly more complicated preconditions for function calls. Differences from OS testing include:

- An object-oriented implementation, meaning that methods are to be tested rather than function calls. This can largely be treated as a syntactic difference.
- A system which requires support for call-backs to objects for testing rather than a simple call to a function to be tested. This was handled with a slight modification to the standard Ballista client test scaffolding.
- Significantly more complex data types. It was feared that a proliferation of data type variants would increase the difficulty of testing them. However, in the end only 13 data types were required for 87 interfaces. And of these data types, 2 were completely re-used from operating system testing, while the rest inherited existing test cases. Thus, performing tests on data types proved moderately scalable. Perhaps just as importantly, these same data types would be used heavily by any HLA application program, and could thus be reused for Ballista testing of such application programs at a future date, resulting in even more effective scaling.
- A system with moderately complicated preconditions for each and every method (for example: to perform an operation, first a so-called federation must be created; then a federate must be created and instructed to join the federation; then the constructors for that federate must be executed depending on data types). Upon further examination, however, it was found that the different methods being tested could be collapsed into only twelve different equivalence classes with respect to test scaffolding. Thus only 10 sets of scaffolding are required (each only a few lines of code long) for 86 modules under test, which as with the data types is a sub-linear scaling with respect to number of methods being tested.
- Support for error reporting by throwing exceptions rather than error return codes. This was done by adding an exception handler to the Ballista test harness, with the requirement that the tester provide a way to distinguish between acceptable exception values and "unknown" exceptions that, when thrown, amount to Abort failures.

5.2. Structure testing

Testing of data structures can quickly become tedious if separate data types must be created to test each different structure. Fortunately, this can be overcome automatically by creating a system that can parse structure definitions and create composite constructors in terms of the primitive components of a structure. As a simple example, a complex number can be treated as a structure containing two floating point numbers, and tests for that data type can be generated simply by providing the structure information, given that floating point numbers can already be tested as a base data type.

It must be kept in mind that a data structure might be pointed to as well as referenced directly, so test values for a structure inherit both pointer tests (*e.g.*, null pointer instead of a pointer to the structure) as well as various data value tests (*e.g.*, pointer to a structure with particular values).

5.3. Finer grain testing -- dials & logical structures

One of the original (and current) goals of Ballista is to automatically generate hardening wrappers based on test results. While that work is still ongoing and beyond the scope of this discussion, it led to an early focus on a need for using testing as a characterization mechanism in addition to merely a quantification mechanism. For example, it is not enough to simply say that a particular module exhibits robustness failures at a certain rate, but also one must know exactly what triggers these failures. Being able to do this requires fairly fine-grained testing. As an example, the file handle tests described earlier are quite course grain, and certainly do not test all possible combinations (for example, they test a file open for write with no data, but not a file open for write with some data already in it). It can be readily seen that without some sort of further decomposition the number of possible test cases grows in a combinational explosion, and loses scalability.

Additionally, it is desirable to have a very large set of potential tests for Ballista to draw upon without having to manually create too many tests. A particular reason to want to do this is to implement randomized testing for the purposes of characterization, as well as adding an ability to discover new, heuristically useful, data type values for testing.

Fortunately a technique to genericize data testing is available in the form of decomposing the constructors for any particular data type test value creation. An analogy can be made to a set of dials that are set in a particular position for a particular test value. The dials are orthogonal (or at least loosely coupled in terms of meaningful sets of values), and each dial is backed by a set of enumerated constructors for particular aspects of a test value. (This approach is similar to the category/choice approach described in [33], but Ballista requires neither inter-category constraints nor specifically described test frames.) As an example, some of the dials for file creations and their settings include:

- File existence: exists, does not exist, deleted after file handle obtained
- File read permissions: read permission, read permission to other than current task, no read permission
- File access: all combinations of open for read, write, read+write, *etc.*

Note that the above dials are influenced by a desire to decouple various aspects of the data value, but remain coupled to the extent required by conveniently writing constructors. Thus, file permissions can be decoupled because they can be set independently after file creation, but file access modes are placed into a single dial because it was found to be awkward to manipulate them independently. In particular applications, the file data type might be expanded to include other dials such as the type of data present in the file.

While the addition of dials seems to complicate the testing situation, it turns out that there is a unifying approach available -- logical structures. Every data type that is decomposed into dials can be logically treated as a data structure for testing purposes (the only difference from a physical structure point of view is that there is no test for a pointer to that data structure, since it only exists logically for the test program, not physically within the MuT). So, to continue the file handle example, testing file handles is done by declaring a file handle to be a logical structure containing a set of dials, and then exploring various combinations of dials in exactly the same way that Ballista would test combinations of values within a physical data structure.

5.4. Potential improvements in characterization

Beyond simply measuring failure rates, Ballista testing has the potential to characterize failure patterns through the use of patterned testing on fine-grain dial-based representations of data values. Previous work in the area of test exploration includes the AETG system [9], which permits testers to specify which sets of parameters in a multi-parameter function calls are closely coupled functionally, and thus should be tested in concert. The TOFU system [6] takes this a step further by adding interaction weightings to the identified parameter tuples.

Clearly the testing approaches from AETG and TOFU can be applied in part to Ballista testing in the form of encouraging testing of one or a few parameters at a time. It is probably undesirable to have a programmer give explicit hints to Ballista with respect to coupling (this reduces scalability, and there is always the chance that the tester will fail to see a subtle coupling and provide an inaccurate hint). However, heuristics are being developed to permit Ballista to automatically discover what couplings may be present, to do exploration around general regions of interest in the boundary between tests that succeed and that fail, and to generally do "smart" testing to characterize failures with a reasonable number of tests.

The current mechanism for making Ballista available is as a web-based testing service rather than as a piece of software that is executed locally. Part of the reason for this strategy is to enable data collection that can be used to improve the quality of characterization approaches.

6. Potential applications to fault tolerance

Traditional fault tolerance techniques are often based on the notion of creating dependable systems out of individually undependable components. The general idea is that if individual component failure rates are known, then a variety of techniques can be used to ensure that a composite system is highly dependable. It is of course unlikely that Ballista testing will produce highly accurate reliability estimates in terms of failures per million operating hours as is done for fielded hardware. Nonetheless, it is probably a worthy goal to produce some relative measure of software component reliability, and a rating of exception handling ability might be a useful starting point.

There are four areas in which a Ballista testing might provide improved quantification for fault tolerance of software-intensive systems: detecting system crashes, detecting violations of fail-stop assumptions, providing information for creating software wrappers, and providing an assessment of software diversity.

In general, it is considered a good idea to build systems that are impossible to crash from "normal" software applications. This is an extension of the traditional fault tolerance approach of having a "hard core" that is as small as possible, and upon which resources are lavished in both design and implementation to ensure its dependability. Outside of that hard core of a processor or operating system kernel, it is to be expected that bugs will occur on a regular basis, generating exceptional situations that must be handled robustly with respect to the system architecture. The particular area of emphasis for Ballista is on exercising exception handling techniques, since it is assumed that normal, correct values are well exercised by normal operational testing.

6.1. Test for overall system crash situations

The most obvious application of Ballista to fault tolerance is to ferret out ways to completely crash a system from unprivileged application software. As the previous results indicate, Ballista can locate some ways to crash an operating system even with the current rather simplistic tests available. Application of a similar methodology should help quantify the extent to which exceptional conditions can trickle down through an application program to reach the operating system as well.

There are four approaches that can improve the effectiveness of Ballista to identify system crashes. The basic techniques required are those discussed in the previous section.

- Use finer grain testing using the dial approach to decomposing parameter test values
- Test primitive functions within the operating system rather than just the POSIX-specified functions.
- Test concurrent function calls, to identify timing-dependent problems such as resource locking bugs.
- Test for the results of resource exhaustion effects, such behaving gracefully when the process table is full or when a memory leak is encountered.

6.2. Test for violations of fail-stop assumption

A second way to apply Ballista to measuring and improving Fault Tolerance is to use it to detect problems with respect to Restart and Silent failures. It is common to base fault tolerance on a fail-fast assumption. However, a Restart failure means that a task is "fail-slow" in that its failure is not recognized until, typically, a time-out period has elapsed (failure to detect a periodic "heartbeat" message, failure to reset a watchdog timer, *etc.*) Furthermore, a Silent failure means that a system has failed somehow, but that the failure is undetected from some period of time. It might be that the Silent failure is not activated, or it might be that it results in a "time bomb" inside the system, such as a NULL pointer to a data structure that is not dereferenced except in an error handling routine.

Restart failures are moderately easy to deal with, and basically are searched for in the same way that catastrophic system failures are searched for as discussed above. A particularly nasty restart failure that was found on a real system was in AIX, in which the core dump facility waited until enough disk space on a nearly full disk was available to dump core, even if core dumping was disabled (the check for disk space came before the check for the maximum amount to dump, which in our case was set to zero).

Silent failures can be identified by using multi-version comparison among different OS test results. This scheme determines declares a result to be a Silent failure if that test case on that OS returns no error indication while that same test case results in an error indication on another OS. This approach works with reasonable accuracy in practice (approximately 80% accurate) [12], but of course requires that there be multiple implementations available. Improving performance for Silent failures takes one of two approaches. In some cases hardware is available that could detect a Silent failure, but is not being used (for example, because memory protection is turned off for page zero of memory to support legacy software). In other cases it is simply that the exceptional parameters are not being checked, and in addition evade detection by hardware mechanisms.

6.3. Generating software wrappers

A possible way to improve software fault tolerance is by using software "wrappers" that encapsulate the modules of a software system. While it is aesthetically more pleasing to fix any exception handling deficiencies in a software module directly, there are times when that is not possible either because of lack of access to the source code or time/budget constraints. Therefore it may be attractive to automatically or semi-automatically generate software wrappers that are interposed between the API implementation and the application. These wrappers can automatically check for exceptional conditions and take action to report them or, in some cases, recover from them.

While a generic capability to create universal software wrappers remains a research issue, there are several strategies that may be employed within a wrapper, such as reporting error return codes, performing retry, and invoking alternate algorithms. A particularly interesting use of wrappers in connection with robustness testing is to use a robustness testing result as a warning that a particular operation is hazardous, and to perform a checkpoint against the need for a later rollback if that operation should fail. This would use failure predictions from robustness testing to lessen the typical cost of checkpointing to those times when it would appear to be most fruitful.

The Xept approach [38] uses software "wrappers" around procedure calls as a way to encapsulate error checking and error handling within the context of a readable program. Given that the fault tolerance community has found that transient system failure rates far outnumber manifestations of permanent system faults/design errors in practice, even as simple a strategy as retrying failed operations from within a software wrapper has the potential to significantly improve system robustness. One could therefore envision using the results of Ballista testing to provide information for error checking within an Xept software wrapper.

6.4. Potential use as measure of diversity for multi-version software systems

A method for using Ballista for Fault Tolerance that does not directly involve robustness testing *per se* is in the area of assessing implementation diversity for multi-version systems. One way to improve dependability is to use multiple, independently-developed versions of software in the hope that different versions are diverse in nature, and thus have differing failure modes [8][1]. This is a way of exploiting inherent design diversity in separately designed systems, in an analogy to exploiting diversity among multiple independently-manufactured hardware subsystems.

One issue with using multi-version software is whether or not such software is truly diverse. There are studies and arguments for both sides of this issue (*e.g.*, [2][4][15][21][25][28]). However, Ballista testing gives a way to shed additional light onto the diversity question. In particular, it can measure the diversity of multiple software versions with respect to exception handling capabilities. (Diversity with respect to correctness would hinge on implementing software assurance abilities discussed later.) It can do so by comparing the results of identical test cases on multiple implementations, and detecting instances in which at least one version detected an exception, indicating that a notional multi-version system could have detected such an exception and responded gracefully even if all systems did not. This is a bit different than traditional multi-version voting in that it suffices for a single version of software to detect an exception, whereas voting typically requires a majority of versions to agree on a correct computational result.

Multi-version assessment of operating systems was performed with Ballista test data [12], and found that OS kernel calls are moderately diverse (but not completely diverse). However, it was

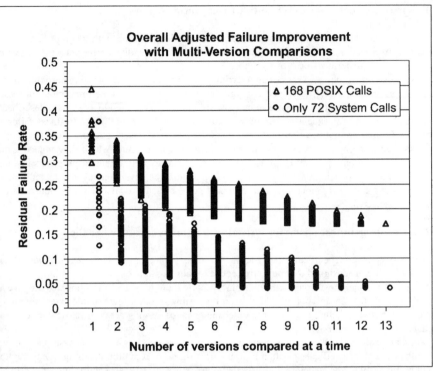

Figure 4. Overall adjusted failure rates for thirteen POSIX operating systems using multi-version failure detection comparison.

also found that C library function calls display a relatively poor level of diversity. Figure 4 shows a scatter plot of the results attained by using all combinations of multi-version detection among thirteen operating systems across 168 function calls [12]. As can be seen, the overall OS interface cannot be improved beyond a 17% failure rate even if all thirteen OS versions are used for comparison. However, if the system call subset is considered in isolation (*i.e.*, those calls not part of the C library), then the failure rate is reduced dramatically (but not eliminated completely) via comparison. This suggests that, at least with respect to exception handling, the C library functions are not particularly diverse.

7. Potential generalization to Software Assurance

Software assurance research has produced many metrics. Some of these metrics are based on measuring the complexity of the software itself. Some of the metrics are more process-based, such as software shipping decision heuristics. And some of the approaches are not metric-based, but rather based on assuring complete correctness, such as with formal methods.

Within the realm of software assurance, Ballista testing is akin to an automated black box testing approach. Since black box testing is about functionality, the question becomes one of how much functionality can be put into the testing while retaining scalability.

7.1. Robustness metric for COTS software component libraries

In a large number of software systems, exception handling is dealt with incompletely in the software specification. This is done intentionally, and usually indicated by phrases such as a behavior being "undefined" or "unspecified."

In some systems, robustness is not an overriding concern, but in others (and in particular ones in which security and fault tolerance are significant concerns), it may be important. In these latter cases Ballista testing can serve to exercise exception handling code as already described, and create a metric for exception handling ability. It should be noted that robustness failures found by Ballista are not necessarily "bugs" or the results of "defects", because those terms can be construed to be with respect to the original software specification, which may indeed state that behavior in a particular situation is "undefined." However, if a general-purpose software component library is being used in a critical system, it may be advantageous to select a library with the best robustness properties, or at least have some measure available of the robustness of the library selected.

7.2. A quality assurance metric for systems with rigorous exception handling

Some systems are specifically designed to be robust. An example is the earlier one of the HLA RTI, which is designed to report error codes for any possible exception. Testing results to date have found that most exceptions are in fact reported, but most software modules do have a few exceptions that go unreported. And, in an interesting result, a few modules were found to have a much higher failure rate than the other modules, suggesting areas of particular concern with respect to system robustness.

Thus, an additional use of Ballista testing for software assurance is a Quality Assurance check on software that is specifically written to implement rigorous exception handling. One way to employ this testing is to generate bug lists that must be fixed. But, especially in cost-sensitive systems, in can be used instead to find the particular modules that for some reason have far worse than average robustness and concentrate available resources on them first. Thus, Ballista testing might be considered a screening tool for which areas to concentrate corrective efforts upon, even if it does not find all existing problems.

7.3. Adaptation to black box testing with customized corner values, etc.

A potentially high impact, but also very difficult, extension of Ballista testing would be to use it to partially automate traditional software testing.

In traditional black box testing, every module is tested with respect to a specification. This approach tends to scale poorly because extra work must be performed to define a specification for every module to be tested, thus scaling effort linearly with the size of the API to be tested. The obvious way to attain scalability is to somehow genericize functionality so that it becomes more object oriented. And, in fact, that approach was taken with pre-Ballista robustness testing [31], but did not achieve scalability. It is possible, however, that in light of work on Ballista, the generic functionality approach could be made to work.

Another approach is to limit correctness testing to properties that can be represented as a linear superposition of test cases for individual parameters. In this approach, correctness tests with postcondition assertions would be added to Ballista testing, and the postconditions would be tested after each test was run. It is difficult to see how this approach could be made to deal with changes to system state caused by a function, because the changes would of necessity be related to functionality. But, the assertions could test for invariants across changes, such as a string remaining null-terminated after any operation.

A simpler, less ambitious, extension would be to included customized test values for boundary testing for a particular module or data type in addition to current Ballista robustness tests. For example, a struct containing an X,Y coordinate pair to a graphics display routine might be tested with the coordinate pair 1024,768 to see whether an appropriate error code is returned for an off-screen point plot attempt. Such an approach might still scale because it is based on a data type that is (presumably) used by multiple software modules.

7.4. Generic behavioral descriptions other than for robustness?

The point at which applying Ballista to software assurance becomes tricky is when one desires to test for properties other than robustness. Beyond trying to apply data-type driven testing to correctness testing, a different way to extend Ballista testing is to find properties that have generic specifications applicable to all (or almost all) software modules, or very simple specifications that can easily be stated for each module. Potential examples of these include:

- Execution time ("module returns in less than X microseconds") where perhaps each module test will need to be annotated with a particular time.
- Memory consumption ("module consumes no more than X bytes of memory from the heap").
- Safety critical state change ("module does not alter any of a predefined set of system variables").

A further type of testing that might be performed would require machine-readable interface specifications to be available, and might thus cross the line into more general software assurance. However, if such specifications are available anyway, the incremental cost to perform Ballista-based testing using them might be reasonable. Example applications might include:

- Checking that all exceptions specified can be generated (failure to generate a documented exception either suggests an addition to the test set or points out something that is not consistent with the current implementation, which may or may not be a problem).
- Checking that exceptions generated are all in the specification (generating an undocumented exception is either a documentation defect or a software defect).
- Using specified pre-condition information to help distinguish between exceptional and non-exceptional tests. Flag any tests which satisfy preconditions but produce exceptional results.
- Using post-condition information to help assess correctness of tests executed under satisfied preconditions (this quickly begins to cross the line into traditional software testing).

If the above examples begin to sound like traditional software testing -- that is because they are. The only significant difference that Ballista testing seems to offer at this point is an object-oriented view to performing testing even on non-object-oriented software.

8. Potential generalization to security

Much of current security testing involves looking for known system vulnerabilities that have been a problem in the past (*e.g.*, the SATAN tool discussed in [35]). Scripts to exercise such problems are useful for ensuring that systems retain a capability to resist previously identified attacks, and can be thought of as a kind of regression testing for new revisions as well as a certification suite for new software.

However, what the security community seems to lack at this point is a systematic ability to detect new security vulnerabilities before they are detected via suffering attacks to exploit them. (There is clearly work to build up a theoretical infrastructure and improve this situation; but that is a difficult problem that will take much effort.) While it is certainly no silver bullet, Ballista testing may be able to add a few tricks to a generic security testing toolkit.

8.1. Bullet-proofing key modules

One classic way to gain entry into a system is to cause a key software subsystem to fail or provide inappropriate access to data, thus circumventing whatever access control may be in place. Current Ballista testing techniques can be used to harden the constituent software modules of such critical subsystems, improving crash resistance at the module level.

An application of existing Ballista testing techniques would be to ensure that interfaces to modules are reasonably hardened. For example, a technique that has enjoyed perennial success is to intentionally submit an overly long string or buffer value to a software module in an effort to get that module to overwrite other, unrelated data causing a security hole (*e.g.*, [36]). While such an attack probably would not be directly detected by Ballista testing, a Ballista test approach could identify that the module does not perform buffer length checking by identifying a separate test case in which an overly long buffer results in an Abort failure, thus indirectly suggesting a vulnerability to an oversized-buffer attack.

At the system level, Ballista has not yet been applied to command-line interfaces and the like. It might be possible to build a parameterized testing approach based on a set of legal and illegal commands, flag values, and so on, but this has not been explored within the Ballista project. (However, the Fuzz project[30] has demonstrated success in robustness testing of command-line interfaces, and should be considered for use in security testing.)

8.2. Generic security behavioral specifications?

As in software assurance, it is possible that Ballista testing can help with some security testing. Possible high-level generic behavioral descriptions to use in detecting failures might be:
• Grants access to a file with insufficient access permissions
• Permits modification of audit logs
• Accesses critical system information (should not be possible with software modules other than a certain few)

As an example, a Ballista test might be set up for the file read command in which the file handle used for testing is created with various forms of permission for access (read-only access, write-only access, no access). However in this case the test result of interest would not be the error return status of the module, but rather whether a read was actually performed, and (via a postprocessing script) whether read permissions were actually set in the test case executed. This amounts to a pre-condition/post-condition comparison, similar to what might be used for a software assurance application (*e.g.*, if pre-condition is "read access permitted" then the read() function satisfies the post-condition of "data read" in the absence of other exceptions).

9. Ballista in perspective: what it does and doesn't do

Although we attempt to suggest several possible extensions of Ballista testing beyond the domain of software robustness, it should be made clear that there are definite limitations on what it can do. And, furthermore, some of the suggestions above might not actually be practical. Bear in mind that software testing is in general a specialized form of software development. Thus, the question of whether software testing can be performed is in most cases of interest not theoretical, but rather, an issue of economics. What is different about Ballista testing is that it attempts to limit the scope of the testing in a way that significantly reduces development cost and effort, while still attempting to measure useful system properties. Thus, it is not a do-all solution, but rather an exercise in attaining limited additional testing or characterization at comparatively low cost.

9.1. The goal: "quantification without tears"

Of course everyone would like to have complete testing or characterization without spending any money or time on it. But, obviously, that isn't going to happen any more than software is going to get developed effortlessly in the first place. So, the real question is, how well does Ballista "scale," where scalability has to do with incremental cost to test additional software modules once an initial set of modules has been tested.

The Ballista approach has proven portable across platforms, and promises to be portable across applications. The Ballista tests have been ported to ten different operating systems. This demonstrates that high-level robustness testing can be conducted without any hardware or operating system modifications. Furthermore, the use of normalized failure reporting supports direct comparisons among different implementations of an API executing on different platforms.

In a somewhat different sense, Ballista seems to be portable across different applications. The POSIX API encompasses file handling, string handling, I/O, task handling, and even mathematical functions. The HLA RTI testing encompasses a large range of object-oriented testing considerations, and required only minor enhancements to the Ballista testing approach. So it seems likely that Ballista will be useful for a significant number of other applications as well.

9.1.1. Testing cost: One of the biggest unknowns when embarking upon a full-scale implementation of the Ballista methodology was the amount of test scaffolding that would have to be erected for each function tested. In the worst case, special-purpose code would have been necessary for each of the 233 POSIX functions tested. If that had been the case, it would have resulted in a significant cost for constructing tests for automatic execution (a testing cost linear with the number of modules to be tested).

However, the adoption of an object-oriented approach based on data type yielded an expense for creating test cases that was sublinear with the number of modules tested. The key observation is that in a typical program there are fewer data types than functions -- the same data types are used over and over when creating function declarations. In the case of POSIX calls, only 20 data types were used by 233 functions, so the effort in creating the test suite was driven by the 20 data types, not the number of functions.

In the case of the HLA RTI, results appear to be that a reasonable level of scalability has also been achieved. The effort involved in preparing for automated testing is proportional to the number of object classes (data types) rather than the number of methods within each class. In fact, one could envision robustness testing information being added as a standard part of programming practice when creating a new class, just as debugging print statements might be added.

A further step in reducing the effort for preparing tests is to add inheritance of test cases. This is conceptually present in the current version of Ballista, but is still being implemented. Each primitive machine type (such as integer or floating point number) has a set of pre-defined tests. Users adding more specific data types (such as "file mode bit pattern" or "enumeration index") can inherit existing generic tests and add more specific test cases as well. Multiple inheritance will help simple creation of pointer data types, for example by inheriting both basic tests for any pointer as well as tests for data values in test cases having a valid pointer.

9.1.2. Effectiveness and system state: The Ballista testing fault model is fairly simplistic: single function calls that result in a crash or hang. It specifically does not encompass sequences of calls. Nonetheless, it is sufficient to uncover a significant number of robustness failures. Part of this may be that such problems are unexpectedly easy to uncover, but part of it may also be that the object-oriented testing approach is more powerful than it appears upon first thought.

In particular, a significant amount of system state can be set by the constructor for each test value. For example, a file descriptor test value might create a particular file with associated permissions, access mode, and contents with its constructor (and, erase the file with its destructor). Thus, a single test case can replace a sequence of tests that would otherwise have to be executed to create and test a function executed in the context of a particular system state. In other words, the end effect of a series of calls to achieve a given system state can be simulated by a constructor that in effect jumps directly to a desired system state without need for an explicit sequence of calls in the form of per-function test scaffolding.

A high emphasis has been placed on reproducibility within Ballista. In essentially every case checked, it was found that extracting a single test case into a stand-alone test program leads to a reproduction of robustness failures. The only situation in which Ballista results have been found to lack such single-call reproducibility is in Catastrophic failures (complete system crashes, not just single-task crashes), and even there results can be reproduced by running a given handful of test cases together.

9.2. Ballista quantifies some aspects of robustness

Ballista has succeeded in providing quantification of some aspects of robustness, specifically the reaction of individual software modules when presented with exceptional parameter values in a single-call context with a moderate amount of associated state information. While we speculate that improving robustness at this simple level will yield benefits at the system level, it is as yet unclear how significant an effect this will be. There is no denying that some system-level problems will be dynamic, involving such emergent behaviors as livelock. But, skeptics have, at various times over the course of the past decade, incorrectly predicted that Ballista and its predecessors would not find any way to crash a system. Given that such system crashes can be found with an admittedly simplistic testing model, it is difficult to say exactly how much remains beyond the reach of a single-threaded Ballista implementation (and, it remains a research topic to figure out how to create a multi-threaded Ballista testing system that retains the characteristics of repeatability and scalability).

There are, of course, not only benefits, but also dangers and pitfalls to be had. The benefits of being able to quantify robustness, albeit in a limited scope, stem from the fact that once something can be measured, it is more readily determined whether that metric becomes better or worse over time. This can lead to the following potential benefits:
- Customers that care about robustness can make more informed purchasing decisions.
- Developers can justify additional resources to improve robustness, since they can now measure the robustness of their system both on an absolute scale and in relation to competitors.
- Development managers can make better-informed decisions about how much effort to devote to robustness (based on measured robustness levels), and measure the effectiveness of those efforts based on resultant robustness improvements.
- From a market-driven point of view, historically only things that can be measured tend to be improved over time. Historically this has included hardware attributes (e.g., MIPS, megabytes RAM, gigabytes disk, megabits/second I/O). For software this has, all too often, meant the length of feature check-off lists. For less performance or functionality-directed attributes, an ability to quantify may mean that they are driven to improvement by market forces as well.

There are, of course, dangers inherent in using any measurement system, and particularly one that produces a single number for comparison:

- A classic management danger is that "you get what you measure." Ballista certainly does not measure every aspect of robustness. Thus, there is a very real danger that consumers will purchase based on "robustness" metrics when the type of robustness they need is not what is being measured, that system designers will optimize for measured robustness at the expense of robustness attributes not measured, *etc.* While this is a very real danger, it is inherent in any measurement technique, and must be addressed by continually improving the measurements in response to such trends. Fear of creating a less-than-perfect measure is no excuse for deciding to measure nothing at all.

- Customers might insist on better robustness numbers even if they do not really need them. While this is a potential pitfall, it is probably no worse than a hobbyist who insists on having the latest CPU model without really needing the performance. And, in both cases, this behavior serves to drive improvement of the metric to the benefit of users who do in fact need it.

- In time, Ballista metrics may suffer from a problem known as the "inoculation effect."

9.3. The inoculation effect requires continuing improvement

A significant concern with Ballista testing is the effect it may have over time on the software it measures (called the "inoculation effect" with respect to software testing [5]). In particular, the issue is, what is to stop a software developer from ensuring that all Ballista tests pass 100%? The first, simple, answer is that reaching that state of affairs is probably desirable, and having a situation in which robustness or other qualities are taken for granted by the marketplace rather than being non-ideal is probably a good thing.

However, there is a more general answer to this issue in that Ballista testing abilities should be made to improve over time, and to adapt to whatever strategies may be used to "game" or otherwise defeat it as a reasonable measurement tool. There is ample experience with this issue in the performance metric arena, where compiler technology has long been used to "break" benchmark programs by using customized optimizations. The response should be not to declare that Ballista testing is pointless because of this almost inevitable outcome, but rather to take it as a challenge to continually improve testing capabilities. Improvement can come in any one of several forms, including:

- Creating richer sets of test data for each data type.
- Improving the abilities of the "dials" metaphor to increase fine-grain testing abilities.
- Improving the search abilities of the testing harness to seek out and identify patterns.
- Adding randomized testing.
- In time, adding concurrent testing abilities.
- In time, increasing the amount of system state that can be set for each test.

Thus, while dealing with the inoculation effect is a legitimate concern, it should be seen as a challenge in a process of ever-improving system quality rather than a stumbling block.

9.4. Scalability is attained by ignoring functional specifications

The key to Ballista's scalability is that it abstracts the functional specification of each module to an extremely high, almost trivial, level. As soon as functionality begins to creep into the testing process, scalability is placed at risk. An immediate reaction of some to seeing Ballista results is to want to apply the approach to displace traditional software testing. While this is naturally a powerful desire (because testing is so expensive), it is simply not what Ballista testing is designed for. It might be possible to encroach on software testing a bit using techniques discussed previously, but ultimately there is a certain amount of essential complexity to software, and that must somehow be represented to the testing system if an automated test generator is to determine whether the actual software artifact meets the specification or not.

9.5. System "state" is a deeper issue than at first suspected

The whole issue of system state has turned out to be far more slippery than originally anticipated. In the original vision of what Ballista would do, system state was explicitly stated to be outside the scope of research. Additionally, it was feared that per-module scaffolding might be required for each function, but at least it was hoped that per-module functional specifications might be avoided.

However, the object-oriented testing approach has permitted per-module scaffolding to be largely eliminated, and a moderate amount of system state to be included in each test. Both of these goals were accomplished by the subsumption of all testing information into the data types. It is currently unclear how far these concepts can be pushed. The initial design did not permit setting any system state, yet that was eventually incorporated via constructors when complex data types such as file handles were incorporated. Preliminary results on operating systems did not show how the techniques could be expanded to encompass object-oriented software testing. Yet that was accomplished with the HLA RTI application. Later results did not show how parameterless functions could be tested, yet that was later accomplished with so-called phantom parameters, that are passed as dummy parameters by the Ballista testing harness, but stripped before calling the actual function [13]. And, although it has not yet been implemented, it is clear that phantom parameters to set things such as remaining disk space can help with larger chunks of system state than previously anticipated.

Finally, it is a commonly held notion that to find all but the most trivial of bugs a sequence of calls must be executed. The results on operating systems have shown that this is not necessarily true -- Ballista testing can find ways to crash an entire system with a single function call. But at a deeper level, what Ballista has done is replaced the notion of a sequence of calls (a control-flow thought model) with the notion of setting system state prior to a single call (an object-oriented thought model). In fact, Ballista *does* make a series of calls via test value constructors -- it is simply the case that these calls are hidden from the user and not considered part of the actual test sequence. Additionally, since Ballista executes tests in batches under a harness, a moderately large number of system calls are made in a row that might tend to flush out state-dependent failures. However, experience has shown that the sequences of calls across different test cases are largely irrelevant -- the single-call testing model has proven to be a useful one.

Thus, as research on Ballista has progressed, we have continually been surprised at the effectiveness of, and the amount of system state that can be set by, a deceptively simple "single-call" testing model.

10. Conclusions and future work

The Ballista testing approach has possible applications to fault tolerance, software assurance, and computer security. It is based on a pair of key approaches that can be applied to these three areas:

- Limiting the scope of testing to those areas in which a generic functional specification can be used across all modules being tested.
- Using an object-oriented approach to creating test values in which all tests are determined by the data types of parameters rather than any genericization of module functionality.

The results of Ballista testing on operating systems have indicated that this generic approach is sufficient to test for and identify significant numbers of robustness failures in a highly scalable manner. Automated testing identified ways to crash commercial operating systems, ways to hang tasks, ways to cause abnormal terminations, and "Silent" errors in which no indication of failure is given. These results have direct applicability to various areas of computing, and scale to applications beyond operating systems.

Beyond the current results, it may be possible to expand the idea of Ballista testing in several directions. In fault tolerance it may prove possible to use Ballista testing to help create software wrappers, to evaluate diversity for multi-version software applications, and to reduce the average cost of checkpointing by providing a warning of potentially hazardous operations. In software assurance, it can be used to evaluate exception handling abilities, and perhaps to provide partially automated testing for boundary conditions. In security it might be used to assure robustness of critical modules, and also to test for general security properties of all modules.

Potential future work already underway by the Ballista project team includes exploring the temporal aspects of robustness, porting Ballista to the popular Windows operating system, and generating software wrappers to improve robustness. The other potential applications may be explored in time, but in general are left as an opportunity for others to pursue.

11. Acknowledgments

The graduate students who have worked on the Ballista project have been crucial to its success, and spent many hours writing the system as well as collecting data. The students contributing to the work reported herein are: Nathan Kropp, John DeVale, Jiantao Pan, and Kim Fernsler. Additionally, Dan Siewiorek and his students laid the groundwork for Ballista in the early 1990s with previous fault injection projects. Dan in particular has offered sage advice and inspired several interesting twists in the research direction. This research was sponsored by DARPA ITO contract DABT63-96-C-0064.

12. References

[1] Avizienis, A., "The N-version approach to fault-tolerant software", *IEEE Transactions on Software Engineering*, SE-11(12): 1491-501, Dec. 1985.

[2] Avizienis, A., Lyu, M., Schutz, W., "In Search of Effective Diversity: A Six-Language Study of Fault-Tolerant Flight Control Software," *The Eighteenth International Symposium on Fault Tolerant Computing*, p. 15-22, 1988.

[3] Barton, J., Czeck, E., Segall, Z., Siewiorek, D., "Fault injection experiments using FIAT," *IEEE Transactions on Computers*, 39(4): 575-82, Apr. 1990.

[4] Brilliant, S.S., Knight, J.C., Leveson, N.G., "Analysis of Faults in an N-Version Software Experiment", *IEEE Transactions on Software Engineering*, 16(2): 238-47, Feb. 1990.

[5] Beizer, B., *Black Box Testing*, New York: Wiley, 1995.

[6] Biyani, R. & P. Santhanam, "TOFU: Test Optimizer for Functional Usage," *Software Engineering Technical Brief*, 2(1), 1997, IBM T.J. Watson Research Center.

[7] Carrette, G., "CRASHME: Random input testing," (no formal publication available) *http://people.delphi.com/gjc/crashme.html* accessed July 6, 1998.

[8] Chen, L., Avizienis, A., "N-Version Programming : A Fault Tolerance Approach to Reliability of Software Operation," *The Eighth International Symposium on Fault Tolerant Computing*, p. 3-9, 1978.

[9] Cohen, D., Dalal, S., Fredman, M. & Patton, G. "The AETG System: an approach to testing based on combinatorial design," *IEEE Transactions on Software Engineering*, 23(7): 437-44, Jul. 1997.

[10] Cristian, Flaviu, "Exception Handling and Tolerance of Software Faults," In: Michael R. Lyu (Ed.) *Software Fault Tolerance*. Chichester: Wiley, p. 81-107, Ch. 4, 1995.

[11] Dahmann, J., Fujimoto, R., & Weatherly, R, "The Department of Defense High Level Architecture," *Proceedings of the 1997 Winter Simulation Conference*, Winter Conference Board of Directors, San Diego, CA, p. 142-9, 1997.

[12] DeVale, J. & Koopman, P., "Comparing the Robustness of POSIX Operating Systems," *29th Symposium on Fault Tolerant Computing (FTCS-29)*, June, 1999, in press.

[13] DeVale, J., Koopman, P. & Guttendorf, D., "Ballista Software Robustness Testing Service," *Testing Computer Software conference (TCS-99)*, June 1999, in press.

[14] Dingman, C., *Portable Robustness Benchmarks*, Ph.D. Thesis, Electrical and Computer Engineering Department, Carnegie Mellon University, Pittsburgh, PA, May 1997.

[15] Eckhardt, D.E. & Lee, L.D., "Fundamental differences in the reliability of N-modular redundancy and N-version programming," *Journal of Systems and Software*, 8(4): 313-318, Sept. 1988.

[16] Hartz, M., Walker, E. & Mahar, D., *Introduction to Software Reliability: A State of the Art Review*, Reliability Analysis Center report SWREL, Rome NY, December 1996.

[17] *IEEE Standard Glossary of Software Engineering Terminology*, IEEE Std 610.12-1990, IEEE Computer Soc., Dec. 10, 1990.

[18] *IEEE Standard for Information Technology - Portable Operating System Interface (POSIX) Part 1: System Application Program Interface (API) Amendment 1: Realtime Extension [C Language]*, IEEE Std 1003.1b-1993, IEEE Computer Society, 1994.

[19] Jones, E., (ed.) *The Apollo Lunar Surface Journal, Apollo 11 lunar landing*, entries at times 102:38:30, 102:42:22, and 102:42:41, National Aeronautics and Space Administration, Washington, DC, 1996.

[20] Kanawati, G., Kanawati, N. & Abraham, J., "FERRARI: a tool for the validation of system dependability properties," *1992 IEEE Workshop on Fault-Tolerant Parallel and Distributed Systems*. Amherst, MA, USA, p. 336-344, July 1992.

[21] Knight, J.C., Leveson, N.G., "A reply to the criticisms of the Knight and Leveson experiment", *SIGSOFT Software Engineering Notes*, 15(1): 24-35, Jan. 1990.

[22] Koopman, P., Sung, J., Dingman, C., Siewiorek, D. & Marz, T., "Comparing Operating Systems Using Robustness Benchmarks," *Proceedings Symposium on Reliable and Distributed Systems*, Durham, NC, p. 72-79, Oct. 22-24 1997.

[23] Kropp, N., Koopman, P. & Siewiorek, D., "Automated Robustness Testing of Off-the-Shelf Software Components," *28th Fault Tolerant Computing Symposium*, p. 230-9, June 23-25, 1998.

[24] Lions, J.L. (chairman) *Ariane 5 Flight 501 Failure: report by the inquiry board*, European Space Agency, Paris, July 19, 1996.

[25] Lyu, M.R., "Software Reliability Measurements in N-Version Software Execution Environment," *Proceedings of the Third International Symposium on Software Reliability and Engineering*, p. 254-63, 1992.

[26] Lyu, M. (ed.), *Handbook of Software Reliability Engineering*, IEEE Computer Society Press/ McGraw Hill, 1996.

[27] McCabe, T.J., *Structured testing: A software testing methodology using the cyclomatic complexity metric*, Nat. Bur. Stand., Washington, DC, USA, Dec. 1982.

[28] McAllister, D.F., Sun, C., Vouk, M.A., "Reliability of Voting in Fault-Tolerant Software Systems

for Small Output-Spaces," *IEEE Transactions on Reliability*, **39**(5): 524-34, Dec. 1990.

[29] Miller, B.P., Fredriksen, L. & So, B., "An empirical study of the reliability of Unix utilities, *Communications of the ACM*, **33**(12): 32-43, Dec. 1990.

[30] Miller, B., Koski, D., Lee, C., Maganty, V., Murthy, R., Natarajan, A. & Steidl, J., *Fuzz Revisited: A Re-examination of the Reliability of UNIX Utilities and Services*, Computer Science Technical Report 1268, Univ. of Wisconsin-Madison, May 1998.

[31] Mukherjee, A. & Siewiorek, D.P., "Measuring software dependability by robustness benchmarking, *IEEE Transactions on Software Engineering*, **23**(6): 366-78, June 1997.

[32] Numega. BoundsChecker. *http://www.numega.com/products/aed/vc.shtml*, accessed 6/1/99.

[33] Ostrand, T.J. & Balcer, M.J., "The category-partition method for specifying and generating functional tests," *Communications of the ACM*, **31**(6): 676-86, June 1988.

[34] Purify. *http://www.pureatria.com/products/purify/index.html*, accessed 8/28/98.

[35] Ram, P. & Rand, D.K., " Satan: double-edged sword," *Computer*, **28**(6): 82-3, June 1995.

[36] Spanbauer, S., "Pentium Bug, Meet the IE4 Flaw," *PC World*, p. 55, Feb. 1998.

[37] Tsai, T., & R. Iyer, "Measuring Fault Tolerance with the FTAPE Fault Injection Tool," *Proceedings Eighth International Conference. on Modeling Techniques and Tools for Computer Performance Evaluation*, Heidelberg, Germany, Springer-Verlag, p. 26-40, Sept. 20-22 1995.

[38] Vo, K-P., Wang, Y-M., Chung, P. & Huang, Y., "Xept: a software instrumentation method for exception handling," *The Eighth International Symposium on Software Reliability Engineering*, Albuquerque, NM, USA, p. 60-69, 2-5 Nov. 1997.

Practical Techniques for Damage Confinement in Software

David J. Taylor
Department of Computer Science
University of Waterloo
dtaylor@uwaterloo.ca

Abstract

In a large software system that is required to be dependable, preventing the spread of damage from one system component to another is important. Damage confinement both allows damage to be assessed in a reasonable way once an error is detected and prevents a fault in a single component from causing sudden collapse of the entire system. This paper examines techniques for constraining the spread of damage, both the kinds of constraints required and the means for enforcing those constraints. Techniques developed primarily or exclusively for uses other than fault tolerance are described and examined for suitability in confining damage. The influence on damage confinement of the level of dependability required, e.g., for safety-critical systems versus other systems, is also discussed.

1. Introduction

One of the four phases in the classical decomposition of fault tolerance is damage confinement and assessment [13]. Damage confinement attempts to constrain the spread of errors from one part of the system to another, to simplify damage assessment and error recovery. Damage confinement must include designing the system with constraints intended to limit the spread of damage. "The extent to which such constraints are present in the operational system and hence are able to *confine* the damage caused by a fault is an important consideration" [13, p. 124].

Thus, both the design of appropriate constraints and the use of mechanisms that enforce those constraints are important issues in developing dependable systems. Although the fundamental problem is the same in hardware and software, hardware often allows physical isolation of components to be used as an effective technique for damage confinement. In software, the need to use shared resources, notably main storage and facilities in the operating system, makes such physical isolation impractical for most systems.

For these reasons, damage confinement is a challenging problem in software. The use of backward recovery, which can remove damage that has not been located, mitigates the problem to some extent; however, even if backward recovery is used, in large systems it may be impractical to roll back the entire state and arbitrary spread of damage can also greatly complicate the problem of fault identification and removal.

The problem of damage confinement appears to have received significantly less attention than many other aspects of fault tolerance. The author conducted an unscientific survey, of the last four Fault-Tolerant Computing Symposia and the most recent special issue on dependable computing of *IEEE Transactions on Computers* (January 1998). No papers had a significant emphasis on damage confinement in the special issue or the 1996 or 1997 Symposia, although four papers in the 1998 Symposium and one in 1995 did.

This paper attempts to provide a basis for damage confinement in large-scale software systems, drawing from previous work both in fault-tolerance and in other areas, such as operating systems, distributed systems, and computer security. Section 2 describes some principles for designing constraints to confine damage, although many such constraints are necessarily application-specific. Section 3 describes means for ensuring that the constraints are enforced, including techniques designed both for fault tolerance and for other purposes. Section 4 discusses the applicability of the constraint-enforcement techniques described in the preceding section, particularly the suitability for fault tolerance of those techniques not designed with that as their purpose. The suitability is discussed with reference to the varying requirements for fault tolerance that exist in different systems. Finally, Section 5 provides a summary and suggests aspects of damage confinement that need to be pursued further.

2. Damage-confinement constraints

For damage confinement to be meaningful, a system must be made up of separate components, with the objective being to contain the effects of a fault within the component containing the fault. Of course, such a decomposition may be used recursively and the ideal is to contain the effects of a fault within the lowest-level component possible.

If the system is at all large, the design will presumably include direct interaction between some pairs of components but exclude direct interaction for most pairs of components. Such restriction is likely to be a natural result of other aspects of good system structuring and is also necessary to avoid the conceptual complexity of having every component interact with nearly every other component. When two components are intended to interact, that interaction may cause damage to propagate from one component to the other if damage initially exists within either component. Damage may also spread as the result of entirely unintended interactions, but that problem is the subject of the next section.

Clearly, a basic principle for limiting the spread of damage is for interacting components to be mutually suspicious. For example, if the interaction takes the form of passing parameters from component A to component B and a result in the reverse direction, then B should thoroughly check the parameters and A should thoroughly check the result. Although the checking of parameters may be time-consuming for B, it is a reasonably well defined problem, at least if the interface of B is well defined. However, for A the problem is much more difficult. Particularly if B does not maintain persistent state, B can likely avoid difficulty fairly easily; however, A essentially needs to determine whether the result returned by B is correct. It is, however, not universally agreed that such checking is desirable. Meyer argues [15, pp. 115-123] that redundant checking, e.g., by A before it calls B and B immediately after being called, is undesirable because it causes "conceptual pollution" of the system. Although his arguments have considerable merit, they do not consider fault tolerance. In particular, they assume that proving a property of a component provides full assurance of its behaviour at run time. The situation here is a particular example of the general need to make tradeoffs carefully between redundancy to improve fault tolerance and the resulting increase in complexity of the system.

An obvious, but expensive, solution to the problem described in the preceding paragraph is to use multiple copies of B and "vote" the multiple results obtained, i.e., use N-version programming [2]. Since we are considering software, these separate versions of B must have diverse designs for the scheme to be useful. Aside from the expense in both construction and execution, this approach becomes very difficult if B does contain persistent state. Sharing the persistent state between different versions of B is difficult and if the state is maintained separately, once a version of B has returned a result believed to be incorrect, its internal state becomes suspect and must be corrected before it is reasonable to use it again [25].

A somewhat different approach is the use of a law-governed architecture (LGA) [16, 17]. In general, this externalises the constraints on interactions between components into a set of rules that are enforced at run time. The rules can be simple, static conditions such as "module A is allowed to call module B" but can be much more complex. In general, the facilities that enforce the rules may contain their own state, so rules can have forms such as "method X of object Y may be invoked only if this process holds the token." Rules of this latter type can be used to enforce global properties of a system, such as mutual exclusion, in addition to rules with obvious local checkability.

In principle, an LGA may be used to enforce rules of arbitrary complexity, based on arbitrary inputs to the rules. In practice, it appears best suited to types of enforcement generally similar to those suggested above—controlling which entities in the system are allowed to interact with which other entities, under what conditions. It appears less well suited to examining the parameters of function calls or the content of messages, in order to determine their validity, although the structure of LGA certainly does not rule out such uses.

It is also possible to provide much weaker checking at interfaces, with the objective essentially being to ensure that the data passed across the interface does not cause the receiving component to fail spectacularly (dividing by zero, accessing invalid addresses, etc.). If the component fails by producing incorrect results, eventually some other component must perform sufficient checking to discover that an error exists and then perform damage assessment using information about which weakly checked interfaces might have been involved in the spread of damage to the point at which it was found.

Unfortunately, there is evidence that simply making extensive use of error checks, such as those discussed above, may not provide effective damage confinement [6]. An experiment, using fault injection, with the Postgres database system found 7% of the faults resulted in spread of damage to the persistent database state before an error was detected and the system halted. Because the system in question is a database, the transaction mechanism can be used to back out changes made by the transaction that was executing at the time of the error, which reduced the spread of faults into persistent storage to 2%.

Most of the above discussion on confinement constraints is very general, since the constraints themselves tend to be quite application-specific. As a trivial example, a function that computes square roots needs to check that its input is non-negative whereas an *arcsin* function needs to check that its input is in the range $[-1, 1]$. A few papers have attempted to discuss the issue more generally, in particular by developing models for interaction and enforcement of interaction constraints. These papers often work with models for confinement that are based on work in the security community, such as the Bell-LaPadula model [3], in which information can flow from lower to higher levels, but not vice versa.

If a system contains multiple components with different dependability requirements, the Bell-LaPadula model can be applied, to a certain extent, fairly directly. One paper [24] discusses mechanisms to constrain the flow of damage in a manner similar to that used to constrain the flow of information in a secure system. In this case, the objective is to prevent the spread of damage from low-integrity to high-integrity components of the system. Unlike security, in which information is generally constrained absolutely to flow in one direction only, here there must also be provisions for flow from low to high integrity, with appropriate checking to ensure that such flows do not spread damage.

If there is not a significant gradation of dependability among components, the Bell-LaPadula model is less directly applicable, but other security models can be considered. For example, a successor the the Bell-LaPadula model allows information to flow from one "domain" to another, but does not require that this relationship between domains be transitive [20]. Although this is more flexible, it may also not map very well onto the general requirements for damage confinement in a large system.

A model proposed recently in the context of civil-aviation aircraft with activities of varying criticality taking place on a single processor [8] is quite relevant to the general problem of damage confinement. In the situation discussed in that paper, it is clearly vital that other activities not interfere with activities having a high level of criticality. The model is based on the notion that activities should generally not interact with each other at all, regardless of their level of criticality. The model takes the realistic view that some interaction will be required but that it must be carefully controlled. The objective is to demonstrate the absence of *unintentional* interference between activities.

3. Enforcing confinement constraints

The material in the preceding section concerns the spread of damage through intended interactions between software components, via function calls, message passing, or explicitly shared data. If faults can produce damage flows that bypass these intended interactions, the flow of damage may be completely unconstrained, possibly producing rapid complete failure of the system and definitely making damage assessment extremely difficult. There are various mechanisms that can produce such flows. For example, the use of a corrupted pointer or an illegal subscript may cause a store into a data structure entirely different from the one intended. Similarly, illegal operations related to allocating and freeing storage can affect any other component that uses dynamically allocated storage from the same storage pool.

The problem of limiting the scope of activity for a component occurs in contexts that are not explicitly fault-tolerant. For example, preventing unwanted activity by code downloaded over the Internet is a problem of great current interest. Another, less prominent, example is the use of kernel extensions that are not trusted by the kernel itself. This section describes techniques for enforcing confinement, both those developed explicitly for fault-tolerance and those developed for other situations. The use of strongly typed languages, which attempts to solve the confinement problem at compile time, is considered first. Then, various run-time mechanisms, principally those found in operating systems are considered.

3.1. Strongly typed languages

A frequently proposed solution for enforcing confinement is the use of a strongly typed language, with the language restrictions guaranteeing the absence of unintended flows. The Hermes language [23] was designed to provide strong constraints and a fine division into components. In Hermes, what would be a function in other languages is a process and what would be an ordinary procedure call in other languages is (effectively) a remote procedure call. In addition, services such as input/output that are usually implicitly available wherever desired are only available if a process has explicitly imported the necessary interface, usually at process initiation. Java, which is currently attracting a great deal of attention, also has the necessary strong typing to constrain unintended information flow [10]. As well, its use of garbage collection rather than explicit freeing of storage avoids one specific source of difficulty. In addition, Java's intended uses include dynamically loaded applets, with the source of the program not necessarily trusted by the user whose workstation will execute code. Thus, Java is intended to allow the execution of code that is strongly constrained not to access or affect any system resources except those explicitly intended for its use. One further example is the language Modula-3 [11], which provides strong typing, but also provides an "escape" mechanism that allows explicitly unsafe code. Thus, Modula-3 needs to be restricted to its safe subset to obtain the desired benefits of strong typing.

An important issue with strong typing is whether the checking takes place statically, during compilation, or dynamically, at run time. In practice, a mixture of the two is likely, with as much checking done statically as can reasonably be managed and the rest done dynamically. If very little of the checking needs to be done dynamically, execution will be quite efficient, but if much dynamic checking is required, the execution-time penalty can be substantial. An obvious example is that if a language implementation allows but does not require bounds checking on array subscripts, it is common to turn off bounds checking for production execution. Of course, this is done in order to increase execution speed. However, if bounds checking is done by a combination of static and dynamic checking, the cost could be reduced substantially.

3.2. Separation of components

An extreme solution for enforcing confinement would be to isolate each component on its own private processor and allow interaction only by message passing. With its own processor, main storage, main-storage free list, and operating system, a component could achieve arbitrary damage confinement by providing as extensive checks as necessary on incoming messages. Clearly, very few systems could practically be constructed in such a fashion, even with a very coarse division into components.

If off-the-shelf components are used, it may be difficult to achieve an appropriate combination of confinement and high-bandwidth communication. A recent paper considers the problem of building a fault-tolerant multiprocessor system based on the VME bus [27]. The difficulty is that the shared memory provided via the VME architecture presents an opportunity for spreading damage in spite of the separation of component execution onto separate processors. The paper proposes a scheme in which a layer of software uses the shared memory to implement a message-passing scheme and constrains access to prevent other, arbitrary use. Fortunately, the VME-bus-interface chip contains the necessary facilities to provide hardware enforcement of read-only access to local memory by remote processors.

The concept of an application "shell" has been proposed [12] as a general mechanism for dealing with system components, primarily software, that are not sufficiently dependable, including the use of off-the-shelf software. Of the three types of shell described, the "protection shell" is most relevant here. The idea of a protection shell is that the dependability of the system will be determined by characteristics of the shell, rather than of the component the shell encloses. By monitoring all communication into and out of the component it surrounds, the protection shell is explicitly intended to prevent flow of damage into or out of the component.

In order to provide a maximally robust implementation, application shells should operate on different machines from the component they surround but, as suggested above, the provision of separate processors is likely to be considered too expensive for most applications. An alternative is to execute the shell simply as a separate process, in which case the implementation becomes dependent on protection mechanisms provided by the underlying system.

3.3. Operating-system mechanisms

As just suggested, an obvious possibility is to use operating-system facilities to constrain the operation of components directly at execution time. One alternative is to make each component a separate process and limit interactions to message passing or other explicit mechanisms provided by the operating system. Unfortunately, a fine-grained division into components will result in very frequent crossing of protection boundaries and that is likely to produce a very high overhead. It is particularly unfortunate that modern RISC processors seem to have made the cost of crossing the user/kernel boundary substantially higher (relative, say, to integer performance) than in earlier CISC processors [1]. Thus, sophisticated approaches are required to provide such run-time confinement at acceptable cost.

One possibility is to reduce the overhead caused by crossing domain boundaries. The obvious way to achieve this is to reduce the cost of crossing the boundary [4]. An alternative is to avoid crossing the boundary for every call. "Futures" are commonly used to increase concurrency by allowing a client to continue execution after making a request of a server, not blocking until the value of the future is required. It is possible to combine the concept of futures with batching of calls to obtain the effect of executing several calls with only one crossing (in each direction) of the domain boundary [14, 28]. The novel ideas in this work are to allow futures to be used as parameters of subsequent calls without waiting for the future and the ability to pass limited control structures with a set of calls, so that effects in addition to a straight-line execution of calls can be achieved inside the server, with only a single "batched" call.

The above has considered facilities provided by, potentially, a large monolithic operating system. Work in the security area has examined the possibility of building an operating system with facilities for constraining information flow as the lowest level of the operating system. Such an implementation then also constrains the remainder of the operating system itself.

A general concept for providing strong guarantees limiting flow of information among processes is the reference monitor [7]. The specific idea is that the reference monitor mediates all accesses to data in order to guarantee security. The reference monitor must correctly implement the security policy, control all data accesses, and be tamper-proof. Clearly, the same kind of control over data access is useful in many other contexts. A reference monitor may be implemented by a security kernel, which is provided as the lowest level of an operating system.

Rushby has suggested isolating the portion of the security kernel that provides separation between domains, allowing only controlled communication, as a component he calls a separation kernel [19]. The remaining functions of a security kernel are then provided by monitors responsible for various classes of resources. A separation kernel more accurately reflects the needs of damage confinement than a security kernel, since the latter has concepts specific to multi-level security embedded in it.

3.4. Constrained kernel extensions

If faults in the operating system are a concern (as they should be, given the complexity of operating systems), there is a problem that any data in main storage could be corrupted by the operating system. Most operating systems run large parts of their code in privileged mode, making such damage significantly likely. This is a particular concern if the system contains a large quantity of main storage, with the intention of using that storage to retain data that would traditionally have been stored on disk. Of course, data on disk can also be corrupted by operating-system faults, but it is significantly simpler to corrupt data in main storage. One possible solution is to conceal part of main storage from the bulk of the operating system, with access to it mediated by a very small kernel [9]. If appropriate hardware facilities exist to "hide" the memory effectively, then flow of damage into the hidden memory depends only on explicit access operations and the correctness of the small kernel.

Many operating systems now allow kernel extensions to be loaded dynamically and some research operating systems use kernel extensions as a major technique for extending a minimal micro-kernel. In many of these cases the extensions are not trusted by the kernel proper. Such a design has obvious advantages for fault tolerance, since only the micro-kernel has the potential for causing arbitrary damage, provided the extensions are properly constrained. Various mechanisms, sometimes quite elaborate, have been used to constrain the extensions.

The mechanisms used in VINO [22] include a transaction mechanism to back out changes on failure, limits on lock-holding time, limits on resource consumption, and limitations on the use of kernel services. Unfortunately, the techniques just mentioned have a strong orientation to the specific application intended and are largely unsuitable for the more general cases that must be handled in building a dependable application. Some of the other techniques do have a more general applicability.

Another paper considers a slightly more general problem, although again with a strong orientation toward providing untrusted extensions on an untrusted base [26]. The technique used is referred to as "sandboxing" and involves modifying the machine code of an untrusted module in order to confine it to its own fault domain. These modifications primarily concern access to main storage, e.g., they work by forcing the high bits of each address to contain a particular value and hence allowing only access to a particular segment of memory. They also discuss constraining access to operating-system services, essentially by forcing such accesses to go through an intermediate, trusted module that determines whether the system call should be allowed to take place. Results indicate that the modified code runs only slightly more slowly than the unmodified code (about 4%) and that for a particular test application, involving extensions to the Postgres database manager, the overhead was substantially less than for the use of separate memory-protection domains.

VINO also uses the sandboxing technique, but uses specialised techniques rather than a trusted intermediate module to restrict access to other code. One technique is simply that kernel functions invoked from an extension check their parameters in the same way that parameters passed in from user space are checked. The other is that the set of functions that can be invoked is restricted. As much as possible, a static check is used, but when static checking is not possible, the function address is checked at run time against a table of legal function entry points.

The SPIN operating system [5] relies on the use of Modula-3 for writing kernel extensions. The strong typing in Modula-3 is claimed to provide adequate isolation of the extensions and to produce essentially no overhead. They do need to rely on the correctness of the compiler and to check that executables have been signed by the compiler.

The sentry mechanism [21] is intended to guard the flow in and out of a server. It provides an organised means for adding required checking and doing it both dynamically and on a per-process basis rather than globally. Although there are some advantages in general, notably in avoiding excessive complexity in the servers, the scheme is most beneficial when the "server" is the operating system and can not be readily modified. The test environment investigated in the paper is the UX server, which provides UNIX services in Mach.

Another alternative that has been explored for kernel extensions is proof-carrying code [18]. The idea is that code is proven to have a set of required safety properties and that proof is attached to the executable code. Generating the original proof may be very difficult but it is possible to check very quickly whether the code satisfies the proof. The result is that the code does not need to be signed and there is no need to trust a compiler or other tool. One concern with this work is that the examples used were packet filters and are quite small pieces of code: the largest example is 1K bytes. For these small examples, the proof-validation times were quite short, all being less than 2.5 msec (on a 175 MHz DEC Alpha 3000/600). It seems unlikely that a system could be divided into components that were all this small, so the scaling of verification times is a concern. Since the verification needs to be carried out only once, during initialisation, the time required may not be a major concern; the difficulty of constructing the proofs for complex components may be a serious obstacle, however.

4. Confinement constraints for fault tolerance

Generally, improved damage confinement implies higher execution-time overheads or added complexity in writing application code. Thus, an appropriate choice of damage confinement must be based on the overall need for reliability and availability in the system, and the importance of various components to those global system properties.

A distinction is often made between safety-critical systems and others, but "safety" may not capture the relevant property. A better term may be simply "critical systems," including systems that would result in massive economic dislocation if they suffered major failures, such as some financial systems. For such critical systems, substantial hardware and software resources are likely to be necessary to achieve the required level of reliability and availability. Techniques such as application shells are suitable as an organised approach for improving the reliability and availability of such systems. In safety-critical systems, the use of added hardware, the slowdown caused by frequent protection-boundary crossings, and so on, are all likely to be tolerated because of the overall design goals for the system. In other critical systems, these should probably also be tolerated although it is not clear that they are. There are clearly also many systems for which a high level of reliability and availability is desired but for which such large expenditure of resources cannot be justified. Such systems may be used, for example, in environments in which computer-system dependability provides competitive advantage but high computer-system cost results in a competitive disadvantage.

Techniques such as security kernels and separation kernels are likely to produce significant costs, although it is not clear what the minimum costs are if a separation kernel is used rather than a security kernel. A major problem with any such "kernel" approach is that it must be built into the lowest levels of the system from the outset. In most cases, an off-the-shelf operating system must be used and most do not provide the needed facilities.

Several of the techniques described in the preceding section are designed explicitly to have low cost and therefore are potentially suitable for systems in which dependability is important, but the system is not critical. The techniques were not intended, principally or even at all, to provide fault tolerance, so it is important to verify whether the techniques are suitable for use in providing fault tolerance. In their original intended application, the principal concern is malice on the part of system users or intruders. It is generally assumed, however, that the hardware and system software operate correctly. For fault tolerance, malice is usually not assumed, although it sometimes is. More significantly, faults in the hardware, the system software, and so on, need to be considered.

For critical systems, the categories of faults just mentioned must be considered. For non-critical systems running on modern hardware and operating systems, that may not be necessary. In particular, the failure rate of a modern CPU using ECC main storage is extremely low and the failure rate for some operating systems is also extremely low in many environments. In such cases, the failure rate of the application software may dominate all other failure rates and be the only significant source of concern in improving reliability and availability. If that is the situation, techniques originating in other areas are likely as suitable for fault tolerance as for their original purposes.

An issue with enforcing information-flow constraints via a strongly typed language is that any damage occurring to the executable code, while stored on disk or while it is resident in memory for execution, bypasses the intended mechanism completely. As discussed above, this may not be a significant concern for a large class of systems.

Another issue concerning strongly typed languages is that reliance must be placed on a great deal of mechanism and the mechanism may itself be subject to faults. For some languages, enforcement relies strongly on the compiler and compilers are very complex software systems. For Java, there is no reliance on the compiler, only on the bytecode interpreter. For the same reason, damage to the executable is not an issue. Unfortunately, pure interpretation has obvious efficiency difficulties, which motivates compilation, at some point, into native machine code. There is then reliance on that compiler and damage to the compiled code is again a concern. Another concern is that if a user program is ultimately executed as native machine code, imperfections in the type enforcement can have major consequences. In the case of interpretation, unless the user program manages to break out of the interpreter completely, imperfections in type enforcement are likely to have more limited effects.

The proof-carrying-code technique essentially represents the use of program-proving combined with a fast means of checking the proof when code is executed. Its primary benefit is in situations in which executable code is not trusted, although the proof checking also helps verify that code has not been damaged prior to being loaded into main storage. It appears unlikely that it represents a good technique for detecting disk-storage errors. It can have value for dependability, however, because it factors out issues of compiler correctness. If the mechanism that verifies the proof when the code is loaded can be trusted, then faults in any of the earlier components involved in creating the executable code and the associated proof are not a concern.

The use of protection boundaries to constrain damage is hardly a novel idea. Techniques, such as those described in the preceding section, for decreasing the total cost of crossing protection boundaries are worth exploring. As long as the techniques do not compromise the boundary itself, they are as applicable to improving dependability as for other purposes.

The sandboxing technique shares with the use of strongly typed languages the difficulty that it is intended to create an executable with certain properties and damage to the executable may cause unnoticed loss of those properties. As discussed above, such damage to the executable may not be an issue in many environments. Thus, sandboxing may be a useful technique for fault tolerance, although some issues need further exploration. One is the overhead it induces, which is reported to be low in most cases, but use for kernel extensions may not be typical of other uses. Another issue is that, although a protection boundary can be crossed very cheaply it appears that parameter passing presents problems. Passing parameters by value is inefficient if parameters are at all large but passing by address is problematic if caller and callee are both constrained to access their own, non-overlapping address spaces.

The implementation strategies used in the two examples of sandboxing mentioned in the previous section are somewhat different. In both cases, added functionality at compile time produces "sandboxed" code as output. In one case [22] the resulting code has a cryptographic digital signature attached, to ensure that the code has been properly "sandboxed." This may not be an issue in a fault-tolerant system, where the use of "illegitimate" code is not the concern. In the other case [26] the code is checked before it starts execution to ensure that the "sandboxing" has been done properly. This approach avoids problems of compiler bugs, as well as the need to verify the origins of a given executable program.

5. Conclusions and further work

The problem of damage confinement, as an issue in fault-tolerance, has not received a great deal of attention, but related problems in other areas have recently received substantial attention. For different reasons, restricting the permitted activity of code has been a concern both in the Internet and in operating-system research. Some of the techniques developed are quite specialised for their intended purpose, but others appear useful for fault tolerance as well. In particular, techniques for decreasing the cost of crossing protection-domain boundaries and for sandboxing appear to have potential.

In general, it appears that these techniques are more suitable for systems which do not have the extreme reliability and availability requirements of critical systems. If failure of the processor to execute instructions correctly, main-storage errors not detected or improperly corrected by ECC, disk-storage errors not detected by CRC, etc., are a concern, then fault-tolerance techniques likely need to be developed from the beginning with such possibilities in mind. Because such failures are very infrequent, they may be legitimately neglected in the construction of many dependable systems. For such systems, techniques developed in other areas have much greater likelihood of being suitable.

A problem with some of the techniques is that they assume a software system is being built "from scratch," starting with the lowest level of the operating-system kernel. In practice, this is rarely the case. Unfortunately, the hardware and software generally available for use may have undesirable properties for damage confinement and remedying such problems, if the underlying system is not modifiable, may be essentially impossible.

Clearly, actual use for fault-tolerance of the techniques identified is needed to determine their costs and effectiveness in practice. As well, other techniques for damage confinement should be sought in additional areas of computer-science research outside the traditional boundaries of fault tolerance.

References

[1] T. Anderson, H. Levy, B. Bershad, and E. Lazowska. The interaction of architecture and operating system design. In *Proceedings, Fourth International Conference on Architectural Support for Programming Languages and Operating Systems*, pages 108–120, Santa Clara, California, April 8–11 1991.

[2] A. Avizienis. The N-version approach to fault-tolerant software. *IEEE Transactions on Software Engineering*, SE-11(12):1491–1501, December 1985.

[3] D.E. Bell and L.J. La Padula. Secure computer system: Unified exposition and Multics interpretation. Technical Report MTR-2997, Rev. 1, MITRE Corp., Bedford, Mass., March 1976.

[4] B. Bershad, T. Anderson, E. Lazowska, and H. Levy. Lightweight remote procedure call. *ACM Transactions on Computer Systems*, 8(1):37–55, February 1990.

[5] B. Bershad et al. Extensibility, safety and performance in the SPIN operating system. In *Proceedings of the Fifteenth Symposium on Operating Systems Principles*, pages 267–284, Copper Mountain Resort, Colorado, December 3–6 1995.

[6] S. Chandra and P. M. Chen. How fail-stop are faulty programs? In *Digest of Papers, Twenty-Eighth Annual International Symposium on Fault-Tolerant Computing*, pages 240–249, Munich, Germany, June 23–25 1998.

[7] Department of Defense. *Department of Defense Trusted Computer System Evaluation Criteria*, December 1985. DOD 5200.28-STD.

[8] B. L. Di Vito. A model of cooperative noninterference for integrated modular avionics. In *Proceedings of the Seventh International Working Conference on Dependable Computing for Critical Applications*, San Jose, California, January 6–8 1999.

[9] F. Eskesen, M. Hack, A. Iyengar, R. P. King, and N. Halim. Software exploitation of a fault-tolerant computer with a large memory. In *Digest of Papers, Twenty-Eighth Annual International Symposium on Fault-Tolerant Computing*, pages 336–345, Munich, Germany, June 23–25 1998.

[10] J. Gosling, B. Joy, and G. Steele. *The Java Language Specification*. Springer-Verlag, Wien, 1996.

[11] S. P. Harbison. *Modula-3*. Prentice-Hall, Englewood Cliffs, New Jersey, 1992.

[12] J. C. Knight, R. W. Lubinsky, J. McHugh, and K. J. Sullivan. Architectural approaches to information survivability. Technical Report CS-97-25, Department of Computer Science, University of Virginia, Charlottesville, Virginia, September 1997.

[13] P. A. Lee and T. Anderson. *Fault Tolerance: Principles and Practice*. Springer-Verlag, Wien, second, revised edition, 1990.

[14] B. Liskov, A. Adya, M. Castro, and Q. Zondervan. Type-safe heterogeneous sharing can be fast. In *Proceedings, Workshop on Persistent Objects (POS-7)*, pages 1–10, Cape May, New Jersey, May 1996.

[15] B. Meyer. *Object-Oriented Software Construction*. Prentice-Hall, New York, 1988.

[16] N. H. Minsky. Law-governed regularities in object systems; Part 1: An abstract model. *Theory and Practice of Object Systems*, 2(4):283–301, 1996.

[17] N. H. Minsky and V. Ungureanu. Regulated coordination in open distributed systems. In *Proceedings, Coordination Languages and Models, Second International Conference (COORDINATION '97)*, pages 81–97, Berlin, Germany, September 1–3 1997.

[18] G. C. Necula and P. Lee. Safe kernel extensions without run-time checking. In *Proceedings of the Second Symposium on Operating Systems Design and Implementation (OSDI '96)*, pages 229–243, Seattle, Washington, October 28–31 1996.

[19] John Rushby. Kernels for safety? In T. Anderson, editor, *Safe and Secure Computing Systems*, pages 210–220. Blackwell Scientific Publications, Oxford, 1989.

[20] John Rushby. Noninterference, transitivity, and channel-control security policies. Technical Report CSL-92-02, Computer Science Laboratory, SRI International, Menlo Park, California, December 1992.

[21] M. Russinovich, Z. Segall, and D. Siewiorek. Application transparent fault management in fault tolerant Mach. In *Digest of Papers, The Twenty-Third International Symposium on Fault-Tolerant Computing*, pages 10–19, Toulouse, France, June 22–24 1993.

[22] M. I. Seltzer, Y. Endo, C. Small, and K. A. Smith. Dealing with disaster: Surviving misbehaved kernel extensions. In *Proceedings of the Second Symposium on Operating Systems Design and Implementation (OSDI '96)*, pages 213–227, Seattle, Washington, October 28–31 1996.

[23] R. E. Strom et al. *Hermes: A Language for Distributed Computing*. Prentice-Hall, Englewood Cliffs, New Jersey, 1991.

[24] E. Totel, J.-P. Blanquart, Y. Deswarte, and D. Powell. Supporting multiple levels of criticality. In *Digest of Papers, Twenty-Eighth Annual International Symposium on Fault-Tolerant Computing*, pages 70–79, Munich, Germany, June 23–25 1998.

[25] K. S. Tso and A. Avizienis. Community error recovery in N-version software: A design study with experimentation. In *Digest of Papers, Seventeenth Annual International Symposium on Fault-Tolerant Computing*, pages 127–133, Pittsburgh, Pennsylvania, July 6–8 1987.

[26] R. Wahbe, S. Lucco, T. E. Anderson, and S. L. Graham. Efficient software-based fault isolation. In *Proceedings of the Fourteenth Symposium on Operating Systems Principles*, pages 203–216, Asheville, North Carolina, December 5–8 1993.

[27] M. F. Younis, J. X. Zhou, and M. Aboutabl. Strong partitioning protocol for a multiprocessor VME system. In *Digest of Papers, Twenty-Eighth Annual International Symposium on Fault-Tolerant Computing*, pages 176–185, Munich, Germany, June 23–25 1998.

[28] Q. Y. Zondervan. Increasing cross-domain call batching using promises and batched control structures. Technical Report MIT/LCS/TR-658, Laboratory for Computer Science, MIT, Cambridge, Mass., June 1995.

Towards a Discipline of System Engineering: Validation of Dependable Systems

Andrea Bondavalli*, Alessandro Fantechi**, Diego Latella* and Luca Simoncini***

*CNUCE-CNR, Pisa, Italy
**University of Florence and IEI-CNR, Italy
***University of Pisa and CNUCE-CNR, Italy

Abstract

Complex systems require the use, of an integrated and best balanced set of components. The integration and the balanced set are crucial issues, which require some sort of verifiable compositionality property of component parts that contribute structurally, functionally, non functionally and interactionally to the total quality of the system design. This is even more important when dealing with the design of highly dependable systems. The concept of verifiable compositionality is much more demanding than the usual approach based on composition of building blocks. It implies the preservation of properties and the ability of verifying them, as well as those that are added (which mainly deal with interactions among parts) in the process of designing and building a system made of components. Economic reasons push towards the use of COTS (Commercial Off the Shelf) and towards the re-use of available components and this trend poses new problems.

Integration, compositionality and re-use appear to be the very challenging issues in the validation (of both design and implementation) of complex systems, in particular dependable ones used for controlling critical applications, and require a special effort towards the emergence of a new discipline - System Engineering - which will encompass and integrate the current design disciplines.

This paper aims at a discussion in the direction of identifying possible advanced approaches to the validation of dependable systems.

1: Introduction

Computer controlled systems are used in many fields of applications, with different levels of criticality requirements. A common characteristic of such systems is the increasing complexity in intrinsic terms (management of distribution, redundancy, layering of functionalities, etc.) and of the in-the-field operation (interfaces towards the environment, timing constraints, criticality of the controlled applications, etc.). This increasing complexity rarely can be completely mastered and usual design practices often suffer from partial approaches, overlooked details, inadequate modelling, insufficient prototyping, limited design tools or techniques available; not to deal with incorrect or incomplete or not understood user requirements, which are often the cause of the final failure of a design or system [58].

The solution to this situation is far away to be reached, but for sure requires the development and the testing in the field of design processes which address the "system" in its entirety and integrate as many as possible relevant requirements, *including* the interactions with the environment.

The current disciplines of hardware, firmware, software, application engineering, commonly considered as separated issues have to evolve towards a discipline of "system engineering" which encompasses all the previous ones, if we have to rely on systems which control critical environments [60].

Mil-STD-499B has defined System Engineering as: "an interdisciplinary approach to evolve and verify an integrated and optimally balanced set of product and process designs that satisfy user and society needs and provide information for management decision making."

This definition is the evolution (and abstraction at a certain level) of the definition given in MIL-STD-499A:

"the application of scientific and engineering efforts to
- transform an operational need into a description of system performance and a system configuration through the use of an iterative process of definition, synthesis, analysis, design, test, and evaluation;
- integrate related technical parameters and ensure compatibility of all physical, functional, and program interfaces in a manner that optimises the total system definition and design;
- integrate reliability, maintainability, safety, survivability, human engineering, and other such factors into the total engineering effort to meet cost, schedule, supportability, and technical performance objectives."

Another interesting definition of System Engineering is the one by Joe DeFoe and Jim McAuley: "the processing of building real things to solve real problems within technological, environmental, economic, legal, ethical, cultural, and institutional constraints." [52]

Although sounding philosophical, this definition is focused on the different types of constraints which a system has to fulfil.

Having this in mind, we can concentrate on the definition given by Mil-STD-499B, which has the merit of pointing out:
- **the interdisciplinary approach used to satisfy user needs**; computer engineers have to interact with other engineers (like mechanical or chemical etc.) and mainly with the final users and the society (who will present all kinds of needs – environmental, legal, ethical etc.);
- **the evolution and verification of product and process designs**; the quality of a product design is dependent on the quality of the process in which is inserted, and these qualities have to be verified; the product-in-a-process approach is an evolving one and changes and modifications have to be taken into account;
- **the evolution and verification of an integrated and optimally balanced set** of product and process designs; if the word "optimally" is taken literally, only techniques which allow quantitative measures of quality parameters, and their combination, could be applied and this would limit the applicability of a system engineering approach (simply consider a system to be designed for high security). Probably the current status of the art is better represented by rephrasing with "best balanced set", which allow the inclusion of all best-effort techniques. The "integration" and "the balanced set" are crucial points, which requires some sort of "verifiable compositionality" property of component parts that contribute to the total quality of the system from the points of view of structure, functionality, non-functional properties and interaction. The concept of "verifiable compositionality" is completely different from and much more demanding than the usual

approach based on composition of building blocks. It implies the preservation of properties (both structural, functional and non-functional) and of the ability of verifying them, as well as those that are added (mainly interactional), in the process of building a complex system made of components.

- **the provision of information for management decision making**; this point is of prevalent importance in the product-in-a-process approach and is self explaining.

Based on these considerations, the INCOSE (International Council on System Engineering) - SE Practice Working Group - Subgroup on Pragmatic Principles has issued on January 21, 1993 a document, edited by J. C. DeFoe, ""Pragmatic Principles" of Systems Engineering", which present a list of points to be followed for a correct product-in-a-process approach [52]. The complete list is reported in Appendix A.

The points of the list covers the entire spectrum of the product-in-a-process approach and we limit ourselves to the discussion on those points which relate intrinsically to the system engineering approach applied to the validation of dependable system architecture design. We are aware that a total quality product and process design cannot overlook the points that we do not discuss, but our opinion is that something beneficial can be obtained even with our limited discussion.

Our attention will therefore be focused on the points indicated in the section E) of the list in appendix A.

2: Validation of dependable system architecture design.

The increasing complexity of computer controlled systems has exposed the limits of the validation techniques traditionally used in industry, like code review, testing, Fault Trees or Failure Mode Error Analysis to cope with the increasingly demanding dependability requirements asked to these systems.

Moreover, new technologies such as Object-Oriented Design and Programming, Advanced User Interfaces, Hardware-Software Codesign, the use of COTS (Commercial Off the Shelf) software components, all present new challenges for the validation process.

The traditional validation techniques are being more and more complemented with advanced validation techniques, such as Formal Verification, Model based Dependability Evaluation, Schedulability Analysis, Fault Injection, which are individually discussed later in this section.

These techniques are not aimed to replace the traditional validation techniques, but should rather be integrated with them.

2.1: Formal verification

Formal verification is a hot topic nowadays in the field of system engineering, specially for the development of critical dependable systems. The use of formal methods for the specification and verification of properties of systems is one methodological improvement of the system production process, which, together with other techniques, can make it possible to reach high quality standards: the use of formal methods is increasingly required by the international standards and guidelines for the development of safety critical computer-controlled systems.

Formal methods are mathematically-based techniques that can offer a rigorous and effective way to model, design and analyse computer systems, and they have been a topic of research for many years and the question now is whether these methods can be effectively used in industrial applications. Tool support is necessary for a full industrialisation process and there is a clear need for improved integration of formal method techniques with other software engineering practices.

Several approaches to the application of formal methods in the development process have been proposed, differing for the degree of involvement of the method within the development process, ranging from the mere use of formal specifications in order to write rigorous specifications, to the (more or less automated) generation of code from the formal specification, to the use of formal verification as an additional validation technique aimed to reach a high level of confidence of the correctness of the system.

Industrial acceptance of formal methods is strictly related to the investment needed to introduce them, to the maturity of tool support available, and to the easy of use of the techniques and tools. The use of graphical representation is often preferred, even if some formality is lost. So, despite some successful experience of application of development processes built around a specific formal method (see for a main example [35]), the industrial trend is currently directed towards the use of graphical specification formalisms (a notable example is SDL [83]), which nevertheless have a (almost completely) formal semantics; due to the lower costs of training and innovation, industries are more keen to accept formal verification techniques assessing the quality attributes of their products, obtained by a traditional life cycle, rather than a fully formal life cycle development.

Formal verification methods and tools can be roughly classified into two categories, the so-called model-theoretical approaches and proof-theoretical ones.

In the proof theoretical approaches, the system state is modelled in terms of set-theoretical structures on which invariants are defined, while operations on the state are modelled by specifying their pre- and post-conditions in terms of the system state. Properties are described by invariants, which must be proved to hold through the system execution, by means of theorem proving.

Model theoretical approaches, on the other hand, work on a finite state representation of the behaviour of the system. Verification is usually carried out by checking the satisfiability of some desired properties over the model of the system by model checking algorithms or equivalence relations. In particular, safety requirements may be expressed as temporal logic formulae and may be checked on the model of the system.

Model theoretical approaches give a direct automatic verification method of system properties. Unfortunately, this approach suffers of the so called "State Space Explosion" problem: systems composed of several subsystems can be associated to a finite state model with a number of states which is exponential in the number of the component subsystems. Moreover, systems which are highly dependent on data values, share the same problem producing a number of states exponential in the number of data variables. Hence, traditional "model checking" techniques [30], have shown themselves not powerful enough to cope with many "real" systems.

Recent advances to cope with the state-explosion problem have seen the use of symbolic manipulation algorithms inside model checkers: the most notable example is the SMV model checker [21]. In SMV the transition relations are represented implicitly by means of Boolean formulae and are implemented by means of Binary Decision Diagrams (BDDs, [20]). This usually results in a much smaller representation for the systems' transition relations thus allowing the maximum size of the systems that can be dealt with to be significantly enlarged. This kind of tools have been successfully applied to very large state spaces in the realm of hardware verification.

On the converse, proof-theoretic approaches, which can exploit their generalisation capability in order not to be affected by the state explosion problem, require in general more skill in the use of theorem proving tools, and, therefore, more investment, in terms of know-how and training. This is because proofs usually need to be guided by humans and so the theorem proving process is not totally automatic. A consequence of this is that the proof details cannot be hidden to the user.

The last years have seen some effort in the integration of model-checking and theorem-proving approaches [66], and this seems to be the most interesting perspective.

2.2: Model based dependability validation

Various methods and tools for dependability modelling and analysis have been developed which provide support to the analyst, during the phases of definition and evaluation of the models. In general, model types used for dependability analysis are usually classified in two categories; combinatorial types and state-space based ones, which include both Markov models and high level approaches which have an underlying Markov model [61].

Combinatorial models: these include reliability block diagrams, fault trees and reliability graphs. It was shown in [61] that Fault Tree with Repeated Events (FTRE) is the most powerful type. A method that combines the simplicity of Fault-Trees with the more powerful representative capabilities of state based approaches has been proposed in [37].

Markov chains: The approach to the modelling based on Markov processes has been widely accepted in the dependability community because of their powerful representative capabilities, and the relatively cheap solution techniques. Constant failure rates are used. While this seems to be natural and has always been accepted for hardware elements it has also been applied to software failures. A failure rate λ_j for software can be computed as a product of a constant execution rate of the software and its failure probability:

$$\lambda_j = P_j \lambda$$

where λ is the execution rate, and P_j is a failure probability.

Such an approach for modelling software fault tolerance architectures has been adopted in [6] and many subsequent papers. The service of the system is modelled through execution rates and the fault manifestation process by failure probabilities.

High-level modelling: Markov-based approaches for dependability modelling and evaluation must face with the increasing complexity of systems, and consequently of the models. The state space combinatorial growth leads to a dramatic increase in the size of Markov chain models, which tend to become difficult to define and computationally intensive to solve. A solution is offered by modelling tools at a higher level than Markov chains, like Queuing Networks, Stochastic Process Algebras, and Stochastic Petri nets. All exhibit the ability to deal with different abstraction levels of the analysis. Usually, the solution of these models is based on a direct transformation to Markov models. However, high-level models have advantages in the model generation phase, because very compact models can be given even for complex systems, and can enjoy efficient state space reduction algorithms in the solution phase as well.

Those based on Petri nets models are becoming more and more popular due to the appealing graphical visualisation of the models and the natural way in which concurrency, competition and synchronisation are all easily represented within the formalism.

Many different classes of Petri nets have been proposed over the past decade. The basic untimed class of place/transition Petri nets was augmented with the time for the sake of quantitative analysis of performance/dependability attributes, thus defining the class of Stochastic Petri Nets (SPN) [63]. SPNs only consider activities whose duration is an exponentially distributed random variable. This limitation was overcame with the introduction of

Generalised Stochastic Petri Nets [1] (GSPN), which allow for both exponential and instantaneous activities. The stochastic process underlying a SPN and a GSPN model is a discrete space continuous-time homogeneous Markov process, which must be solved to derive the measures of interest for the system.

Nearly all the tools for dependability modelling and evaluation that are based on Petri net models can be used to define and solve GSPNs. What may be different from one tool to the other is merely a matter of the syntax used to define the model; in this sense, GSPN models can be seen as a standard language which is understood by the majority of the tools for the automated evaluation of dependability attributes, like SURF-2 [57], UltraSAN [79], SPNP [29], GreatSPN [26], TimeNET [44].

GSPN extensions: Several extensions of the GSPN class of Petri nets have been further introduced. These extensions can be distinguished in two classes, depending whether the representative power of the extended models is increased beyond that of GSPNs.

For the extensions that do not increase the representative power, the stochastic processes underlying the models are still Markov processes. In this case the extensions provide useful shorthand notations to represent in a concise way complex dependencies among the elements of the model. The Stochastic Activities Networks (SAN) [72] and the Stochastic Reward Nets (SRN) [77] are two classes of Petri nets that include such extensions. UltraSAN and SPNP are the automated tools for the solution of SANs and SRNs, respectively.

On the other hand, there are classes of Petri nets whose underlying stochastic process is not a simple Markov process. For instance, consider the class of Deterministic and Stochastic Petri Nets (DSPN) [2]. DSPN include transitions having exponentially distributed, immediate and deterministic firing time, and are therefore able to represent models GSPNs can not deal with. The tool TimeNET [44] was especially developed to solve DSPN models. An even more powerful class of Petri nets is represented by the Markov Regenerative Stochastic Petri Nets (MRSPN) [28], which allow for transitions having generally distributed firing times. No automated solution tool exists for MRSPNs, yet.

The quantitative analysis of the dependability attributes of computer systems using stochastic modelling is a process that requires ability and experience. Building the model of a system needs the introduction of assumptions, simplifications and *abstractions*, whose impact on the final results can not be estimated a priori. Also, slight variations in the value of a crucial parameter might cause dramatic changes in the final measures. Actually, analytical models had always as their usual target mechanisms or specific parts of the systems. When they have been used for modelling entire complex systems (e.g. [56, 64]) several problems have been encountered like subtle interactions between hardware and software, stiffness of the models (i.e. when the rates of transitions differ by several orders of magnitude) and primarily state explosion. Despite modularity in defining the model can be achieved, the model has to be solved in its entirety to maintain the Markovian properties. Unless more powerful methods can be used, it is not possible to define hierarchies of models where sub models can be separately solved and the results obtained plugged in a higher level model of the hierarchy. Therefore models of real - even rather simple - systems tend to be very abstract and usually do not account for (maybe important) details. This need of carefully selecting the characteristics to be represented is probably also the cause of the extreme difficulty in the automatisation (or even the definition of rigorous methodologies) of the process of model definition.

2.3: Schedulability analysis

In real-time systems, a failure of a system can be caused not only by a functional fault or by an hardware fault, but also by its inability to perform the needed computations within the time limits established for them. Such inability is typically due to the attempt of executing too many different tasks with limited computational resources.

The validation of temporal constraints mainly consists in the search of a *feasible* schedule, i.e. an ordering of the execution of the tasks admitted to the system and for which it can be proved that each task will complete before its deadline. Scheduling has been studied for long time and many proposals exist for static scheduling and (much fewer) dynamic approaches.

Without entering in details on the individual algorithms [74] it is remarkable to note that guarantees (absolute or probabilistic) are given by making many, often unrealistic, assumptions on the number of tasks, their maximum execution time, precedence constraints and resource conflicts, etc. Moreover very restrictive assumptions are often made on the admitted faults so that a few works exists on real-time fault-tolerant systems [43, 76, 81].On the other hand, modern design languages, including those based on the OO paradigm, require restrictions to the computational models, i.e. the allowed interactions among tasks, for allowing to design system with real-time requirements.

For these reasons, until recently no commercial tool supporting schedulability analysis were available. In the recent times, tools like PERTS from TriPacific Software [67] and TimeWiz from TimeSys [78] devoted to the early schedulability analysis have supplemented the avaialble low level debugging or execution tracing tools. What is actually missing is an overall integrated design environment that, within a coherent design methodology, allows to evaluate the impact of the different priority schemes and scheduling algorithms on the real-time system performance and functionality, already at the design level. One step in this direction has been taken by the HRT-HOOD [HOOD 1992] design methodology, which addresses explicitly the design of hard real-time systems in an object based framework, providing means for the verification of their performance. The overall methodology can be supported by automated tools, such as HRT-HoodNICE [53].

2.4: Validation based on fault injection

Despite the continuous advances in systems modelling, several limits remains on the possibilities offered by analytical approaches. Therefore a specific experimental effort remains necessary to test the behaviour, in presence of faults, of fault tolerance mechanisms of the systems. The fault injection is an activity aiming at measuring the characteristic parameters of fault treatment and error treatment mechanisms. Fault injection experiences contribute to the estimation of the coverage and efficacy of fault tolerance and complement the analytical techniques previously described.

Independently of the abstraction level applied, fault injection campaigns contribute to the 'Fault Forecasting' by studying either error propagation [24, 27, 75], or error latency [25, 42] or the coverage of fault tolerance mechanisms [70, 80]. Many techniques and methods have been developed and integrated in tools specific for fault injection, e.g. [3, 23, 55].

As previously mentioned, fault injection is particularly tailored for estimating the coverage of fault tolerance techniques. In particular, the notion of coverage can be applied to errors, specifically to trace the efficacy trough the different steps characterising error treatment. Moreover one should also consider the dynamic dimension of the treatment process leading to the definition of coverage as a function of the time at which the expected treatment is performed. Despite many studies dealt with both coverage and latency, only a few tried an integration by considering them in a unified way, see [5, 38, 62].

The imperfect coverage of fault tolerance mechanisms is due to two main causes:
- the wrong definition/application of the mechanisms with respect to the considered fault assumptions, which results in a lack of the coverage of the mechanisms

- wrong assumptions on the faults which are different from those that hit the system in operation, which results in a lack of coverage of the assumptions

Fault injection is particularly good in revealing imperfections due to the former cause. To estimate coverage of the fault assumption other kind of analyses are required.

Two main criteria must be considered for the experimental validation of fault tolerant systems: the system abstraction level and the form in which injection is applied. For what concerns the system abstraction level it is possible to distinguish the case in which a physical system is available from a simulation model describing the structure and or the behavior of the system. The form in which injection is applied can be either physical injection - faults are directly introduced on physical components through mechanical or electromagnetic alterations, or logical injection - alteration of Boolean variables or data.

Most studies on physical injection used pin-level injection although other techniques like heavy-ion radiation have been used for specific systems. Despite problems of the doubtful representativeness of the injection on the pins of integrated circuits, the other main problem arising is the accessibility of the physical component themselves, due to higher and higher integration and clock rate. The main solution is then represented by the usage of hybrid injection - faults are injected at the logical level of the physical components.

Fault simulation is heavily used for developing test cases in industrial environments, e.g. for quality control of integrated circuits. Still currently there are only a few examples of evaluation of the coverage of fault tolerant mechanisms performed by using simulation models.

As a last comment about fault-injection, we notice that the same principle can be applied also at a more abstract level: in the framework proposed in [10] for the formal validation of fault-tolerance mechanisms, specific anticipated faults are injected in the specification of the mechanisms, with the aim of analysing the behaviour of the specified mechanism in case of faults, and to guarantee that the mechanism satisfies given correctness properties even in case of faults.

2.5: Needs for integration of validation

The discussed validation techniques are separated and not integrated among them; that is, each technique requires to define a particular model of the system, each focused on those aspects which are specific of the technique itself, with no relation with the other models built to apply the other validation techniques.

In a coherent "system engineering" approach the application of these techniques cannot be seen as a mere juxtaposition of unrelated techniques, but rather as an integration of techniques using different, but semantically related models.

In the next two sections we discuss what has been done in this respect in two recent European projects, GUARDS and HIDE. While GUARDS is a very updated best effort example of use of different advanced techniques for design validation, HIDE tries to propose a possible approach to integration.

3: The GUARDS validation framework

In this section we first recall the GUARDS validation framework and discuss its limitations regarding *integration*. GUARDS [68] is an effort, partially supported by the European Community as ESPRIT Project 20716, to design and develop a Generic Upgradable Architecture for Real-Time Dependable Systems, together with its associated development and validation environment. GUARDS aims at reducing the life cycle costs of such embedded systems. The intent is to be able to configure *instances* of a generic architecture that can be shown to meet the very diverse requirements of critical real-time application domains. The cost of validation and certification of instances of the architecture thus becomes a critical factor. The effort to reduce this cost has exploited:

- re-use of already-validated components in different instances
- the support of software components of different criticalities
- and focus validation obligations on a minimum set of critical components.

The GUARDS validation strategy considers both a short-term objective which is the validation of the design principles of the architecture and a long-term one being the validation of instances of the architecture for specific requirements. Different methods, techniques and tools contributed to these validation objectives.

The validation environment that supports the strategy is depicted in Figure 1, which illustrates also the relationship between the components and their interactions with the architecture development environment.

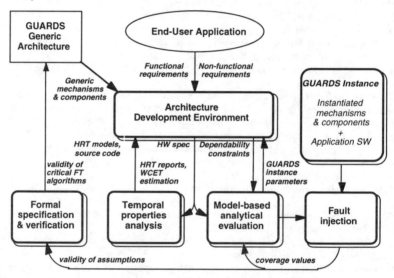

Figure 1 — Main interactions between architecture development and validation (from [68])

The figure explicitly identifies the main validation components: formal verification, model-based evaluation, fault injection and the methodology and the supporting toolset for schedulability analysis. The figure also depicts the complementarity and relationships among the validation components. In particular, fault injection, carried out on prototypes, complements the other validation components by providing means for: a) assessing the validity of the necessary assumptions made by the formal verification task, and b) estimating the coverage parameters included in the analytical models for dependability evaluation.

3.1: Formal verification

Formal approaches were used both for specification and as a design-aid and applied for the verification of critical dependability mechanisms, namely: a) clock synchronisation, b) interactive consistency, c) fault diagnosis, and d) multi-level integrity. The first three mechanisms constitute basic building-blocks of the architecture, and the fourth one corresponds to a major innovation.

The formal approaches that have been applied included both theorem proving and model checking.

The work carried out on the verification of clock synchronisation relied heavily on PVS (*Prototype Verification System*) [66]. It led to the development of a general theory for averaging and non-averaging synchronisation algorithms [73].

The verifications concerning interactive consistency [7, 9], fault diagnosis [8] and multi-level integrity [40] were all based on model checking using the JACK (*Just Another Concurrency Kit*) toolset [14] and on the framework introduced in [10] to deal with dependable systems. This integrated environment provides a set of verification tools that can be used separately or in combination. Due to the complexity of the required models, the toolset was extended to include a symbolic model checker for ACTL [39].

3.2: Model-based dependability evaluation

Model-based dependability evaluation in the GUARDS context posed several of the modelling problems discussed previously ("stiffness", combinatorial explosion, etc.).

To master them, different modelling activities have been carried on, choosing modelling details and levels to fit the specific evaluation objectives. This was achieved by focusing either on generic or specific architectural features, or on selected dependability mechanisms. The "focused" models addressed several issues concerning the analysis of generic mechanisms (e.g., α-count [11]) and of specific features for selected instances (phased missions, for space prototype instances [13], intra-channel error detection for railway prototype ones).

Then, elaborating on previous related work (e.g., [56]), an incremental approach proposing modular constructs has been devised. This second viewpoint aims to establish a baseline set of models of the prototype instances of the architecture [69]. A general notation is introduced that allows for a consistent interpretation of the model parameters (layers, correlated faults, etc.). This work guides the choice of a particular instantiation of the architecture, according to the dependability requirements of the end-user application. Last, a third viewpoint was considered that aims to provide detailed models needed to allow for a more comprehensive analysis of the behaviour of the instances (dependencies, error propagation, etc.). Specific work has addressed hierarchical modelling with the aim of mastering the complexity attached to the development of such detailed models [54]. This work is directed mainly at: a) enforcing the thoroughness of the analysis, b) helping the analyst (i.e., a design engineer who is not necessarily a modelling expert).

Although different tools have been used all modelling is based on Stochastic Petri nets to allow re-use of the results of the various studies (both models and modelling methodology).

3.3: Schedulability analysis

The design and development of a GUARDS software application are centred on a hard real-time (HRT) design method, which allows real-time requirements to be taken into account and verified during the design. The method also addresses the problem of designing replicated, fault-tolerant architectures, where a number of computing and communication boards interact for the consolidation of input values and output results.

Despite GUARDS does not force the selection of a specific method, a survey and an analysis of design methods have shown that only HRT-HOOD [22] addresses explicitly the design of *hard* real-time systems, providing means for the verification of their performance. Therefore, HRT-HOOD was selected as the baseline design method and HRT-HoodNICE adopted as supporting tool [53].

To deal with the design of *distributed* systems, HRT-HOOD was extended to include the concept of *Virtual Nodes*, similar to that in the HOOD 3.1 method [50]. The HRT-HoodNICE toolset has been accordingly enhanced.

The application tasks (i.e., HRT objects) are mapped onto the infrastructure architecture. They are coupled with the real-time models of the selected components, in order to analyse and verify their schedulability properties. This is done by the Temporal Properties Analysis toolset, which analyses the performance of the resulting distributed software system.

The Temporal Properties Analysis toolset includes a Schedulability Analyser and a Scheduler Simulator, based on those available in HRT-HoodNICE. They have been enhanced to provide a more precise and realistic analysis (by taking into account the concept of thread offsets) and to cope with the specific needs of a redundant fault-tolerant architecture (by allowing the analysis of the interactions over the ICN).

A further result is that, on the basis of the real-time models produced by the verification tools, the critical interactions among software functions on different channels are scheduled in a deterministic way. The transfer slots allocated to them and a set of pre-defined exchange tables are produced automatically.

3.4: Fault injection

Fault injection has been considered in GUARDS as an experimental verification activity to be carried on prototype instances. Its main objectives are: a) to complement the formal verification of GUARDS mechanisms by overcoming some of the behavioural and structural abstractions made, especially regarding the failure mode assumptions, and b) to support the development of GUARDS instances by assessing its overall behaviour in the presence of faults, in particular by estimating coverage and latency figures for the built-in error detection mechanisms [4].

Both for cost-effectiveness and flexibility, the fault injection environment is based on the software-implemented fault injection (SWIFI) technique [51]. Although available tools could have been used — albeit with some extensions — a specific fault injection toolset (FITS) is being developed. Such a toolset is made available to support end-users in the development of specific instances of the generic architecture.

Besides injecting specific fault/error types, FITS allows injection to be synchronised with the target system by monitoring trigger events. Of course, the observations depend on the targeted mechanisms. While it is primarily intended to inject on a single channel, observations are carried out on all channels.

3.5: Discussion

The GUARDS validation framework has been based on a set of advanced techniques that cover all the aspects mentioned in section 2. However, it is pretty clear that the used validation techniques have been separately applied, with very little integration. The only relation linking different models (dependability models, formal models, HRT diagrams, code) are mostly constituted by written documents.

On the other hand, it could not be in the scope of the project to provide such a strict integration, which requires a much deeper research effort. One of the aims of the project was, certainly, to define a validation environment as a set of support tools, what can be called a "tool kit", rather than a really integrated environment, since it was not possible to create a common theoretical framework in which to unify the different modelling techniques adopted.

In this sense, the validation policy of GUARDS is not so different from the best current industrial practice, where different techniques are applied to different validation phases, at best linked by an appropriate requirement tracing mechanism, sometimes supported by a dedicated tool. In GUARDS, more advanced techniques and tools (but this means also academic, prototypal and less mature tools) were employed within an overall validation policy aimed to provide a wide validation *coverage*.

Really integrating the adopted techniques along a System Engineering approach requires a step further, that is working on the models underlying the different techniques.

4: The HIDE approach to integration of validation

One step towards integration of different validation techniques within a common framework is represented by the ESPRIT Project 27493, HIDE (High-level Integrated Design Environment for Dependability) [47]. The main objective of HIDE is the development of an integrated environment for system design via the Unified Modelling Language (UML). The step forward which allows a more integrated validation is represented by the choice of using a semi-formal design description language (UML) for describing the entire systems under design. This allows to develop models for analyses which can be suited to the different properties of interest. Obviously the design language has to offer mechanisms for decomposing the system into manageable parts. Once the approach proposed within HIDE has been fully implemented it can be used for the validation of systems like GUARDS, provided the effort to describe the entire system with UML is undertaken.

The UML is a standard modelling language. It may be used for visualising, specifying, constructing and documenting several aspects of - or views on - systems. It is based on the object-oriented paradigm and it is heavily graphical in its nature. Different diagrams are used in order to describe different views on a system. For instance, Class Diagrams show sets of classes and their relationships thus addressing the static design view on systems. On the other hand, Statechart Diagrams show state machines thus addressing the dynamic behaviour of systems and their components.

It is outside the scope of this paper to further analyse the UML. We refer the interested reader to [41, 71].

A key point of the HIDE philosophy is to assist the practitioner designer by offering her/him basically a UML interface while providing translations from such a notation to mathematical models suitable for different kinds of validation. This way, the designer can easily validate her/his design since the bulk of the validation technicalities are hidden to her/him. Automatic or semi-automatic translations into the individual mathematical models for the particular validation, or validations, of concern will take care of such technicalities. The results of such validations will be presented back to the designer in the form of annotations in the original UML model.

Usually, each translation focuses on those components of the UML model which are relevant for the validation of concern, possibly enriched with some external information needed for the validation itself. Whenever possible, such enrichment is itself modelled using UML. In the following we shall briefly describe a couple of translations defined within the context of HIDE, as examples of the overall approach.

A first translation maps UML Structural Diagrams to Timed and Generalised Stochastic Petri Nets for dependability assessment [12].

Dependability modelling and analysis of complex systems consisting of a large number of components poses formidable problems. The most important is complexity. The existing tools are not able to deal with the state explosion problems, which plague big size models. To master complexity, a modelling methodology is needed so that only the relevant aspects are detailed, still enabling numerical results to be computable. A feasible strategy to cope with complexity considers starting from simple models, and making them more and more complex and detailed by including refinements of those parts of the system which are reputed to be relevant .

The translation from UML structural diagrams to timed Petri nets in order to keep small the size of the models, tries to capture only the features relevant to dependability leaving aside all other information. It

- allows a less detailed but system-wide representation of the dependability characteristics of the analysed systems.
- provides early, preliminary evaluations of the system dependability during the early phases of the design. This way, a designer can easily verify whether the system that is being built satisfies predefined requirements on dependability attributes.
- deals with various levels of detail, ranging from very preliminary abstract UML descriptions, up to the refined specifications of the last design phases. UML higher level models, (structural diagrams) are available before the detailed, low levels ones. The analysis on these rough models provides indications about the critical parts of the system which require a more detailed representation. In addition, by using well defined interfaces, such models can be augmented by inserting more detailed information coming from refined UML models of the identified critical parts of the system. These might be provided by other transformations dealing with UML behavioural and communication diagrams.

It is important to point out that not only the UML diagrams that form the input of such transformation do not have a formal semantics, but also the specification this set provides might be incomplete or ambiguous. Therefore, a "formalization" of the transformation in the sense of formal correctness cannot be provided.

The second translation maps a subset of UML Statechart Diagrams to Kripke Structures (or in general transition systems) for formal verification of functional properties [59].

This translation defines a reference formal operational semantics for UML Statechart Diagrams within HIDE. Formal semantics are obviously necessary whenever formal verification is at issue: they are a necessary prerequisite for any sensible formal verification or analysis, which is the ultimate goal of the translation. In particular, the Kripke Structure resulting from the translation of a Statechart Diagram can be conveniently used as a basis for model checking. To that purpose it is of course necessary to specify the requirements against which the model has to be checked. Such requirements are usually expressed by a temporal logic formula or by another Kripke Structure or automaton. In the first case the formula is not part of the UML model, since the UML does not provide an explicit notation for temporal logic. In the second case, the requirement can be expressed again as a (simple) Statechart Diagram and its resulting semantics be used for model checking the (semantics) of the original Statechart Diagram.

A nice aspect of the translation definition proposed in [59] is that it is *parametric* in aspects which are not (yet) completely defined for UML. In particular, parametricity of the semantics definition w.r.t. transition priorities makes it suitable for describing the behaviour of systems under different priority schemes. A different approach for the definition of a semantics of UML Statechart Diagrams and for their model checking has been proposed in [18, 82].

5: Discussion

A first, maybe obvious, benefit of the HIDE approach is integration as such. Integration brings homogeneity and uniformity which, in turn, help in managing complexity. The possibility of having a unique model of the system to which reference can be done during different phases of system design certainly helps the designers in dealing with all technical aspects of such a design, and also with documentation issues. This is specially true when the modelling technique allows designers to define different views on the system, as is the case with the UML. All this is moreover beneficial because it makes it easier to compare different designs, and thus to evaluate different alternative approaches to the design of a system. HIDE goes a step further in the sense of 'opening further views' on the system, in the form of functions to proper validation domains.

Another advantage of the HIDE approach is the fact that the typical designer is not necessarily concerned with all the mathematical issues on which a particular validation approach is based, neither with the technicalities of the related validation tool(s). On the other hand, such a driving philosophy of HIDE, although attractive in theory, still needs experimental evidence.

Moreover, the use of an automatic (or semi-automatic) translation may suffer of a classical problem, i.e. efficiency; it is extremely difficult to automatically generate validation models which are more efficient, in terms of size, than those generated manually, by skilled experts. One way to tackle this problem is to use powerful optimisation techniques in the representation of validation models. In the case of formal verification it is worth mentioning the already cited BDD technology and the various compression techniques described in [49].

Another issue is the level of integration. In the HIDE experience, in the end, such a level is not very high: different translations usually work on different kinds of UML diagrams, i.e. on different views, and there is not much integration *between* different mappings. This alone is not enough. The level of integration should be increased by allowing also the specification of functional as well as non-functional (e.g. quantitative) aspects within the same kind of diagrams in order to derive integrated models for different validations. An example of this could be the possibility of annotating Statechart Diagrams with deterministic-time and/or stochastic-time and/or probability information and then translate them into enriched semantic models like timed and/or stochastic and/or probabilistic automata.

Similar work has already been done in the context of other formalisms for the specification and verification of systems. Notable examples are Petri Nets and their quantitative extensions mentioned in Sect. 2.2, and Process Algebras and their timed, probabilistic and stochastic extensions [16, 17, 33, 34, 45, 46, 48, 65] .

The possibility of having both functional and quantitative aspects of (a critical part of) a system within the very same notation is extremely interesting and convenient since it fills the gap which usually separates formal verification from quantitative validation. Usually, these two aspects of dependability assessment make reference to completely different models and there is no proven guarantee that such models are consistent in some sense. The use of enriched notations equipped with enriched semantic models like those mentioned above may help in providing rigorous definitions of what consistency means and related formal proofs. The advantage of applying such an approach to Statechart Diagrams, comes from the fact that Statechart Diagrams naturally offer simple and effective *abstraction* as well as *composi-*

tion mechanisms. Both features are extremely useful or even essential for clean and manageable system specifications, specially when non-functional aspects are considered.

Compositionality allows the time/probability information to be assigned locally to the components of concern, leaving the composition of such information to the semantics definition, i.e. to the translation function. The opposite approach, namely decorating with time/probability information the semantic model is impractical for systems of reasonable size, because of the monolithic nature of such a model. However compositionality appears to be a property very hard to achieve in the context of model based dependability validation. In fact, Markovian models can be composed just by connecting sub models but a hierarchical composition results in loosing the Markovian property. In order to achieve hierarchical compositionality it is necessary to resort to more powerful formalisms such as Markov regenerative processes (see Section 2.2) which require the development of techniques to limit and control state explosion and of new efficient tools.

Abstraction is even more important. As stated above, it is simply unthinkable to have a detailed model of the system behaviour enriched with quantitative information because of its prohibitive size. It is then important to be able to produce abstractions of components of the systems in such a way that they are correct with respect to behavioural semantics and preserve the non-functional properties of such components. This way, one can specify different (critical) components separately, translate them into the enriched semantic models, build conservative abstractions of those models and compose them with the (abstract) models of other components.

The use of proper behavioural relations developed in the context of process algebra and automata theory, like bisimulation and its quantitative extensions, can be useful for formally dealing with such abstractions. Additionally, proper techniques, like abstract interpretation may be of great help [19, 31, 32, 36].

The problem of relating different views of the same system has been addressed also in the work done about the formalization of consistency between different viewpoints of the Open Distributed Processing computational model [15].

References

[1]   M. Ajmone Marsan, G. Balbo and G. Conte, "A Class of Generalized Stochastic Petri Nets for the Performance Analysis of Multiprocessor Systems," ACM TOCS, Vol. 2, pp. 93-122, 1984.

[2]   M. Ajmone Marsan and G. Chiola, "On Petri nets with deterministic and exponentially distributed firing times," Lecture Notes in Computer Science, Vol. 226, pp. 132-145, 1987.

[3]   J. Arlat, "Fault injection for the experimental validation of fault-tolerant systems," in Proc. Workshop on Fault-Tolerant Systems, Kyoto, Japan, 1992, pp. 33-40.

[4]   J. Arlat, M. Aguera, L. Amat, Y. Crouzet, J.-C. Fabre, J.-C. Laprie, E. Martins and D. Powell, "Fault Injection for Dependability Validation — A Methodology and Some Applications," IEEE Trans. Software Engineering, Vol. 16, pp. 166-182, 1990.

[5]   J. Arlat, A. Costes, Y. Crouzet, J. C. Laprie and D. Powell, "Fault injection and dependability evaluation of fault-tolerant systems," IEEE Transactions on Computers, Vol. 42, pp. 913-923, 1993.

[6]   J. Arlat, K. Kanoun and J.C. Laprie, "Dependability Modelling and Evaluation of Software Fault-Tolerant Systems," IEEE Transactions on Computers, Vol. 39, pp. 540-513, 1990.

[7]   C. Bernardeschi, A. Fantechi, S. Gnesi and A. Santone, "Formal Specification and Verification of the Inter-Channel Consistency Network," PDCC, Pisa, Italy ESPRIT Project 20716 GUARDS Report, April 1998.

[8]   C. Bernardeschi, A. Fantechi, S. Gnesi and A. Santone, "Formal Specification and Verification of the Inter-Channel Fault Treatment Mechanism," PDCC, Pisa, Italy ESPRIT Project 20716 GUARDS Report, May 1998.

[9]   C. Bernardeschi, A. Fantechi, S. Gnesi and A. Santone, "Formal Validation of Fault Tolerance Mechanisms," in Proc. Digest of FastAbstracts - 28th Fault-Tolerant Computing Symposium (FTCS-28), Munich, Germany, 1998, pp. 66-67.

[10]   C. Bernardeschi, A. Fantechi and L. Simoncini, "Validating the Design of Dependable Systems," in Proc. 1st IEEE Int. Symposium on Object-Oriented Real-Time Distributed Systems - ISORC'98, Kyoto, Japan, 1998, pp. 364-372,.

[11]   A. Bondavalli, S. Chiaradonna, F. Di Giandomenico and F. Grandoni, "Discriminating Fault Rate and Persistency to Improve Fault Treatment," in Proc. 27th IEEE FTCS - International Symposium on Fault-Tolerant Computing, Seattle, USA, 1997, pp. 354-362.

[12]   A. Bondavalli, I. Majzik and I. Mura, "Automated Dependability Analysis of UML Designs," in Proc. ISORC'99 - 2nd IEEE International Symposium on Object-oriented Real-time distributed Computing, Saint Malo, France, 1999, pp. 139-144

[13]   A. Bondavalli, I. Mura and M. Nelli, "Analytical Modelling and Evaluation of Phased-Mission Systems for Space Applications," in Proc. 2nd IEEE High Assurance System Engineering Workshop (HASE'97), Bethesda, MD, USA, 1997, pp. 85 - 91.

[14]   A. Bouali, S. Gnesi and S. Larosa, "The Integration Project for the JACK Environment," Bulletin of the EATCS, Vol. 54, pp. 207-223 (See also http://rep1.iei.pi.cnr.it/projects/JACK), 1994.

[15]   H. Bowman, E. A. Boiten, J. Derrick and M. W. A. Steen, "Viewpoint Consistency in ODP, a General Interpretation," in Proc. First IFIP International Workshop on Formal Methods for Open Object--based Distributed Systems, FMOODS'96, Paris, France, 1996.

[16]   E. Brinksma, J-P. Katoen, R. Langerak and D. Latella, "A stochastic causality-based process algebra.," The Computer Journal, Vol. 38, pp. 552-565, 1995.

[17]   E. Brinksma, J-P. Katoen, R. Langerak and D. Latella, "Partial Order Models for Quantitative extensions of LOTOS," Computer Networks and ISDN Systems, Vol. 30, pp. 925-950, 1998.

[18]   J.M. Broersen and R.J. Wieringa, "Interpreting UML-statecharts in a modal m-calculus," in Proc. Submitted to Fundamental Approaches to Software Engineering (FASE'99), 1999.

[19]   G. Bruns, "A practical technique for process abstraction.," in Proc. CONCUR'93, LNCS 715, 1993, pp. 37-49.

[20]   R.E. Bryant, "Graph Based algorithms for boolean function manipulation," IEEE Transaction on Computers, Vol. C-35, 1986.

[21]   J.R. Burch, E.M. Clarke, K.L. McMillan, D. Dill and J. Hwang, "Symbolic Model Checking 10^{20} states and beyond," in Proc. LICS, 1990.

[22]   A. Burns and A. Wellings, "HRT-HOOD: A Structured Design Method for Hard Real-Time Ada Systems," Real-Time Safety Critical Systems, Elsevier, Vol. 3, 1995.

[23]   J. Carreira, H. Madeira and J.G. Silva, "Xception: Software Fault Injection and Monitoring in Processor Functional Unit," in Proc. Fifth International Working Conference on Dependable Computing for Critical Applications, Urbana-Champaign, U.S.A., 1995, pp. 135-149.

[24]   R. Chillarege and N. S. Bowen, "Understanding large system failures - a fault injection experiment," in Proc. 19-th International Symposium on Fault-Tolerant Computing (FTCS-22), Chicago, Il, USA, 1989, pp. 356-363.

[25]   R. Chillarege and R. K. Iyer, "Measurement-based analysis of error latency," IEEE Transactions on Computers, Vol. 36, pp. 529-537, 1987.

[26]   G. Chiola, "GreatSPN 1.5 Software Architecure," in Proc. 5th Int. Conf. on Modelling Techniques and Tools for Computer Performance Evaluation, Torino, Italy, 1987.

[27]   G. S. Choi and R. K. Iyer, "FOCUS: an experimental environment for fault sensitivity analysis," IEEE Transactions on Computers, Vol. 41, pp. 1515-1526, 1992.

[28]   H. Choi, V. G. Kulkarni and K. S. Trivedi, "Markov regenerative stochastic Petri nets," Performance Evaluation, Vol. 20, pp. 337-357, 1994.

[29]   G. Ciardo, J. Muppala and K. S. Trivedi, "SPNP: stochastic Petri net package," in Proc. International Conference on Petri Nets and Performance Models, Kyoto, Japan, 1989.

[30]   E.M. Clarke, E.A. Emerson and A.P. Sistla, "Automatic Verification of Finite--State Concurrent Systems Using Temporal Logic Specification," ACM Transaction on Programming Languages and Systems, Vol. 8, pp. 244-263, 1986.

[31]   E.M. Clarke, O. Grumberg and D.E. Long, "Model Checking and Abstraction.," ACM Toplas, Vol. 16, pp. 1512-1542, 1994.

[32]   P. Cousot and R. Cousot, "Refining Model Checking by Abstract Interpretation," Automated Software Engineering, Vol. 6, pp. 1-28, 1999.

[33]   P.R. D'Argenio, J-P. Katoen and E. Brinksma, "An algebraic approach to the specification of stochastic systems," in "Programming Concepts and Methods", D. Gries and W.-P. de Roever Ed., Chapman and Hall, 1998.

[34]   P.R. D'Argenio, J-P. Katoen and E. Brinksma, "General purpose discrete-event simulation using SPADES," in Proc. 6th Int. Workshop on Process Algebras and Performance Modelling, 1998.

[35]   C. Da Silva, B. Dehbonei and F. Mejia, "Formal Specification in the Development of Industrial Applications: Subway Speed Control System," in "Formal Description Techniques, V (C-10)", M. Diaz and R. Groz Ed., Elsevier Science Publishers B, V, (North-Holland), 1993.

[36]   D. Dams, O. Grumberg and R. Gerth, "Abstract Interpretation of Reactive Systems," ACM Toplas, Vol. 19, pp. 253-291, 1997.

[37]   J. B. Dugan and M. R. Lyu, "Dependability modeling for fault-tolerant software and systems," in "Software fault-tolerance", M. R. Lyu Ed., Wiley & Sons, 1995, pp. 109-137.

[38]   J. B. Dugan and K. S. Trivedi, "Coverage modeling for dependability analysis of fault-tolerant systems," IEEE Transactions on Computers, Vol. 38, pp. 775-787, 1989.

[39]   A. Fantechi, S. Gnesi, R. Pugliese and E. Tronci, "A Symbolic Model Checker for ACTL," in Proc. FM-Trends'98: International Workshop on Current Trends in Applied Formal Methods, Boppard, Germany, 7-9 October, 1998.

[40]   A. Fantechi, S. Gnesi and L. Semini, "Formal Description and Validation for an Integrity Policy Supporting Multiple Levels of Criticality," in Proc. DCCA-7 - 7th IFIP Int. Conference on Dependable Computing for Critical Applications, San Jose, Ca, USA, 1999.

[41]   M. Fowler and K. Scott, "UML Distilled. Applying the Standard Object Modeling Language," Addison-Wesley, ISBN 0-201-32563-2, 1997 1997.

[42]   R. Geist, M. Smotherman and R. Talley, "Modeling recovery time distributions in ultrareliable fault-tolerant systems," in Proc. 20-th International Symposium on Fault-Tolerant Computing (FTCS-20), Newcastle-Upon-Tyne, UK, 1990, pp. 499-504.

[43]   M. Gergeleit and H. Streich, "TaskPair-Scheduling with Optimistic Case Execution Times - An Example for an Adaptive Real-Time System," in Proc. 2nd IEEE Int. Workshop on Object-oriented Real-time Dependable Systems, Laguna Beach, California, February 1-2, 1996.

[44]   R. German, C. Kelling, A. Zimmermann and G. Hommel, "TimeNET: a toolkit for evaluating non-Markovian stochastic Petri nets," Performance Evaluation, Vol. 24, 1995.

[45]   N. Gotz, U. Herzog and M. Rattelbach, "TIPP - Introduction and application to protocol performance analysis," in "Formale Beschreibungstechniken fur verteilte Systeme. FOKUS series", H. Konig Ed., Saur Publishers, 1993.

[46]   P. Harrison and B. Strulo, "Stochastic Process Algebra for Discrete Event Simulation.," in "Quantitative Methods in Parallel Systems, ESPRIT Basic Research Series", F. Baccelli, A. Jean-Marie and I. Mitrani Ed., Springer, 1995., pp. 18-37.

[47]   HIDE, "Esprit LTR 27439 HIDE," Public home page: https://asterix.mit.bme.hu:998/ 1998.

[48]   J. Hillston, "A Compositional Approach to Performance Modeling," Distinguished Dissertation in Computer Science, Cambridge University Press, 1996.

[49]   G. Holzmann, "The model checker SPIN," IEEE Transactions on Software Engineering, Vol. 23, pp. 279-295, 1997.

[50]   Technical Group HOOD, "HOOD Reference Manual, Release 3.1.1," 1992.

[51]   M.-C. Hsueh, T. K. Tsai and R. K. Iyer, "Fault Injection Techniques and Tools," IEEE Computer, Vol. 40, pp. 75-82, 1997.

[52]   INCOSE, "http://www.incose.org/," 1998.

[53]   Intecs-Sistemi, "HRT-HoodNICE: a Hard Real-Time Software Design Support Tool," Intecs Sistemi, Pisa, Italy ESTEC Contract 11234/NL/FM(SC), Final Report, 1996.

[54]   E. Jenn, "Modelling for Evaluation," Technicatome, Aix en Provence, France ESPRIT Project 20716 GUARDS Report, January 1998.

[55]   G. A. Kanawati, N. A. Kanawati and J. A. Abraham, "FERRARI: a flexible software-based fault and error injection system," IEEE Transactions on Computers, Vol. 44, pp. 248-260, 1995.

[56]   K. Kanoun, M. Borrel, T. Morteveille and A. Peytavin, "Modelling the Dependability of CAUTRA, a Subset of the French Air Traffic Control System," in Proc. 26th IEEE Int. Symposium on Fault Tolerant Computing, Sendai, Japan, 1996, pp. 106-115.

[57]   LAAS-CNRS, "SURF-2 User guide," LAAS-CNRS 1994.

[58]   J.-C. Laprie, J. Arlat, J.-P. Blanquart, A. Crouzet Costes, Y., Y. Deswarte, J.-C. Fabre, H. Guillermain, M. Kaaniche, K. Kanoun, C. Mazet, D. Powell, C. Rabejac and P. Thevenod, "Dependability Guidebook," Toulouse, Cepadues-Editions, 1995.

[59]   D. Latella, I. Majzik and M. Massink, "Towards a Formal Operational Semantics of UML Statechart Diagrams," in Proc. IFIP TC6/WG6.1 Third International Conference on Formal Methods for Open Object-Oriented Distributed Systems,, Florence, Italy, Feb. 15-18, 1999.

[60]   G. Le Lann, "The Ariane 5 Flight 501 Failure - A Case Study in System Engineering for Computing Systems," INRIA Research Report, December 1996.

[61]   M Malhotra and K. S. Trivedi, "Power-hierarchy among dependability model types," IEEE Transactions on Reliability, Vol. 43, pp. 493-502, 1994.

[62]   J. McGough, M. Smotherman and K. S. Trivedi, "The conservativeness of reliability estimates based on instantaneous coverage," IEEE Transactions on Computers, Vol. 34, pp. 602-609, 1985.

[63]   M. K. Molloy, "Performance analysis using stochastic Petri nets," IEEE Transactions on Computers, Vol. 31, pp. 913-917, 1982.

[64]   M Nelli, A. Bondavalli and L. Simoncini, "Dependability Modelling and Analysis of Complex Control Systems: an Application to Railway Interlocking," in Proc. EDCC-2 European Dependable Computing Conference, Taormina, Italy, 1996, pp. 93-110.

[65]   X. Nicollin and J. Sifakis, "An Overview and synthesis on Timed Process Algebras," in Proc. Real-Time: Theory and Practice. REX Workshop, LNCS 600, 1991, pp. 526-548.

[66]   S. Owre, S. Rajan, J. M. Rushby, N. Shankar and M. K. Srivas, "PVS: Combining Specification, Proof Checking, and Model Checking," in Proc. Computer-Aided Verification - CAV'96, LNCS 1102, New Brunswick, NJ, USA, 1996, pp. 411-414.

[67]   PERTS, "http://www.tripac.com/html/products.html,"

[68]   D. Powell, J. Arlat, L. Beus-Dukic, A. Bondavalli, P. Coppola, A. Fantechi, E. Jenn, C. Rabéjac and A. Wellings, "GUARDS: A Generic Upgradable Architecture for Real-time Dependable Systems," IEEE Trans. on Parallel and Distributed Systems, .1999.

[69]   D. Powell, J. Arlat and K. Kanoun, "Generic Architecture Instantiation Guidelines," LAAS-CNRS, Toulouse, France ESPRIT Project 20716 GUARDS Report, Apr 22 1998.

[70]   D. Powell, E. Martins, J. Arlat and Y. Crouzet, "Estimators for fault tolerance coverage evaluation," in Proc. 23-th International Symposium on Fault-Tolerant Computing (FTCS-23), Toulouse, France, 1993, pp. 261-274.

[71]   J. Rumbaugh, I. Jacobson and G. Booch, "The Unified Modeling Language Reference Manual," Addison-Wesley, ISBN 0-201-30998-X 1999.

[72]   W. H. Sanders and L. M. Malhis, "Dependability evaluation using composed SAN-based reward models," Journal of parallel and distributed computing, Vol. 15, pp. 238-254, 1992.

[73]   D. Schwier and F. von Henke, "Mechanical Verification of Clock Synchronization Algorithms," Design for Validation, ESPRIT Long Term Research Project 20072: DeVa 2nd Year Report, pp. .287-303, LAAS-CNRS, Toulouse, France, 1997.

[74]   J.A. Stankovic, M. Spuri, M. Di Natale and G.C. Buttazzo, "Implications of Classical Scheduling Results for Real-Time Systems," IEEE Computer, Vol. 28, pp. 16-25, 1995.

[75]   A. Steininger and H. Schweinzer, "A model for the analysis of the fault-injection process," in Proc. 25-th International Symposium in Fault-Tolerant Computing (FTCS-25), Pasadena CA, USA, 1995.

[76]   H. Streich, "TaskPair-Scheduling: An Approach for Dynamic Real-Time Systems," Int. Journal of Mini & Microcomputers, Vol. 17, pp. 77-83, 1995.

[77]   L. A. Tomek and K. S. Trivedi, "Analyses using stochastic reward nets," in "Software fault-tolerance", M. R. Lyu Ed., Wiley & Sons, 1995, pp. 139-166.

[78]   TW, "http://www.timesys.com/,"

[79]   UltraSAN, "User Manual," Center for Reliable and High-Performance Computing Coordinated Science Laboratory, University of Illinois, Urbana, USA. 1994.

[80]   C. J. Walter, "Evaluation and design of an ultrareliable distributed architecture for fault-tolerance," IEEE Transactions on Reliability, Vol. 39, pp. 492-499, 1990.

[81]   W. Wang, K. Ramamrithan and J.A. Stankovic, "Determining Redundancy Levels for Fault Tolerant Real-Time Systems," IEEE Transactions on Computers, Vol. 29, pp. 720-731, 1995.

[82]   R.J. Wieringa and J. Broersen, "A Minimal Transition System Semantics for Lightweight Class and Behavior Diagrams," in Proc. ICSE98 Workshop on Precise Semantics for Software Modeling techniques, Muenchen, Germany, 1998.

[83]   Z.100, "Specification and Description Language SDL," ITU-T, June 1994.

Appendix A. The list of "Pragmatic Principles" of system engineering.

A). Know the problem, the customer, and the consumer

1. Become the "customer/consumer advocate/surrogate" throughout development and fielding of the solution.
2. Begin with a validated customer (buyer) need - the problem.
3. State the problem in solution-independent terms.
4. Don't assume that the original statement of the problem is necessarily the best, or even the right one.
5. When confronted with the customer's need, consider what smaller objective(s) is/are key to satisfying the need, and from what larger purpose or mission the need derives; that is, find at the beginning the right level of problem to solve.
6. Determine customer priorities (performance, cost, schedule, risk, etc.).
7. Probe the customer for:
   • new product ideas
   • product problem/shortfall identification
   • problem fixes
8. Work with the customer to identify the consumer (user) groups that will be affected by the system.
9. Use a systematic method for identifying the needs and solution preferences of each consumer group.

10. Don't depend on written specifications and statements of work. Face to face sessions with the different customer/consumer groups are necessary.
11. State as much of the each need in quantified terms as possible. However, important needs for which no accurate or quantified measure exists, still must be explicitly addressed.
12. Clarify each need by identifying the power and limitations of current and projected technology relative to the customer's larger purpose, the environment, and ways of doing business.

B). Use effectiveness criteria based on needs to make system decisions

1. Select criteria that have demonstrable links to customer/consumer needs and system requirements.
   - Operational criteria: mission success, technical performance.
   - Program criteria: cost, schedule, quality, risk.
   - ILS criteria: failure rate, maintainability, serviceability.
2. Maintain a "need based" balance among the often conflicting criteria.
3. Select criteria that are measurable (objective and quantifiable) and express them in well known, easily understood units. However, important criteria for which no measure seems to exist still must be explicitly addressed.
4. Use trade-offs to show the customer the performance, cost, schedule, and risk impacts of requirements and solutions variations.
5. Whenever possible, use simulation and experimental design to perform trade-offs as methods that rely heavily on "engineering judgement" rating scales are more subject to bias and error.
6. Have the customer make all value judgements in trade-offs.
7. Allow the customer to modify requirements and participate in developing the solution based on the trade-offs.

C). Establish and manage requirements

1. Identify and distinguish between specified (fundamental or essential), allocated, implied and derived requirements.
2. Carry analysis and synthesis to at least one level broader and deeper than seems necessary before settling on requirements and solutions at any given level. (Top-down is a better recording technique than it is an analysis or synthesis technique.)
3. Write a rationale for each requirement. The attempt to write a rationale for "requirement" often uncovers the real requirement.
4. Ensure the customer and consumer understand and accept all the requirements.
5. Explicitly identify and control all the external interfaces the system will have - signal, data, power, mechanical, parasitic, etc. Do the same for all the internal interfaces created by the solution.
6. Negotiate interfaces with affected engineering staff on both sides of each interface and get written agreement by the two parties before the customer approves the interface documentation.
7. Document all requirements interpretations in writing. Don't count on verbal agreements to stand the test of time.
8. Plan for the inevitable need to correct and change requirements as insight into the need and the "best" solution grows during development.

9. Be careful of new fundamental requirements coming in after the program is underway. They invariably have a larger impact than is obvious.
10. Maintain requirements traceability.

D). Identify and assess alternatives so as to converge on a solution

1. Take the time to innovate by generating a wide range of alternative solutions to satisfy the need. (A common mistake is to converge a "comfortable design" concept too early because of time constraints.)
   - Consideration of seemingly bizarre alternatives often yields
   - additional insight into the requirements and provides a
   - reasonableness check for trade-off criteria and weights.
   - Include the "do nothing solution" in the system level solution
   - trade-off to provide a measure of the value-add the new system will
   - bring the customer/consumers.
2. Use a systematic architecture/design method.
   - Abstract the requirements to identify the essential design
   - problems.
   - Establish functional structures.
   - Search for solution principles to fulfill the sub-functions.
   - Combine the solution principles to fulfill the overall functions.
   - Select suitable combinations.
   - Firm combinations into conceptual alternatives.
3. Evaluate each alternative against the requirements and the effectiveness criteria. Determine the alternative that provides the best weighted value combining:
   - effective
   - efficient
   - safe
   - reliable
   - producible
   - testable
   - maintainable
   - easiest to learn
4. Elaborate the customer's top-level concept of operations to show how the consumers will use each solution alternative to satisfy the consumers' and the customer's needs. This detailed concept of operations must be reflective of the design aspects of the system's operation.

E). Verify and validate requirements and solution performance

1. Quality must be designed in, it cannot be tested in.
2. Use preplanned peer reviews and inspections.
3. Prototype critical elements.
4. Use models to demonstrate feasibility before bending metal and writing code.
5. Explicitly identify and sanity check all model assumptions.
6. Work the critical and controversial requirements and design areas first.
7. Plan the verification and validation for every requirement.
8. Know the expected results before testing.

F). Maintain the integrity of the system

1. Maintain a systems engineering presence throughout the program (even though SE staff starts to drop off after PDR and more after CDR) to provide technical oversight of the ongoing design process and to resolve requirements/technical issues that invariably arise, including resolution of test discrepancies/anomalies.
2. Prevent process and product contamination.
3. Ensure the system design meets the requirements, satisfies the need, and reflects the voice of the customer.
4. Ensure the requirements address not only the operational objectives but all the life-cycle objectives for the system.

G). Use an articulated and documented process

1. Start with established principles - avoid reinventing the wheel and really learn from "lessons learned" investigations.
2. Use the principles to develop a process tailored to the need, the system, the customer, and the development organization.
3. Use the process consistently across the program.
4. Train the development staff in the process and its application - technical education is one key to productivity, quality, and cost reduction.
5. Use standardized analysis techniques, document formats, design review formats, etc. to reinforce the consistent application of the process.
6. Use readily available automated tools wherever appropriate.
7. Maintain process integrity but never let the process prevent the "best" solution from being discovered or used - do whatever it takes to build in product quality.

H). Manage against a plan

1. Use a "tasks are executed to produce useful work products" focus for the plan.
2. Prepare a plan that is success oriented, achievable, defendable, and cost-effective but which can absorb the changes that will come.
3. Have a contingency plan for each identified risk.
4. Develop a plan that reflects organizational commitment to systems engineering.
5. Look for and abolish fraction-of-a-job situations.
6. Perform each task according to the plan.
7. Change the plan as soon as experience shows a better way to do a task.
8. Remember: micromanagement is not planning.
9. Remember Dwight D. Eisenhower's words: "Plans are nothing. Planning is everything."

Security and Dependability: Then and Now

Catherine Meadows
John McLean
Center for High Assurance Computer Systems
Naval Research Laboratory
Washington, DC 20375

Abstract

We survey security research from the point of view of the dependability taxonomy developed by IFIP Working Group 10.4 and discuss changes since a similar survey was performed four years ago.

1 Introduction

Four years ago, the first author of this paper published a paper [Mea96] which compared the approach to assurance that was then taken in the security community with the approach recommended by IFIP Working Group 10.4 in [Lap92] to ensuring dependability. According to [Lap92], "dependability" refers to the trust that can be placed upon a system to deliver the services that it promises. Dependability comprises not only security, but a number of other system properties, such as reliability, safety, quality of service, and so forth. This makes sense since all of these properties have a family resemblance to one another. As such, one would expect that techniques recommended for assuring dependability would be applicable to assuring security. However, what we found was that the work being done in computer security encompassed only a small part of the techniques recommended for assuring dependability. The paper recommended a number of different ways in which security research and practice could be improved by the incorporation of the techniques described in [Lap92].

In the four years since that paper was published security has changed greatly. The continuing increased reliance on networks and the World Wide Web has continued to change the focus of security from securing individual computers and operating systems to ensuring the connections between them. The demise of the Orange Book [Nat85] has left the security community without an overriding paradigm governing research and practice, and so the types of solutions proposed and implemented have become much more

diverse. These new techniques have also tended to focus on more lightweight security devices rather than the traditional A1 approach. This reflects a change in orientation from DoD security to industrial and personal security. Industry cannot afford security techniques that would delay product time to market. Businesses can use their increased market share, as well as insurance and legal mechanisms, to offset any additional loss they may sustain as a result of decreased security. These options are not available to DoD, although DoD itself has been forced to accept new security techniques that are based more on risk mitigation rather than risk avoidance. This has stemmed from the proliferation of commercial off the shelf products within DoD.

Given these changes to the security landscape, it made sense to take another look at the dependability taxonomy and see how security stacked up now. As might be expected, we found a number of formerly empty places in the taxonomy that are now heavily populated. We also still found some significant gaps, and most interestingly, at least one instance of security research covering an important aspect of assuring dependability that was not covered in the dependability taxonomy.

2 The Dependability Taxonomy

The taxonomy in [Lap92] begins by dividing the things that can go wrong in a computer system into three types: faults, errors, and failures. A failure occurs when the delivered service no longer complies with its specification. An error is that part of the system state which is liable to lead to subsequent error. A fault is the judge or hypothesized cause of the error.

An example of a failure from multilevel security is the case in which information classified at a high security level is released at a lower security level. An example of an error that could lead to that failure would be a malicious process operating at a high level communicating with another malicious process operating at a low level via a covert channel, An example of a fault would be the covert channel itself, as well as the system development/distribution/maintenance/operation process that allowed the hostile processes to enter in the first place.

Note that there are a number of different ways that the above error could have been prevented. The communication between the hostile process could be detected and stopped. The existence of the hostile processes could be detected and the processes removed. The hostile process could have been prevented from entering the system in the first place. The covert channel could be detected and removed. Or the covert channel could remain, but noise could be added to either it in particular or the system in general, so that it could no longer be used as an effective communication device.

By the same token, there are a number of different ways of preventing failures by preventing or neutralizing errors and faults. The taxonomy divides these into four categories: fault prevention, fault tolerance (providing service in the presence of faults), fault removal, and fault forecasting. The taxonomy does not have much to say about fault prevention, which it considers outside its scope, but it divides the other three up as follows:

Fault Tolerance Fault tolerance is divided into two subcategories, error processing, that is, removing errors from the computational state, and fault treatment, or preventing faults from being activated again.

Error processing can be carried out in two ways: (1) error recovery, or the substitution of an error-free state for the erroneous one, and (2) error compensation, in which the erroneous state contains enough redundancy to enable delivery of an error-free service even though an internal state is erroneous. Error compensation can be applied when the error is known, by use of a self-checking component either in hardware or software or it can be applied systematically, even when errors or not present, in which case it is known as fault masking. An example of fault masking is majority vote.

Fault treatment is divided into two steps: fault diagnosis, which consists of determining the cause of errors (that is the faults), and fault passivation, that is, preventing the faults from being activated again, by removing the faulty components and possibly reconfiguring the system.

Fault Forecasting Fault forecasting is the evaluation of system behavior with respect to future fault occurrence or activation. It is divided into two kinds: non-probabilistic, e.g. fault-tree analysis, or probabilistic, expressing the future behavior in terms of probabilities associated to the attributes of dependability. Thus, mean-time-to-failure is an example of probabilistic fault forecasting. Much of this type of forecasting is based on knowledge of the past behavior of the system.

Fault Removal Fault removal is composed of three steps: verification, diagnosis, and correction. Verification is the process of checking whether faults are present. This can be done via static verification, which includes both formal verification and code walk-throughs, or dynamic verification, which includes symbolic execution and testing. The taxonomy does not give any breakdown of fault diagnosis or correction.

3 Fault Tolerance and Security

The area of fault tolerance is the one in which security has shown the most growth, partly because of a conscious decision by funding agencies to encourage work in this area, and partly because security is becoming more integrated with other system properties. When [Mea96] was first written we found relatively little work in this area; this time we found a great deal of work in almost all aspects of fault tolerance. In this section we will go through each part of the taxonomy for fault tolerance and describe what research and practice in security corresponds to it.

3.1 Error Processing

3.1.1 Error Detection and Recovery

Under error detection we can place the substantial amount of work that is being done on intrusion detection. Intrusion detection systems detect if the system is an erroneous state (that is, undergoing an intrusion) that could lead to a failure (e.g., denial of service or someone having unauthorized access to the system).

Surprisingly, there seems to be relatively little systematic work on error recovery. One notable exception is database security, where recovery techniques used for non-security related errors can be extended to recovering from intrusions [AJMB97]. This may be partly because real-time intrusion detection is still largely an unsolved problem, so that at this point there is little application for fast recovery mechanisms. The relative lack of interest in recovery may also be due to the fact that intrusions are currently treated as criminal acts, not acts of war. Because computer intrusion is a crime, it is necessary to keep the scene of the crime untouched so that evidence may be gathered by investigators.[1] If computer intrusion were conducted as part of information warfare, the emphasis would be more on recovering rapidly than on gathering evidence, and we can expect, with the growing interest in information warfare, a corresponding growing interest in recovery mechanisms.

However, even in the area of information warfare, error recovery is hampered by a lack of a clearly acceptable responses. Detection of an intruder or virus in a network

---
[1] We owe this point to Judy Froscher.

component may lead us to isolate that component until the problem can be fixed. However, this may lead to a degradation of service, which may have been the real purpose of the intrusion or infection in the first place.

3.1.2 Error Compensation

Much work on error compensation and security has concentrated on fault masking, either by use of some form of majority vote, or by use of self-checking components (e.g. wrappers). One example of the use of majority vote is the DICOTS database project which runs multiple vendor back end databases and returns an output that is obtained by a majority vote among these back-ends, thus making it harder for a single-vendors Trojan Horse to affect the database's response to a query [MF97]. Another is the application to mobile agent security proposed in [KV98b], where agent integrity is supported by having multiple agents vote on a trusted platform.

Yet another possibility is the use of cryptographic techniques to compensate for errors. A *k out of n threshold scheme* [Bla79, Sha79] divides a secret into n parts so that any k of them could be used to reconstitute the secret, but that no k-1 reveal any information. They can also be designed so that corrupted shares may be detected. Thus threshold schemes can be used to compensate both for attacks on secrecy (that is, compromise of a share) and of attacks on integrity (loss of corruption of a share). It is also possible to trade off the degree of secrecy protection against the degree of integrity protection [BM84]. Recent results in threshold cryptography [Des94, Des97] have made it possible to use key shares to encrypt, decrypt, and authenticate data without making it necessary to reconstitute the key, thus eliminating a single point of failure, and making threshold schemes even more attractive as a means of providing secrecy and integrity within a single error compensation mechanism.

The use of self-checking components to achieve error compensation, although, originally not used much, has now become more prominent with the use of wrappers. A wrapper is a small program that sits between a component (usually COTS with so particular security functionality) and the program executing it. The wrapper can detect input that violates the security policy (that is, erroneous input) and disallow it. Thus the wrapper has the effect of providing security functionality to the wrapped component. The wrapper can also prevent the component from providing faulty output to the environment. In general, wrappers are software-based, as in [FBF99], but it is also possible to conceive of hardware analogues of wrappers. The NRL Pump, for example, sits between untrusted database components operating at different security levels and prevents a Trojan Horse in the high database from exploiting covert channels that exist in update acknowledgments from the low database [KMM98]. Firewalls can likewise be thought of as hardware-based wrappers.

Most wrappers only serve to protect the component against the program using it, not the other way around. Thus, they solve only part of the security problem. In particular, they do not protect against the case in which the wrapped component is itself under hostile control. Moreover, as is pointed out in [Sch99], even if the wrapped component is not hostile, but its functionality is merely poorly understood, problems can result, as in the case of a component originally designed for a single human user being requested to deal with input from an entire network. However, with the increasing use of COTS, the continued use of poorly understood legacy systems, and the increasing number of applications for which moderate assurance is apparently adequate, wrappers are becoming more popular.

3.2 Fault Treatment

Much of the ongoing work in survivability makes use of fault treatment techniques. This work concentrates on identifying faulty components, removing them, and reconfiguring the system so that it runs in the absence of the faulty components. Thus, for example, Millen [Mil99] develops algorithms for constructing reconfiguration policies that will allow a system to carry on its operations even when some components have been disabled. Counterattack and litigation also may fall under this area since its purpose it to prevent future intrusions. However, counterattack is limited by legal issues and by technical issues that hamper the identification of the source of the attack.

4 Fault Forecast and Security

Fault forecast was another area we found underrepresented in our original survey. The situation now has changed somewhat, but not completely.

There is a substantial interest in forecast in security, but most of it might be rather be described as failure forecast rather than fault forecast; people seem to be more interested in calculating the risks of using a system with known bugs rather than predicting the occurrence of new bugs. Our conjecture is that the most likely reason for this is that most security problems are either the result of software faults, which are extremely difficult to predict, or basic design flaws, which are extremely difficult to repair.

Most of the systems designed for risk analysis in security are fairly ad hoc. The user is given a set of parameters to which to assign numerical or other types of values. The system then uses some built-in formulas to calculate the level of risk based on the values of these parameters. Since the values given as inputs to these systems are tend to be arbitrary, there is little reason to trust the output. Further, even if we had correct outputs for individual components, it's not clear how to combine these into a correct output for the entire system.

There are also some research systems that use a more systematic version of this approach. The work described in [ODK98] uses fault trees to develop a set of possible attacks on UNIX systems, and assigns numerical levels of difficulty to each edge in the tree. It then uses a Markov model to calculate the calculate the effort required to cause a security failure.

A related area is that of *trust metrics* or *authentication metrics* [RS97]. These are usually assigned, not to systems, but to authenticators (that is, public key certificates), and are computed using paths of certification authorities. Here the numerical values are assigned to the authorities themselves, and the degree of trust in a public key certificate is computed using the certification paths to it. Although this work has a somewhat different context than the risk management work, the techniques and the overall goal are similar: to calculate a numerical measure of the degree of trust you are willing to put into a system or certificate. However, trust metrics appear to provide a more tractable, limited problem than risk analysis in general, and thus more progress appears to have been made in trust metrics than in risk analysis for systems.

5 Fault Prevention and Removal and Security

We put fault prevention and removal together because many of the techniques that apply to fault removal (e.g. static verification) also apply to prevention. In our original survey we found the most security work concentrated in this area. This time around we found that interest had not gone away, but that the focus had changed greatly.

We note that the array of techniques for fault prevention and removal have not changed, e.g. sound system design, formal verification, testing, etc. What has changed is the uses to which they may be put in convincing another party that a system is in fact fault-free. This has a lot to do with changes have taken place in the way a decision is made to allow software to execute on one's system. Formally, the decision to allow software to execute on one's system was essentially a procurement process. One decided to buy a piece of software much the same way one decided to buy a car or vacuum cleaner, or (if in the military) a helicopter. The decision to buy was a relatively long, drawn-out process in which one could consult several authorities as to the safety of the software. Although that process was often abrogated, it was nevertheless available.

With the advent of mobile code, all this has changed. The user of a system is no longer aware exactly what software is running on that system, nor where it is from. The decision whether or not to run a piece of software must be made by the system itself, and must be made on the fly. We can execute the code in a vendor supplied sandbox, but then we are reduced to trusting a third party sandbox to protect us from a third party program. Another approach is to embed our own runtime checks into the code, but this approach has also limits, since the runtime checks could be tampered with [KV98a].

A different approach to this problem is provide digital certificates for the code. For example, a certificate could say who the developed the code, what it should be used for, and what privileges it should have. For added assurance, the certificate could be cryptographically sealed to the code using digital signatures. The is the approach followed, for example, by ActiveX. A system could then agree or disagree to run the code based on that system's policy.

The use of certificates provides added assurance, but still requires the system to put its trust in the originator of the code. Another approach is to give the system the means of verifying for itself that the code is correct, as in the case of Java type-safety checking [GJS96]. The most extreme example of this approach is in Necula's proof carrying-code [Nec97], where the code carries its own proof of correctness with it, which is then verified by the system on which it runs. In this approach, the trust required by the system is minimal.

We see that the changing computing environment has led to a drastic change in the way we make decisions to use code, which in turn has led to research and new techniques for guaranteeing to other parties that code is safe to use. Given the importance of this area, we believe that it is important to make *convincing another party that a system is free from faults* a part of the dependability taxonomy, that is, that the trilogy of verification, diagnosis, and correction, should be changed to verification, diagnosis, correction, and convincing.

6 Conclusion

As we expected, we have found numerous areas of the 10.4 taxonomy that were relatively unpopulated by security research that are heavily populated today. This is especially true for the area of fault tolerance; given our increasing reliance on COTS and legacy systems that we know contain faults, fault tolerance is becoming a necessary feature of any secure system. What was more surprising that, in the case of fault prevention and removal emerging work on security describes new ways that the taxonomy can be extended. We would expect a more thorough study would turn up other ways in which both the taxonomy and security research could be enriched.

170

References

[AJMB97] P. Ammann, S. Jajodia, C. McCollum, and B. Blaustein. Surviving information warfare attacks on databases. In *Proceedings of the 1997 IEEE Symposium on Security and Privacy*, pages 164–174. IEEE Computer Society Press, May 1997.

[Bla79] G. R. Blakley. Safeguarding cryptographic keys. In *Proceedings of the National Computer Conference*, pages 313–317. American Federation of Information Processing Societies, AFIPS Press, 1979.

[BM84] G. R. Blakley and C. A. Meadows. Security of ramp schemes. In G. R. Blakley and David Chaum, editors, *Proceedings of Crypto '84*, pages 242–268. Springer-Verlag LNCS 196, 1984.

[Des94] Yvo Desmedt. Threshold cryptography. *European Transactions on Telecommunications*, 5(4):449–457, July-August 1994.

[Des97] Yvo Desmedt. Some recent research results in threshold cryptography. In E. Okamoto, G. Davida, and M. Mambo, editors, *Information Security, Proceedings*, pages 158–173. Springer-Verlag LNCS 1396, 1997.

[FBF99] T. Fraser, L. Badger, and M. Feldman. Hardening COTS components with generic software wrappers. In *Proceedings of the 1999 IEEE Symposium on Security and Privacy*, pages 2–16. IEEE Computer Society Press, May 1999.

[GJS96] James Gosling, Bill Joy, and Guy Steele. *The Java Language Specification*. Addison-Wesley, January 1996.

[KMM98] Myong Kang, Andrew Moore, and Ira Moskowitz. Design and assurance strategy for the NRL Pump. *IEEE Computer Magazine*, 31(4), April 1998.

[KV98a] Lora Kassab and Jeffrey Voas. Agent trustworthiness. In *Procceings of ECOOP Workshop on Distributed Object Security and 4th Workshop on Mobile Object Systems Secure Internet Mobile Computations*, pages 121–134, Brussels, July 20-21 1998. INRIA.

[KV98b] Lora Kassab and Jeffrey Voas. Towards fault-tolerant mobile agents. In *Proceedings of Distributed Computing on the Web Workshop*, pages 96–106. Univ. of Rostock Press, 1998.

[Lap92] Jean-Claud Laprie, editor. *Dependability: Basic Concepts and Terminology*, volume 5 of *Dependable Computing and Fault-Tolerant Systems*. Springer-Verlag, 1992.

[Mea96] Catherine Meadows. Applying the dependability paradigm to computer security. In *Proceedings of the 1995 New Security Paradigms Workshop*. IEEE Computer Society Press, 1996.

[MF97] John McDermott and Judith Froscher. Practical defenses against storage jamming. In *Proceedings of the 13th Annual Computer Security Applications Conference*, pages 265–273, San Diego, CA, December 1997.

[Mil99] Jonathan Millen. Local reconfiguration policies. In *Proceedings of the 1999 IEEE Symposium on Security and Privacy*, pages 48–56. IEEE Computer Society Press, May 1999.

[Nat85] National Computer Security Center. *Trusted Computer System Evaluation Criteria*, December 26 1985. DoD 5200-STD.

[Nec97] George Necula. Proof-carrying code. In *Proceedings of 21st Annual ACM SIGPLAN-SIGACT Symposium on Principle of Programming Languages (POPL '97)*. ACM, January 1997.

[ODK98] R. Ortalo, Y. Deswarte, and M. Kaaniche. Experimenting with quantitative evaluation tools for monitoring operational security. In M. Dal Cin, C. Meadows, and W. H. Sanders, editors, *Dependable Computing for Critical Applications 6*, pages 307–328. IEEE Computer Society, 1998.

[RS97] M. K. Reiter and S. Stubblebine. Toward acceptable metrics of authentication. In *Proceedings of the 1997 IEEE Symposium on Security and Privacy*, pages 10–20. IEEE Computer Society Press, May 1997.

[Sch99] Fred B. Schneider, editor. *Trust in Cyberspace*. National Academy Press, 1999.

[Sha79] Adi Shamir. How to share a secret. *Communications of the ACM*, 22:612–613, 1979.

Diversity against Accidental and Deliberate Faults

Yves Deswarte[1], Karama Kanoun and Jean-Claude Laprie
LAAS-CNRS
7 avenue du Colonel Roche
31077 Toulouse cedex 4 – France
{deswarte, kanoun, laprie}@laas.fr

Abstract

The paper is aimed at examining the relationship between the three topics of the workshops that gave rise to this book: security, fault tolerance, and software assurance. Those three topics can be viewed as different facets of dependability. The paper focuses on diversity, as a desirable approach for addressing the classes of faults that underlay all these topics, i.e., design faults and intrusion faults.

1. Introduction

The paper is aimed at examining the relationship between the three topics of the workshops that gave rise to this book: security, fault tolerance and software assurance. Those three topics can be viewed as different facets of dependability [29, 33], (see also the paper by Brian Randell in this volume). The second section is devoted to a fault classification, which identifies three major classes of faults: physical faults, design faults, (human-machine) interaction faults, where the latter two classes can be either accidental or deliberate. The classes of faults that come into play, when considering simultaneously security, fault tolerance and software assurance are the design faults and the interaction faults. Contributions of fault tolerance to security and software assurance necessitate diversity. Diversity can take place at a number of levels in a system: execution support (hardware plus operating system), execution conditions or design of the application software, human-machine interface, and operators. The third section is devoted to a close examination of these possibilities, with indications on their effectiveness with respect to the classes of faults of interest. Diversity is also commonly used for the validation of dependable systems all along its development, as presented in the fourth section. However, some faults can defeat fault-tolerance techniques (e.g., those faults resulting from tradeoffs between security and usability, or faults giving rise to common-mode failures). It is thus necessary to make an evaluation of the risk that is incurred, which is the topic of the fifth part of the paper.

---

[1] Yves Deswarte is currently on sabbatical at Microsoft Research, Cambridge, UK.

2. Faults [29, 33]

Faults are the adjudged or hypothesized causes of system failures, i.e. deviations from delivery of correct service to the system user(s). Faults and their sources are extremely diverse: a) their phenomelogical cause can be physical or human-made, b) they can be accidental or deliberate, with or without malicious intent, c) they can be created or occur during the system development or during its operational life, d) they can be internal or external to the system, and e) they can be permanent or transient. However, the many resulting classes of faults can be grouped into three major categories (Figure 1): physical faults (adverse physical phenomena), design faults, interaction faults (operational misuses).

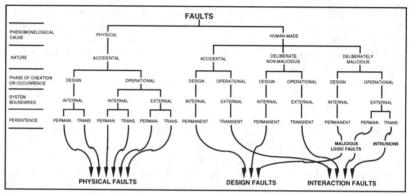

Figure 1 - Classes of faults

The causal chain from faults to failures (figure 2) involves errors, i.e. that part of system state that may lead to subsequent failure.

Figure 2 - Causal chain from faults to errors, to failures

Failures can be classified according to a) their domain, i.e. value or timing, b) their perception by system users, i.e. consistent or inconsistent, usually called Byzantine, c) their consequences upon system environment, from minor to catastrophic, with usually intermediate grading, such as significant or major. From the very existence of the causal chain from faults to failures, it is relatively common usage to classify faults according to the failures they cause.

The ability to identify the activation pattern of a fault that caused one or more errors is the activation reproducibility of a fault. Faults can be categorized according to their activation reproducibility: faults whose activation is reproducible are called solid, or hard, faults, whereas faults whose activation is not systematically reproducible are elusive, or soft, faults. Most residual design faults in large, complex, software are elusive faults (or "Heisenbugs"[23]): they are subtle enough that their activation conditions depend on equally subtle combinations of internal state and external solicitation, which occur rarely and can be very difficult to reproduce.

Situations involving multiple faults and/or failures are frequently encountered. Given a system with defined boundaries, a single fault is a fault caused by one adverse physical event or one harmful human action. Multiple faults are two or more concurrent, overlapping, or sequential single faults whose consequences, i.e., errors, overlap in time, that is, the errors due to these faults are concurrently present in the system. Consideration of multiple faults leads one to distinguish a) independent faults, which are attributed to different causes, and b) related faults, which are attributed to a common cause. Related faults generally cause similar errors, i.e., errors that cannot be distinguished by whatever detection mechanisms are being employed, whereas independent faults usually cause distinct errors; it may however happen that independent faults lead to similar errors [5], or that related faults lead to distinct errors. The failures caused by similar errors are common-mode failures.

3. Diversity for fault tolerance

Many techniques commonly used in security or safety critical application domains can be identified as different means of implementing diversity for fault-tolerance. All these techniques are aimed at tolerating some kind of design faults, but they can be classified according to where they are implemented:
- at the level of users or operators,
- in the human-computer interfaces,
- at the application software level,
- at the execution level, or
- at the hardware or operating system level.

In this section, we identify these levels, and for each of them we analyze the fault classes they intend to tolerate.

Since every good concept is better if recursive, diversity can be successfully applied at diverse levels. For instance, the AIRBUS A-300/600 digital fly-by-wire system [41] is run by two classes of computers, with different microprocessors (designed independently and provided by different vendors), the application software being developed by two different companies, using different languages (and compilers), each computer being self-checking with independent channels for functional processing and monitoring. If we add the fact that a) some pilot interfaces implement diversity, b) two pilots are in the cockpit and c) the diverse computers control different axes of the plane (one controls the pitch axis and the other the roll axis), this example covers all levels of diversity implementation.

3.1. Diversity at the level of users or operators

If some privileged users or operators are not blindly trusted[2], or if they can be impersonated by some intruders, it is useful to require the cooperation of several independent users or operators to perform a sensitive operation. This can be interpreted as an application of the diversity approach to users and operators: as long as there is no

---

[2] In a recent survey by Ernst and Young concerning computer-related fraud involving 1200 companies in 32 countries, 66% of the surveyed companies had experienced at least one computer-related fraud in the previous 12 months; 17% of the companies had even experienced more than 5 such frauds. The survey reported that 84% of frauds were perpetrated by company employees.

common-mode failures of these independent persons (i.e., collusion), the system remains secure. On the contrary, if a single user or operator can perform such a sensitive operation, you system is insecure if this user is not perfectly trustworthy.

The *separation of duty* proposed by Clark and Wilson [13] is one implementation of user-level diversity. In the separation of duty model, complementary roles are assigned to different users, and a sensitive operation can be realized only by the successive executions of several programs that can be run only by different roles. A direct implementation of this approach can tolerate the malicious behavior of some users (at least commission faults, rather than omission faults), but no other class of faults (e.g., physical faults or software design faults, including malicious logic).

Distributing trust is another user-level diversity implementation. In this approach, sensitive operations, e.g. authentication and access control, can only be realized by running similar programs on different machines under the control of independent operators [16, 37]. In this case, the operators have similar privileges, and an operation is securely realized if at least a majority of the program copies are executed correctly. No single operator is trusted, but there is a reasonable confidence that a majority of them are not malicious. Secret sharing [40], and more generally "threshold cryptography" can also be viewed as a cryptographic implementation of trust distribution. This approach is able to tolerate the malicious behavior of a minority of operators (omission faults as well as commission faults), but also accidental interaction faults (operator mistakes) and physical faults. Design faults are tolerated only if diversity is also applied at the application software level and/or at the support level (see Sections 3.3 and 3.5).

Trust distribution approach is efficient against malicious operators, but its efficiency against external attacks depends on the difficulty for the intruder to gain the control of a majority of the machine pool running the sensitive operation before being detected and neutralized. To increase this difficulty, it is advisable to implement also some sort of execution diversity (see Section 3.4).

Operator-level diversity is also commonly used in safety-critical applications to tolerate operator disability or mistakes. This is, for instance the reason of the presence of two pilots in commercial airplane cockpits. More generally, teamwork is often organized to prevent and tolerate independent operator errors [38].

3.2 Human-computer interface diversity

Operator-level diversity necessitates the cooperation of multiple operators. But even if only one operator is involved, diversity can be applied to human-computer interfaces to counter interaction deficiencies. These deficiencies can be caused by interface design faults, but also by possible operator inability to interact correctly[3]. Another cause of deficiency is the intrinsic inefficiency of some -human-computer interfaces. For instance, authentication mechanisms are based on something the user knows (e.g., a password), something he owns (e.g., a token) or something he is (biometric authentication). All these mechanisms have their limits: passwords can be guessed or

---

[3] If the operator misinterprets displayed data or is unable to enter correct information in time, this may be due to bad interface design. Accident cause analysis is the source of endless arguments on responsibility sharing between interface design faults and operator mistakes.

disclosed deliberately, tokens can be stolen or borrowed, and all biometric techniques have some false positive (authenticating the wrong person) and false negative (not authenticating the right person) rates. The most efficient authentication systems use diverse mechanisms, e.g. smartcard activated by keying a Personal Identification Number (PIN), or fingerprint matching with patterns stored on a smartcard (this kind of techniques can also ease privacy concerns raised by uncontrolled storage of biometric data).

Diverse interfaces can also provide back-up facilities to cope with physical faults affecting some parts of the interfaces.

3.3 Application software diversity

This is the most common form of diversity. The notion of software diversity has been formulated in the seventies [11, 22, 36]. It has been significantly used in safety-critical systems to provide either a fail-halt property or service continuity.

The fail-halt property, with respect to design faults, can be simply achieved by self-checking modules consisting of two parts: a functional part and a monitor part running an acceptance test based on assertions checked on input data, intermediate data or result data. Acceptance test can also be implemented by comparing two versions of the functional part. If the acceptance test detects an error, the component is isolated or halted, in order to prevent disturbance of other parts of the system.

Continuity of service can be provided by recovery blocks [36], N-version programming [4] or N-self-checking programming [30].

Application software diversity is of course primarily targeting at (accidental or deliberate) design faults in the application software. But they can be efficient also to tolerate physical faults [30], and also some hardware or operating system design faults. For instance, the ELEKTRA railway interlocking control system [28] is composed of two channels: one channel executes the interlocking control software, the other one executes the monitoring software (i.e., the safety bag). Both channels are made of identical hardware, with identical operating systems. According to the very high safety requirements, operating system and hardware cannot be considered as exempt of design faults. But, since the application programs running on the two channels are different, it can be considered as very unlikely that the same (hardware or OS) design fault can be activated at the same execution step on both channels and produce consistent errors leading to an unsafe state.

N-version programming can also be efficient against viruses, if inter-process communications are checked efficiently [26].

3.4. Diversity at the execution level

The same software run on the same hardware but with a different execution context may behave differently with respect to accidental design faults, and this kind of diversity can have a surprising high efficiency. Practical experience of Tandem systems [7, 23] has shown that rollback mechanisms designed to tolerate physical faults turn out to be equally efficient for the software faults, owing to the loose coupling between process executions: since most "Heisenbugs" appear to be context sensitive, those affecting primary execution are very unlikely to be activated during the rollback.

This kind of diversity would deserve more attention.

3.5. Diversity at the hardware and OS level

Diversity can be applied at the hardware level, for instance by designing independently different processors able to run identically the same software [3], and by comparing bit-by-bit the results. This kind of diversity has been primarily intended to tolerate hardware component failures and external physical faults: such faults are very unlikely to produce identical errors on diversely implemented hardware. But nowadays, such diversity should be still more useful to tolerate the numerous design faults induced by the increasing complexity of recent microprocessors. See for instance the Pentium Specification Updates published by Intel®, with many "errata" defined as "design defects or errors".

To tolerate compiler (design or execution) faults, but also to increase the execution diversity, identical application software modules can be compiled by independently developed compilers, as is the case for the Boeing 777.

Operating systems are also prone to design flaws, and diversity can help to tolerate them. In particular, it is possible to run application software replicas on different Commercial-Off-The-Shelf (COTS) operating systems. This should be especially efficient for security critical software, which could be attractive targets for intrusions (e.g., certification authorities, name and directory services, electronic commerce, etc.). Indeed, most intrusions exploit flaws in OS platforms rather than flaws in the security-related software itself. But a particular attention must be given to prevent "correlated faults" which could appear in several COTS OS. For example, the buffer overrun attack is common on many Unix-based systems, as well as on Microsoft Windows-NT. In some cases, such correlated faults cannot be easily avoided, e.g., when they are features of standard protocols. Such features are often exploited by denial-of-service attacks (see for instance [12]).

4. Diversity and validation

This section addresses the role of diversity in the validation process in two ways: on one hand, design diversity aids the validation of the software variants and, on the other hand, a good validation method necessitates a set of diverse verification and validation techniques.

Design diversity is generally used to check the dynamic behavior of the software during execution. In addition to its ability to detect or tolerate faults in operation, it has been observed that design diversity i) aids the validation of software variants, thanks to back-to-back testing and ii) helps in detecting certain errors that are unlikely to be detected with other methods. For example, in a controlled experiment performed in [42], 14 % of faults were detected by back-to-back testing of three variants after extensive individual tests, whereas in [8] nine faults were detected after extensive use of other testing methods. It can be argued that design diversity is costly. However, previous experiments and evaluations showed that design diversity does not double the cost (see e.g., [1, 6, 24, 31]), and more recently a study performed on an industrial software [27] confirmed that the cost of one diverse variant is between 0.7 and 0.85 the cost of a non fault-tolerant software. This is due to the fact that even though some development activities (e.g., detailed design, coding, unit and integration tests) are performed separately for each unit, several activities (e.g., specifications, high level design and system test) are performed globally and even take advantage of the existence of more than one variant.

Considering now, more generally, the validation of software systems. It is well known (and this is confirmed in the survey carried out in [32], Section 2.2.3) that despite the large number of available validation techniques (that are very valuable), none of them is perfect. The authors of this survey argue for the combination of various (i.e., diverse) techniques to obtain a high level of trust. They recommend combining static analysis with testing for all categories of software systems. For critical software, these techniques should be reinforced by formal specification, behavioral analysis and proof-of-correctness. Indeed, the diverse techniques allow different types of faults to be revealed. Static analysis (e.g., walk-through, inspection) can be applied to specifications and code and allow detection of a large number of faults before software execution: they could reveal as high as 84% and 95% of faults in the software (see respectively [10, 39]). Testing uncovers faults that static analyses have failed to reveal. Even within testing, diverse methods are recommended: for example it is worth combining functional and structural testing as well as strategies with randomly selected inputs and deterministic inputs. The behavioral analysis complements the static analysis as the dynamic properties can be verified. Formal specification and proof-of-correctness should be used for critical components. Another matter related to diversity in the validation process is the aim of the various activities. Indeed, even though the overall aim of validation is to check the software correct behavior, static analysis, behavioral analysis and testing aim at uncovering faults (they succeed when they uncover faults), whereas formal specification and proof-of-correctness aim at demonstrating the correct behavior (they fail when they uncover faults). Also, diversity within the same validation activity may be beneficial: in the experiment conducted in [21] two inspection teams, following the same rules, found different types of faults in the same software system (for each team around 75 % of faults were not found by the other team).

5. Efficiency evaluation

Diversity efficiency is mainly limited by the related faults defined in Section 2: even independently developed hardware of software can exhibit faults generating similar errors, as has been experienced by many experimental studies such as [5]. The evaluation of the impact of such faults on the overall dependability of the system can be evaluated as in [31]. This Section examines the efficiency of diversity a) on the development process and b) with respect to security/usability tradeoffs.

5.1 Efficiency of diversity on the development process

High quality software necessitates a controllable and well-defined production process as it assumed that there is a direct relationship between the quality of the development process and the quality of the resulting product. Programs aimed at improving and maturing the development process are usually referred to as reliability improvement programs. Such programs are generally based on several diverse actions: well-defined specification process, combined use of validation techniques, data collection, feedback to the development process and actions performed to improve the process, etc. The evaluation of the efficiency of these methods is needed to check their impact on the product quality and on the development process productivity and efficiency.

Indeed most of the companies that have followed a reliability improvement program have already appreciated the progress accomplished. Among these companies we can quote without being exhaustive: AT&T, Bull, Fujitsu, Hewlett-Packard, IBM, Motorola, NASA, etc. In addition to specific experiences, several papers and books have already been published advocating and defining methods and models for improving software process (see e.g., [25, 34]).

One of the major objections to reliability programs is their cost that has been considered for a long time as increasing with the required dependability level. The relationship between the level of dependability required and the associated cost is further complicated when considering factors such as the supplier's rework cost, the maintenance cost, the consequence of failure for the customer, or the cost of fault correction. For example, past experience has showed that the cost of fixing a fault uncovered during operation to be one or two orders of magnitude higher than the cost of the same fault detected during development [9].

It is worth noting that all the companies that have followed a well-defined program for improving software process and quality agree on the fact that the benefits are important. However, it is very difficult to partition the gains according to the methods used (e.g., the relative impact of fault prevention and fault removal techniques is very difficult to be assessed). Another difficulty comes from the fact that the improvement are usually evaluated by comparing the results of the new methods with respect to the previous ones used by the company. Moreover the criteria of comparison vary from one company to the other. These criteria concern for instance software productivity, fault density in the field, reduction of test duration, etc. It is thus very complicated to draw general conclusions from the published work. The examples presented below are given as indication about some benefits observed; they have to be considered within the context in which they have been obtained.

- The results obtained through the quality program started at AT&T's International DEFINITY PBX [19] (using among other techniques the Cleanroom approach and software reliability objectives) show: a factor-of-10 reduction in customer-reported problems, a factor-of-10 reduction in program maintenance cost, a factor-of-2 reduction in the system test interval, and a 30% reduction in new product introduction interval.

- The experience reported in [20] by IBM, consisting in analyzing reliability-related data (trend tests and reliability growth models) and in the application of an economic model to determine optimal release time, shows that the benefit-to-cost ratio brought by such analyses is 6.14, 11.98, and 78.65 depending on whether the cost of a failure is 500, 5,000, or 50,000 monetary units.

- The experience reported by Fujitsu [2], using the concurrent development approach, shows the release cycle has been reduced by 75%.

- The study carried out over 15 projects by Raytheon Equipment Division [18] shows that the rework cost has shrunk to a quarter of its original value after completion of a five-year program aimed at process improvement.

- Motorola (Government Electronics Div.) [17] has followed an improvement and an evaluation program: they went from Capability Maturity Model (see e.g., [25]) level 2 to level 3 in three years and it took them three more years to reach level 4 for the whole process and level 5 for policies and procedures. From level 2 to 5, the number of faults has been divided by 7, the cycle time by 2.4 whereas productivity has been improved by 2.8.

5.2. Efficiency of diversity with respect of security/usability tradeoffs

In Section 3, it has been shown that diversity can contribute significantly to improve security. But quite often, even if they are implemented with diversity, security mechanisms can be defeated by a careless user, e.g., who writes his PIN on his smartcard.

Indeed, most computing systems users are not motivated sufficiently by security concerns to accept easily the unavoidable discomfort induced by any security measures. It may be difficult for them to imagine that, while they may have no access to sensitive information, their careless attitude can endanger other users who may have to deal with such sensitive data. But this is really true! Many attackers are exploiting badly protected user accounts to gain enough privileges to progress towards more sensitive targets. For instance, they can easily impersonate a careless user and abuse the trust that other persons place in the impersonated user.

In fact, trust relationships should not be transitive: if Alice trusts Bob, and Bob trusts Charlie, this does not mean that Alice trusts Charlie. Nevertheless, when implemented by computer mechanisms, such trust relationships can be transitively abused. For instance, if Alice trusts Bob and grants him the privilege to access her account (e.g., by using .rhosts on Unix), and in the same manner, if Bob gives Charlie an access to his account, Charlie can easily access Alice's account. Yet Alice may not wish to deny Bob's access to her account or Bob deny Charlie's access to his, if these accesses are needed to ease their work. Most operating systems exhibit such facilities, e.g. to improve teamwork or to enable some users to benefit from other users' expertise. If these features are correctly used, they can even improve security (examples are given in [15]).

It is thus important to assess the influence of user behavior on the system security. A quantitative evaluation method has been developed for this purpose [14]. Measurements provided by this approach aim at representing as accurately as possible the security of the system in operation, i.e. its ability to resist possible attacks, or equivalently, the difficulty for an attacker to exploit the vulnerabilities present in the system and defeat the security objectives assigned to the system. This method is based on 1) a theoretical model, the privilege graph, exhibiting the system vulnerabilities, 2) a definition of the security objectives, 3) a mathematical model to compute significant security measures.

In the privilege graph model [15], a node represents a set of privileges owned by a user or a set of users (e.g., a Unix group) and an arc represents a vulnerability. An arc exists from node X to node Y if there is a method enabling a user owning X's privileges to obtain Y's privileges. Most of these vulnerabilities are induced by lax user behavior or by features activated to facilitate information sharing. Weights are assigned to each arc, according to the effort needed for a possible attacker to exploit the vulnerability. In the privilege graph, diversity-implemented security mechanisms are represented by arcs with weights corresponding to the difficulty to break each of these mechanisms.

The security objective definition is mostly used to identify in the privilege graph which nodes represent the privileges of possible attackers and which nodes represent the privileges of possible targets. The mathematical model, based on Markov chains, is used to compute measures representing the global effort associated with all the paths that connect possible attacker node to possible target nodes. A set of software tools has been developed to generate automatically privilege graphs for distributed Unix systems, to define security objectives, and to compute significant security measures [35]. Such tools can help a security administrator to identify those security flaws that can be eliminated for the best security improvement, with the least incidence to users. These tools can also enable the administrator to monitor the evolution of the global system security according to changes in the environment, in the configurations or in the user behavior.

6. References

[1] T. Anderson, P. A. Barrett, D. N. Halliwell, and M. R. Moulding, "Software Fault Tolerance: An Evaluation", IEEE Trans. on Software Eng., vol. SE-11, pp. 1502-1510, 1985.

[2] M. Aoyama, "Concurrent-Development Process Model", IEEE Software, vol. July, pp. 46-55, 1993.

[3] J. Arlat, "Design of a Fault-Tolerant Microcomputer by Means of Functional Diversification", Doctoral Thesis. In French: INP, Toulouse, France, 1979.

[4] A. Avizienis, "The N-version Approach to Fault-Tolerant Systems", IEEE Trans. on Software Eng., vol. 11, pp. 1491-1501, 1985.

[5] A. Avizienis and J. P. J. Kelly, "Fault Tolerance by Design Diversity: Concepts and Experiments", IEEE Computer, vol. 17, pp. 67-80, 1984.

[6] A. Avizienis, M. R. Lyu, W. Schutz, K. S. Tso, and U. Voges, "DEDIX 87 - A supervisory System for Design Diversity Experiments at UCLA", in Software Diversity in Computerized Control Systems, Dependable Computing and Fault-Tolerant Systems, vol. 2, U. Voges, Ed. Vienna, New York, Springer-Verlag, 1988, pp. 127-168.

[7] J. Bartlett, J. Gray, and B. Horst, "Fault Tolerance in Tandem Computer Systems", in The Evolution of Fault-Tolerant Systems (Proc. IFIP Symp. on The Evolution of Fault-Tolerant Computing, Baden, Austria, July 1986), Dependable Computing and Fault-Tolerant Systems, A. Avizienis, H. Kopetz, and J.-C. Laprie, Eds., 1 ed. Vienna, Austria, Springer-Verlag, 1987, pp. 55-76.

[8] P. G. Bishop, D. G. Esp, M. Barnes, P. Humphreys, G. Dahl, and J. Lahti, "PODS — A Project on Diverse Software", IEEE Trans. on Software Eng., vol. 12, pp. 929-940, 1986.

[9] B. W. Boehm, Software Engineering Economics. Englewood Cliffs, NJ: Prentice-Hall, 1981.

[10] M. Bush, "Getting Stared on Metrics - Jet Propulsion Laboratory Productivity and Quality", Proc. 12th International Conference on Software Engineering, Nice, France, 1990, pp. 133-142.

[11] L. Chen and A. Avizienis, "N-Version Programming: a Fault Tolerance Approach to Reliability of Software Operation", Proc. 8th Int. Symp. Fault-Tolerant Computing (FTCS-8), Toulouse, France, 1978, pp. 3-9.

[12] CIAC, "Tools Generating IP Denial-of-Service Attacks", US Department of Energy, Computer Incident Advisory Capability (CIAC), Bulletin I-019, 1997.

[13] D. D. Clark and D. R. Wilson, "A Comparison of Commercial and Military Computer Security Policies", Proc. Proc. Int. Symp. on Security and Privacy, Oakland, CA, USA, 1987, pp. 184-194.

[14] M. Dacier, "Towards Quantitative Evaluation of Computer Security", Doctoral Thesis. In French: INP, Toulouse, 1994.

[15] M. Dacier and Y. Deswarte, "Privilege Graph: An Extension to the Typed Access Matrix Model", Proc. European Symposium on Research in Computer Security (ESORICS 94), Brighton, UK, 1994, pp. 319-334.

[16] Y. Deswarte, L. Blain, and J.-C. Fabre, "Intrusion Tolerance in Distributed Computing Systems", Proc. Int. Symp. on Security and Privacy, Oakland, CA, USA, 1991, pp. 110-121.

[17] M. Diaz and J. Sligo, "How Process Improvement Helped Motorola", IEEE Software, vol. Sept., pp. 75-81, 1997.

[18] R. Dion, "Process Improvement and the Corporate Balance Sheet", IEEE Software, vol. July, pp. 28-35, 1993.

[19] M. Donnelly, B. Everett, J. Musa, and G. Wilson, "Best Current Practice of SRE", in Handbook of Software Reliability Engineering, M. Lyu, Ed., Mc Graw Hill, 1996, pp. 219-254 (Chapter 6).

[20] W. Ehrlich, B. Prasanna, J. Stampfel, and J. Wu, "Determining the Cost of a Stop-Test Decision", IEEE Software, vol. March, pp. 33-42, 1993.

[21] K. El Emam and I. Wieczorek, "The repeatability of Code Defect Classifications", Proc. 9th International Symposium on Software Reliability Engineering (ISSRE'98), Paderborn, Germany, 1998, pp. 322-332.

[22] W. R. Elmendorf, "Fault-tolerant Programming", Proc. 2nd IEEE Int Symp. Fault-Tolerant Computing, Newton, Massashusetts, 1972, pp. 79-83.

[23] J. Gray, "Why Do Computers Stop and What Can be Done About it ?", Proc. 5th Int. Symp. on Reliability in Distributed Software and Database Systems, Los Angeles, CA, 1986, pp. 3-12.

[24] G. Hagelin, "ERICSSON Safety System for Railway Control", in Software Diversity in Computerized Control Systems, Dependable Computing and Fault-Tolerant Systems, vol. 2, U. Vogues, Ed. Vienna, New York, Sringer-Verlag, 1988, pp. 9-21.

[25] W. S. Humphrey, Managing the Software Process: Addison-Wesley, 1989.

[26] M. K. Joseph and A. Avizienis, "A Fault Tolerance Approach to Computer Viruses", Proc. Int. Symp. on Security and Privacy, Oakland, CA, USA, 1988, pp. 52-58.

[27] K. Kanoun, "Cost of Software Design Diversity — An Empirical Evaluation", Proc. 10th Int. Symp. on Software Reliability Engineering (ISSRE'99), Boca Raton, FL, USA, 1999.

[28] H. Kantz and C. Koza, "The Elektra Railway Signaling System: Field Experience with an Activity Replicated System with Diversity", Proc. 25th Int. Symp. on Fautlt Tolerant Computing (FTCS25), Pasadena, CA, 1995, pp. 453-458.

[29] J.-C. Laprie, "Dependability: Basic Concepts and Terminology," in Dependable Computing and Fault-Tolerant Systems, vol. 5, E. J.C. Laprie, Ed. Wien-New York: Springer Verlag, 1992, pp. 265.

[30] J.-C. Laprie, J. Arlat, C. Béounes, and K. Kanoun, "Definition and Analysis of Hardware-and-Software Fault-tolerant Architectures", IEEE Computer Magazine, vol. 23 (7), pp. 39-51, 1990.

[31] J.-C. Laprie, J. Arlat, C. Béounes, and K. Kanoun, "Architectural issues in Software fault Tolerance", in Software Fault Tolerance, M. Lyu, Ed., Wiley, Trends in Software, 1996, pp. 45-80 (Chapter 3).

[32] J.-C. Laprie, J. Arlat, J.-P. Blanquart, A. Costes, Y. Crouzet, Y. Deswarte, J.-C. Fabre, H. Guillermain, M. Kaâniche, K. Kanoun, C. Mazet, D. Powell, C. Rabejac, and P. Thévenod, Dependability Handbook. in French, Toulouse, France: Cepadues - Editions, 1995.

[33] J.-C. Laprie, A. Avizienis, and B. Randell, "Dependability of Computing Systems: Fundamental Concepts, Terminology, and Examples", LAAS-CNRS Report: 99-293, 1999.

[34] J. Musa, Software Reliability Engineering: Computing McGraw-Hill, 1998.

[35] R. Ortalo, Y. Deswarte, and M. Kaâniche, "Experimenting with Quantitative Evaluation Tools for Monitoring Operational Security", IEEE Transactions on Software Engineering, vol. 25, 1999.

[36] B. Randell, "System Structure for Software Fault Tolerance", IEEE Transactions on Software Engineering, vol. SE-1, pp. 220-232, 1975.

[37] M. K. Reiter, "Distributed Trust with the Rampart Toolkit", Communications of the ACM, vol. 39 (4), pp. 71-74, 1996.

[38] L. Rognin and B. Pavard, "Collective activities and Reliability", Proc. XIII Conference on Human Decision Making and Manual Control, June 13-14, Espoo, Finland, 1994, pp. 177-187.

[39] C. Sayet and E. Pilaud, "An Experience of a Critical Software Development", Proc. 20th IEEE Int. Symp. on Fault-Tolerant Computing (FTC-20), Newcastle, UK, 1990, pp. 36-45.

[40] A. Shamir, "How to Share a Secret", Communications of the ACM, vol. 22 (11), pp. 612-613, 1979.

[41] P. Traverse, "Dependability of Digital Computers on Boards Airplanes", in Dependable Computing for Critical Applications, Dependable Computing and Fault-Tolerant Systems, vol. 1, A. Avizienis and J. C. Laprie, Eds., Springer-Verlag, 1987, pp. 133-152.

[42] U. Voges, "Use of Diversity in Experimental Reactor Safety Systems", in Software Diversity in Computerized Control Systems, Dependable Computing and Fault-Tolerant Systems, vol. 2, U. Voges, Ed. Vienna, New York, Sringer-Verlag, 1988, pp. 29-49.

From Security to Safety and Back

Victoria Stavridou and Bruno Dutertre
Computer Science Laboratory, SRI International
333 Ravenswood Avenue, Menlo Park, CA 94025
{victoria,bruno}@csl.sri.com

Abstract

Dependability encompasses different classes of system properties, related to security, reliability, or safety. This paper examines the relevance of the security concept of noninterference to safety-related properties, and, conversely, the applicability of fault-tolerance mechanisms usually applied to provide safety and reliability in the security domain. We suggest promising lines of research in the intersection of safety and security, in the application of security concepts and models to different classes of safety or fault-tolerance properties, and in the theory and practice of fault-tolerant systems applied to intrusion tolerance.

1. Introduction

Safety and security are two attributes of dependability, along with availability and reliability [17]. In broad terms, security is the prevention of unauthorized access to information and unauthorized modification of information. Safety is the avoidance of catastrophic consequences to the environment. Despite their common contribution to dependability, research in computer safety and research on security have followed mostly separate paths. The objective of this paper is to discuss possible connections between the methods and models developed by the two communities.

The computer security community has developed various models of secure systems. The emphasis of such models is usually on confidentiality, that is, on preventing the unauthorized disclosure of information. Early models were based on access control formulations: confidentiality is enforced by restricting the operations that the active entity in a system (the subjects) are allowed to perform on the data repositories of the system (the objects) [2]. Such models have well-known limitations [23, 25]: they do not separate security policy and enforcement mechanisms, they require knowledge of the internals of a system to identify objects and subjects, and, more importantly, they do not consider covert channels. More abstract models have been proposed that address these issues. These security models are all related to the concept of noninterference proposed by Goguen and Meseguer [10]. In such models, security is defined as the absence of unauthorized information flows between users of a system. The security requirements are constraints on the set of sequences of events that can be produced on the input and output interfaces of the system. In the first part of the paper, we give an overview of the different types of information-flow security concepts proposed in the literature, and we examine the application of such concepts in safety-related areas.

In the second part of the paper, we take a reverse point of view. We discuss the possible contribution of fault-tolerance techniques designed to increase system reliability to security. More precisely, we examine whether these techniques can be extended to tolerate intentional attacks rather than accidental faults.

2. Information flow models of security

Informally, there is no information flow between from a user A to a user B of a system if the actions of A have no effect on what B can observe. Many security models have been proposed to make this idea more precise. A survey of these various information-flow models and of other security models is given by McLean in [25]. The ingredients are always the same: a model of computer systems, a definition of users' actions and observations, and a security property that attempts to characterize the absence of information flow between users. The key modeling choices include whether deterministic or nondeterministic systems are considered, and, in the latter case, whether or not probabilistic models are used. Security models also differ in other respects, such as in the representation of time and of input and output events. To illustrate the different variants of information flow models proposed in the literature, we use a trace-based model similar to those used by Wittbold and Johnson and by Gray [44, 13]. Based on this model, we examine three examples of security properties: noninterference [10, 21], nondeducibility [41], and causality [3, 32].

2.1. System Model

A system's interface consists of a set of ports C and a set $\mathcal{D}$ that serves as both input and output alphabet. The set C is split into two disjoint subsets I and O that represent input and output ports, respectively. We assume $\mathcal{D}$ contains a special symbol $\perp$ that represents a null value. We use a discrete time model. A run or trace of the system is represented by an infinite sequence $\sigma = (x_t)_{t \in \mathbb{N}}$ where x_t is the event that occurs at time t. Each event x_t is a mapping from C to $\mathcal{D}$; for a given port c, $x_t(c)$ is either the value present on c at time t or $\perp$ if no value is received or transmitted on c at that time. We denote by $\mathcal{T}_C$ the set of all sequences of events. The system's behavior is characterized by its set of traces $\mathcal{H} \subseteq \mathcal{T}_C$.

Given an event x and a set of ports $A \subseteq C$, we denote by $x \restriction A$ the restriction of x to A. Similarly, $\sigma \restriction A$ denotes the projection of a trace σ on the set A. As above, $\mathcal{T}_A$ denotes the set of sequences of A-events, that is, of mappings from A to $\mathcal{D}$. The set of input traces admissible by the system is

$$\mathcal{H}_I = \{\alpha \in \mathcal{T}_I \mid \exists \sigma \in \mathcal{H} : \sigma \restriction I = \alpha\}.$$

The system is deterministic if a trace σ of the system is uniquely determined by its projection on the input ports:

$$\forall \sigma \in \mathcal{H}, \forall \sigma' \in \mathcal{H} : \sigma \restriction I = \sigma' \restriction I \Rightarrow \sigma = \sigma'.$$

In security contexts, it is often assumed that systems are input total since a system cannot prevent users from sending arbitrary input sequences. In such cases, we have $\mathcal{H}_I = \mathcal{T}_I$. However, the security properties we examine in the sequel can be presented in a more general context.[1]

It is traditional to present security properties in the context of multilevel security. The objective is then to prevent flows of information from a high-clearance user to a low-clearance user, where each user has access to a disjoint subset of the system's ports. In the basic case, a user has access to a set of input ports $A \subseteq I$, another user has access to a set of output ports $B \subseteq O$, and the objective is to prevent information from flowing from A to B.

2.2. Noninterference

---

[1] Strictly, we should also include causality properties in our model. For a given trace $\sigma \in \mathcal{H}$, the output event observed at time t cannot depend on future input events.

Noninterference was originally proposed by Goguen and Meseguer [10] in the context of deterministic systems. McCullough [21] defined *generalized noninterference* as an extension of noninterference to nondeterministic systems. Our definition is slightly weaker than generalized noninterference and is essentially the same as proposed by McLean [26].

In noninterference models, information is considered to flow from A to B if changing the sequence of input values on A while leaving all other input values unchanged can modify the sequence of output values observed on B. More formally, for any input sequence $\alpha \in T_I$, let $Out_B(\alpha)$ be the set of sequences observable on B when α is the input sequence received by the system:

$$Out_B(\alpha) \;=\; \{\beta \in T_B \mid \exists \sigma \in T : \sigma \lfloor B = \beta \wedge \sigma \lfloor I = \alpha\}.$$

Let $\approx_A$ be the equivalence relation on input traces, as follows:

$$\alpha \approx_A \alpha' \quad \text{iff} \quad \alpha \lfloor (I - A) = \alpha' \lfloor (I - A).$$

We then have $\alpha \approx_A \alpha'$ if α and α' are identical except for the values occurring on the ports of A. There is no interference from A to B if the following condition holds:

$$\forall \alpha \in T_I, \alpha' \in T_I : \alpha \approx_A \alpha' \Rightarrow Out_B(\alpha) = Out_B(\alpha').$$

In other words, $Out_B(\alpha)$ does not depend on $\alpha \lfloor A$. The sequence of input events received on A has no influence on the set of event sequences that can be observed on B.

Noninterference can be defined equivalently by using a "purge" function as was done originally by Goguen and Meseguer [10]. Given an input sequence $\alpha \in T_I$, let $purge(\alpha, A)$ be the sequence where all inputs on port of A are replaced by $\perp$ and other inputs are unchanged. For every time t and every port $c \in C$,

$$purge(\alpha, A)(t)(c) \;=\; \begin{cases} \perp & \text{if } c \in A \\ \alpha(t)(c) & \text{otherwise.} \end{cases}$$

Noninterference is then equivalent to the following property:

$$\forall \alpha \in T_I : Out_B(\alpha) = Out_B(purge(\alpha, A)).$$

Intuitively, this means that the set of possible output sequences on B does not depend on whether some input values have been received on A or not.

The two definitions of noninterference above require that if an input sequence α is admissible (i.e. $\alpha \in \mathcal{H}_I$ or equivalently $Out_B(\alpha) \neq \emptyset$) then any α' such that $\alpha \approx_A \alpha'$ is also admissible. A weaker security requirement is the following:

$$\forall \alpha \in \mathcal{H}_I, \alpha' \in \mathcal{H}_I : \alpha \approx_A \alpha' \Rightarrow Out_B(\alpha) = Out_B(\alpha').$$

This is equivalent to the formulation of noninterference used by McLean in [26].

2.3. Nondeducibility

Nondeducibility is an alternative security property proposed by Sutherland [41]. Nondeducibility is based on the observation that there is a flow of information from A to B if, by observing B, one can deduce something about what happened on A. More precisely, we can assume that the behavior of the system, that is, the set of traces $\mathcal{H}$, is known to all users. Observing that an output sequence $\beta \in T_B$ occurred on B tells us that the corresponding global trace is an element σ of $\mathcal{H}$ that satisfies $\sigma \mid B = \beta$. The input presented on A is a sequence α of the form $\sigma \mid A$ for one such σ. For a fixed β, the set of all possible sequences α is given by

$$\mathcal{H}_A(\beta) \;=\; \{\alpha \in T_A \mid \exists \sigma \in \mathcal{H} : \sigma \mid B = \beta \wedge \sigma \mid A = \alpha\}.$$

A priori, we know that any sequence of events on A belongs to the set

$$\mathcal{H}_A \;=\; \{\alpha \in T_A \mid \exists \sigma \in \mathcal{H} : \sigma \mid A = \alpha\}.$$

If $\mathcal{H}_A(\beta)$ is a strict subset of $\mathcal{H}_A$ then observing β gives us some information about α that was not known a priori.

Nondeducibility forbids deductions of the above form. It requires that for all sequences β observable on B, the two sets $\mathcal{H}_A(\beta)$ and $\mathcal{H}_A$ are equal. It is equivalent to require $\mathcal{H}$ to satisfy the following property:

$$\forall \beta \in \mathcal{H}_B, \forall \alpha \in \mathcal{H}_A, \exists \sigma \in \mathcal{H} : \sigma \mid A = \alpha \wedge \sigma \mid B = \beta,$$

where $\mathcal{H}_B$, the sets of sequences observable on B, is defined in the same way as $\mathcal{H}_A$. Nondeducibility requires then that every sequence β observable on B is compatible with every sequence α observable on A. It follows that nondeducibility generalizes to arbitrary sets of ports and that it is a symmetric property. Nondeducibility of the events on A from observing events on B is the same as nondeducibility of the events on B from observing events on A.

2.4. Causality

Roscoe [32] defines two security properties for systems modeled as CSP processes. These security properties are closely related to the notion of causality proposed earlier by Bieber and Cuppens [3]. In both approaches, a system is secure if it appears deterministic to its low-level users. Simpson et al. [39] have recently adapted Roscoe's definition of noninterference to safety and fault tolerance.

Assume that a user has access to a set of input ports A and can observe a set of output ports B. Causality requires that for any sequence α_A sent to the ports A, the system always produces the same sequence of output on B:

$$\forall \sigma \in \mathcal{H}, \sigma' \in \mathcal{H} : \sigma \mid A = \sigma' \mid A \Rightarrow \sigma \mid B = \sigma' \mid B.$$

In other words, the output on B is functionally dependent on the input on A. The system appears deterministic to a user who can observe only the ports of A and B. Input values received on ports not in A have then no influence on what such a user can observe, and there is no information flow from such ports to B.

2.5. Evaluation

The three security properties above are constraints on the sets of event sequences observable on two disjoint sets of ports. In the form given above, the three properties relate input ports A to output ports B. Since the sets A and B do not play the same role in all cases, we have to consider a slightly more general context to compare the three approaches. We consider two users U_1 and U_2 whose interface with the system are given by two pairs of sets (A_1, B_1) and (A_2, B_2), where

$A_1 \cap A_2 = \emptyset$ and $B_1 \cap B_2 = \emptyset$. To prevent communication from U_1 to U_2, we can require any of the following properties[2]:

- Noninterference from A_1 to B_2

- Nondeducibility of A_1 from $A_2 \cup B_2$

- Causality with respect to A_2 and B_2.

For the same security objective, the three security models give three different constraints on $\mathcal{H}$. In general, the causality property is strictly stronger than the noninterference property, which is itself strictly stronger than the nondeducibility property. However, in case $I = A_1 \cup A_2$ and $O = B_1 \cup B_2$ and only deterministic systems are considered, the three above formulations are equivalent.

The key question about any formal definition of security is how much security it provides in practice. For deterministic systems, noninterference is a very good criterion. Millen [29] showed that if there is no interference from A to B in a deterministic system, then the capacity of the communication channel of input A and output B is zero. The only problem is that noninterference is too strong in some cases. In particular, systems that rely on encryption mechanisms to ensure confidentiality can violate noninterference [26].

On the other hand, nondeducibility is a fairly weak property, as shown in by McCullough [21] and by Wittbold and Johnson [44]. Systems that are visibly nonsecure can still satisfy nondeducibility. It may still be useful in certain cases where noninterference and causality do not apply. Since nondeducibility applies to arbitrary sets of ports, it can be used to specify that output sequences on separate output ports are independent. This may be useful if one wants to prevent deductions about secret outputs from the observation of nonsecret outputs. Such a constraint cannot be expressed by using noninterference or causality.

For nondeterministic systems, both noninterference and nondeducibility suffer from the same limitation: they ignore probabilistic inference. For example, nondeducibility examines only the set of input sequences that are compatible with an observed output sequence β. This is clearly insufficient if not all input sequences are equally probable. As discussed by Wittbold and Johnson [44], there are visibly insecure nondeterministic systems that still satisfy noninterference and nondeducibility requirements. Better models have been developed that take probabilities into account [24, 12, 13]. The probabilistic noninterference model defined by Gray [13] achieves the same result as noninterference in the deterministic case. Probabilistic noninterference ensures that the communication channel from a high-level user to a low-level user has capacity zero, that is, information cannot flow from high to low [13]. Causality applies to probabilistic systems as well as nonprobabilistic models. It is in fact a very strong requirements: if causality holds for the low-level user of a system then the system satisfies probabilistic noninterference. Unfortunately, causality may be too strong and is not an adequate property when encryption is used.

All the security models mentioned above give theoretical security criteria intended to prevent any unauthorized flow of information. In practice, it is not clear whether useful systems can be built that satisfy such stringent security requirements. It is not likely that all covert channels in a system can be eliminated. More useful security definitions should allow for some tolerable information leakage. Nonprobabilistic models seem inadequate for this purpose because they

---

[2]The nondeducibility formulation is that U_2 cannot deduce U_1's input by observing both A_2 and B_2. For input-total systems, this is equivalent to nondeducibility of A_1 from B_2 alone.

do not provide any means of measuring the amount of information that can be communicated between users. Probabilistic models and the tools of information theory provide a better approach for dealing with limited information leakage.

2.6. Compositionality

The security models mentioned previously all give definitions of the secure systems with respect to a given confidentiality policy. For these definitions to be useful, there should be practical ways of verifying whether a system satisfies the relevant property. Verification methods have been developed for noninterference and related notions [11, 35, 25, 27], but it is not clear how such methods can scale to large systems. The usual means to fight complexity, namely abstraction and decomposition, do not seem to apply easily to security properties. More exactly, the decomposition mechanisms and abstraction techniques that exist for verifying safety or liveness properties do not work for many security properties. The technical reasons are discussed by McLean [26].

A first difficulty is that many security properties are not preserved under the usual notions of refinement. For example, in our trace-based model, a plausible definition of refinement could be that $\mathcal{H}$ refines $\mathcal{H}'$ if all the input sequences admissible for $\mathcal{H}'$ are also admissible for $\mathcal{H}$ and for any such sequence, any output produced by $\mathcal{H}$ is a possible output of $\mathcal{H}'$. With this definition, $\mathcal{H}$ can be more deterministic than $\mathcal{H}'$ and it follows that neither noninterference nor nondeducibility are preserved by refinement. On the other hand, causality is preserved under refinement and this observation is the main motivation for causality given by Roscoe [32]. If $\mathcal{H}$ satisfies a causality property, then any refinement, that is, any implementation of $\mathcal{H}$, still satisfies the same property.

A second problem is that many security properties are not compositional. Connecting two systems that satisfy the same policy in an apparently secure way may result in an overall system that is not secure [21, 22]. This problem can be solved to a certain extent by strengthening the security properties considered. For example, McCullough [22] defines restrictiveness as a strengthening of generalized noninterference that is preserved under composition. The potential drawback is that the new property may be too strong to be useful. For example, Wittbold and Johnson citeWittbold90 argue that forward correctability, a property similar to restrictiveness, is too strong. Another approach might be to rule out compositions that are known to cause problems, for example, disallow feedback. Under such restrictions, various compositionality results can be obtained [28, 26, 33, 45].

Even when available, these compositionality results are often too limited. In the best case, combining two subsystems that have security property P in a proper way results in a global system that still have P. However, system-level security is an emergent property and relies on a variety of mechanisms such as encryption, authentication, or security kernels. Systems are built out of heterogenous components that may not satisfy P or for which property P is not meaningful. In this context, preservation of a security property under composition is not useful. A more pressing issue is to obtain global security guarantees for systems from more elementary properties of the components. Properties which are relevant at the component level may be different from the overall security property at the system level. See Neumann [30] for further discussion on this topic.

3. Other applications of noninterference

Research in computer security has led to the development of a rich theory of secure systems.

The search for a mathematically precise yet practical definition of security based on information flow was a central motivation for most of this work. The results have been a collection of possible characterizations of security for several classes of systems. The situation is reasonably clear for deterministic systems where noninterference provides an almost perfect security criterion, though sometimes too strong. On the other hand, a practical notion of information flow security for nondeterministic systems has proved much harder to obtain. Probabilistic models provide convincing security definitions but are fairly complex, and few examples of successful applications are available. Nonprobabilistic models are simpler and seem easier to apply, but they can be both too weak to ensure real security and too strong in many applications. As a whole, the various security models remain mostly of theoretical interest, and practical applications are scarce. These security models have had little impact on the way we build computer systems in practice.

Some of the difficulties in applying information flow models in practice are due to their "all or nothing" philosophy. In other words, information flow models aim at defining perfect and absolute security that cannot be achieved in practice. Most models are not adequate for more realistic security goals, such as tolerating covert channels of low capacity. Only the more complex probabilistic models are able to characterize such properties. Another limitation of many existing information flow models is that they promote a centralized view of computer systems. The associated analysis method requires first the construction of a model of the global system's behavior and proof that this global model satisfies the expected properties. Because of noncompositionality, no clear alternative to this naive approach has emerged.

3.1. Fault Tolerance

Despite practical limitations of noninterference and related information-flow models in the security domain, there may be interest in applying such notions to other areas. Recent examples have shown that variants of noninterference can be useful in analyzing fault-tolerance and strong-partitioning mechanisms. Simpson et al. [39] extend the CSP formulation of causality defined by Roscoe to analyze general fault-tolerance mechanisms. The general idea is to ensure that the observable behavior of a system is independent of possible faults triggered by the environment.

As a simple illustration, consider a system with input ports A and output ports B. We can represent the occurrence of faults as additional input events received on a fictitious set of ports E. The behavior of the system, including the effect of faults, can then be modeled as a set of traces $\mathcal{H}$ over the ports of A, B, and E. If $\mathcal{H}$ satisfies the causality property with respect to A and B, then the output on B depends only on the input on A and is therefore unaffected by the input events received on E. In other words, the event sequences observed on A and B do not depend on the presence or absence of faults, and the system is fault tolerant.

Obviously, such a formalization of fault tolerance is too simplistic and too strong a requirement to be practical. It corresponds to a very strong fault-masking property: faults have absolutely no impact on the input-output behavior of the system. Simpson et al. [39] propose more useful classes of fault-tolerance properties, obtained by relaxing the above causality requirement. These fault-tolerance properties also allow one to include assumptions about the number, frequency, and severity of faults to be tolerated, that is, about the event sequence received on E.

3.2. Partitioning in Integrated Modular Avionics

Di Vito [6], Dutertre and Stavridou [7], and Wilding et al. [43] all apply noninterference concepts to integrated modular avionics. In this context, software components performing different avionic functions share common hardware resources and one must show that nontrusted components do not interfere with components performing safety-critical functions.

Traditional avionics systems are based on federated architectures. Independent functions (e.g. autopilot and flight management) are performed by dedicated hardware subsystems with their own power supplies, processors, and communication links. There is only limited communication between the different subsystems, which ensures fault isolation. A fault in a computer system supporting one function or in the software implementing that function is not likely to propagate to other functions.

Integrated modular avionics (IMA) has recently emerged as an alternative to the federated approach. In IMA, a single computer system provides a common computer resource to several functions. IMA architectures require less hardware resource than federated systems, and can lead to significant gains in space, weight, and power requirements, and in maintenance cost. However, IMA does not provide the inherent fault isolation of federated architectures. A faulty function might monopolize the shared resources, corrupt the memory used by other functions or send wrong commands to their actuators. To prevent such interference, an IMA infrastructure must provide strong partitioning to ensure that faults in one function cannot propagate to other functions that use the same resources [36]. The problem is very similar to preventing interference, in the security sense, between distinct users of a computer system.

For example, assume that an IMA system performs two independent control functions. One reads sensor inputs on a set of ports A_1 and produces actuator commands on a set of ports B_1. The other reads input from ports A_2 and produces output on ports B_2. The overall system can be characterized by a set of traces $\mathcal{H}$ and partitioning is achieved if there is no interference from A_1 to B_2 and from A_2 to B_1. As previously, this simplistic formulation is too strong to be useful, but more realistic partitioning models for single-processor systems rely on this general principle [6, 7, 43]. It remains to extend these models to the distributed architectures proposed for real IMA systems. Key issues to address include timing, bus sharing, and controlled communication between components.

3.3. Future Directions

In the above examples, the goal is to ensure that some desirable system property is satisfied despite interference from the environment or from faulty system components. In a sense, noninterference has a more modest role in such applications than in security. In the latter case, noninterference is the top-level system property one tries to achieve; it is essentially taken as the definition of security. In the former case, the overall system property of interest is something else, typically safety, and noninterference is used as an auxiliary concept for verifying mechanisms that contribute to safety. Not surprisingly, noninterference models are easier to define and apply in this more limited context.

Security models make worst-case assumptions about system users and environment. Systems have to resist deliberate attack by a skilled opponent. The attacker is often assumed able to exploit covert channels and to insert Trojan horses in the system. One must then make sure that no information flow exists between two users who are colluding and trying their best to communicate. The properties required to ensure information confidentiality under such pessimistic assumptions are very strong and hard to implement in practice. In the safety domain, the objective is usually to protect against accidental rather than deliberate faults, and one can then make more favorable assumptions. For example, faulty components may be fail-silent or fail-stop or may be assumed to fail independently.

In non-security-related applications, it becomes easier to define a tolerable degree of interference. Essentially, interference can be tolerated as long as the top-level property of interest still holds. For example, the authors [7] consider bounded interference in the temporal domain. There is no need for sophisticated probabilistic models and information-theoretic notions for obtaining noninterference notions that can be achieved in practice. This contrasts with the unrealistic "all or nothing" properties proposed in security models.

The examples above are promising applications of noninterference notions outside of the original security domain. It is unrealistic to expect that all aspects of dependability can be handled by noninterference alone. Attempts by Simpson et al. [39] at systematically characterizing system-level safety by noninterference properties are less convincing than their work on fault tolerance. However, noninterference may still provide a useful framework for specifying and verifying properties and mechanisms related to safety, security, reliability, and availability. Many open problems remain to be solved before such a noninterference framework becomes practical. Verification techniques need to be developed for noninterference notions; in particular, compositionality issues have to be addressed. The challenge is still to be able to decompose systematically high-level system properties into local noninterference properties of components that can be implemented and verified easily.

4. Intrusion tolerance

The complexity of the software systems built today virtually guarantees the existence of security vulnerabilities. When the existence of specific vulnerabilities becomes known, typically as a result of detecting a successful attack, intrusion prevention techniques such as firewalls and anti-virus software seek to prevent future attackers from exploiting these vulnerabilities. However, vulnerabilities cannot be totally eliminated, their existence is not always known, and prevention mechanisms cannot always be built. Intrusion tolerance is the capability to deal with residual security vulnerabilities. An intrusion-tolerant system is able to continue providing service after a penetration. This means that the damage caused by an intruder is contained and possibly automatically repaired. The premise of intrusion tolerance is that it is preferable to continue system operation with possibly degraded characteristics, as opposed to completely withdrawing the system and the service it provides.

Intrusions are only one of the many classes of faults that can affect a system. An intrusion occurs when an attacker gains unauthorized access to the system. Attackers can be outsiders who illegitimately gain access to the system or insiders who misuse their privileges. Intrusion can then be classified as intentional operational faults, in contrast to faults that occur accidentally or during system development. There exist fault tolerance schemes for maintaining system services in the presence of accidental operational faults. In this section, we examine the relevance of such fault-tolerance mechanisms to intrusion tolerance.

4.1. Fault tolerance in distributed systems

The risk of intrusion is of primary concern in computer networks and the fault-tolerance techniques the most relevant to intrusion tolerance are those developed for distributed systems.[3]

---

[3]Replication and therefore distribution are necessary for fault tolerance (at least for tolerating hardware failures). We are interested here in systems that are distributed in the first place, as opposed to conceptually centralized systems that are distributed for fault-tolerance purpose.

Conceptually, such systems can usually be structured in terms of clients and services. The usual objective of fault tolerance for such architectures is to provide high service availability despite possible failures of the server nodes or of the communication network.

The basic mechanism of fault tolerance is redundancy. In distributed systems, servers are replicated on several nodes so that extra resources are available in case one node fails. In order to achieve proper service, the interaction between clients and servers and between servers need to be coordinated via protocols that are themselves fault tolerant. Several approaches exist for managing redundant servers in a distributed system, such as atomic transactions [16], triple modular redundancy, or primary-backup architectures.

A survey of approaches based on active replication is given by Schneider [38]. In such systems, multiple replicas of the same server process the same client requests. The associated coordination mechanisms ensure that the answers from nonfaulty replicas to the same request are identical. This requires deterministic servers and a protocol to ensure that the same requests are received and processed in a consistent order by all nonfaulty replicas.

Another family of redundant architectures uses passive replication. In this approach, one of the replicas acts as the primary server and other replicas as backups, ready to take over if the primary server fails. The associated coordination mechanisms ensure that the failure of the primary server is detected, that a backup server is elected as the new primary server, and that clients are informed of the identity of the current primary server. Coordination is also required between the primary and backup servers to ensure that all the replicas are maintained in consistent states. Primary-backup architectures are less expensive than active replication systems but are not effective against the more severe classes of failures. Passive replication approaches require error detection: backup servers must be able to detect failure of the primary server for reconfiguration to take place.

In all fault-tolerant systems, the complexity of the coordination protocols and the number of replicas required depend on the number and severity of faults to be tolerated [20, 4]. The simplest case corresponds to crash failures, where a failed server simply stops to produce answers. The most complex case corresponds to Byzantine failures, where no assumption is made about faulty servers which can exhibit arbitrary behaviors. Other classes of faults include various kinds of omission and timing failures at the node or network level. Tolerance to Byzantine failures requires active replication and can be achieved only under strong assumptions about the communication network [15]. Systems tolerating such faults are usually reserved for safety-critical applications with very high availability requirements, such as flight control systems. Less expensive approaches such as transaction-based systems or primary-backup architectures are of greater practical interest in common distributed systems.

The basic assumption behind all server-replication techniques is that the same fault does not affect all replicas at the same time. Server nodes are assumed to fail independently. Fault isolation is also required; the failure of a server or client site must not cause the failure of other sites.

4.2. Relevance to intrusion tolerance

Intrusion tolerance can have several objectives, depending on the system's dependability requirements. In many systems, the objectives might be to preserve information confidentiality and integrity after an attacker has penetrated the system. In other applications, ensuring the continuity and quality of service might be more important than confidentiality issues. Intrusion tolerance may also be a concern in safety-critical systems, for example, in air-traffic control or other transportation systems.

Simple replication schemes are of little use for ensuring confidentiality and data integrity after intrusion. Replication can even be detrimental to confidentiality, since it increases the number of nodes where information can be compromised. Existing intrusion-tolerant systems that ensure confidentiality and integrity rely on the distribution of trust and data and use threshold encryption schemes [5, 8]. The authentication mechanisms used in such systems can also provide some protection against denial of service.

The fault-tolerance mechanisms presented previously are mostly relevant if the objective is to ensure that services remain available after intrusion. With this objective, an intrusion-tolerant system based on the client-server model must ensure proper service to honest end users in case of the penetration of one or more servers or clients.

Fault-tolerant schemes can provide such intrusion tolerance, provided the class of intrusions to be tolerated satisfies the relevant fault assumptions. To ensure fault independence, one must assume that penetrating several nodes is much more difficult than penetrating a single site. This assumption may not be very realistic for current computer networks. The same vulnerabilities may exist in nodes running the same version of the same operating system.[4] Control of several sites of the system by the same user can also invalidate the fault-independence assumption. Separation of duties can be used to protect against such internal threats. For example, the server sites could be managed by different system administrators.

Ensuring fault isolation is also an important related issue. Initial intrusion at a node should not enable easy access to the rest of the system. Although illicit access to a server can have a more immediate effect on the service, intrusion tolerance must also take into account possible attacks mounted from a client site. The server replication techniques described above are intended to protect against server failure but for such schemes to work in practice, the servers should be designed so that failures of a client do not propagate to servers. In particular, faulty client requests or misuse of the client-server protocol should not lead to server failure. Protecting servers against rogue clients is even more a concern in the intrusion tolerance context.

The approaches used to protect against accidental faults in distributed systems can provide solutions to intrusion tolerance in case the objective is to maintain service after intrusions. For such solutions to be effective, one must ensure that the underlying assumptions about fault independence and isolation are still valid in the case of intentional faults. These assumptions are more difficult to justify in the case of deliberate attacks than in the case of accidental faults. Proper security measures, such as strong user authentication or separation of duties, must be in place.

In addition, it is not clear whether the classes of faults considered in usual replication schemes, such as Byzantine failures, crashes, or omission failures, are adequate for dealing with intrusions. In the worst case, an intruder can gain full control of a node. The behavior of a compromised node is then arbitrary and intrusions lead to Byzantine failures. Unfortunately, protection against such failures require costly solutions and is difficult to implement in large distributed systems, when not theoretically impossible [9]. On the other hand, an assumption that penetrated nodes are fail-silent or only exhibit omission or timing failures is too optimistic. A better understanding and classification of the behavior of nodes after an intrusion is still needed.

Building intrusion-tolerant systems will require fast detection of intrusion and system reconfiguration techniques. Simple error-detection techniques are not effective against skilled attack-

---

[4]For example, the 1988 Internet worm exploited security weaknesses in common versions of popular operating systems [40].

ers. In the last decade, there has been considerable research on developing intrusion-detection systems. Such systems analyze audit data or message traffic for detecting and reporting suspicious activities in a computer system. There are two broad classes of intrusion-detection approaches. In the first class are systems that recognize the occurrence of known attack patterns in the audit trail. In the second class are systems that first build a profile of normal system or user behavior and then report deviation from this profile as potential intrusion attempts. Intrusion-detection systems rely on diverse tools such as expert systems, neural networks, statistical modeling, or data mining algorithms [19, 14, 18]. Such systems could provide the basic elements of intrusion-tolerant architectures. The key issues of scalability and the timely detection and reporting of anomalies remain to be solved, although recent progress has been made [31].

5. Conclusion

Applying security concepts in the domain of safety-critical systems is not a new idea. For example, Rushby [34] examined the relevance of security kernels to safety in 1989. This work has led to the development and implementation of kernels that provide certain safety guarantees in industrial control applications [42, 1]. Safety kernels have the limitations discussed in the original paper by Rushby but are still a useful concept. New classes of problems have emerged recently, such as the need for strong partitioning in IMA, that have led to a renewed interest in the interplay of security and safety. In addition, recent developments in the theory of secure systems, which are only beginning to be explored, could be valuable contributions om the safety domain. These include causality-based security and the associated verification techniques proposed by Roscoe [32] and new results on the relation between noninterference and different notions of process equivalence [37].

References

[1] P. Ammann. A Safety Kernel for Traffic Light Control. *Proceedings of the Tenth Annual Conference on Computer Assurance (COMPASS'95)*, pages 71–82, Gaithersburg, MD, June 1995.

[2] D. Bell and L.J. La Padula. Secure Computer Systems: Unified Exposition and Multics Interpretation. Technical Report MTR-2997, Mitre Corporation, March 1976.

[3] P. Bieber and F. Cuppens. A Logical View of Secure Dependencies. *Journal of Computer Security*, 1(1):99–129, 1992.

[4] N. Budhiraja, K. Marzullo, F. Schneider, and S. Toueg. The Primary-Backup Approach. *Distributed Systems*, Mullender, editor, pages 199–216. Addison-Wesley, 1993.

[5] Y. Deswarte, L. Blain, and J.-C. Fabre. Intrusion Tolerance in Distributed Computing Systems. *Proceedings of the IEEE Symposium on Research in Security and Privacy*, pages 110–121, Oakland, CA, May 1991.

[6] Ben Di Vito. A Model of Cooperative Noninterference for Integrated Modular Avionics. *Dependable Computing for Critical Applications (DCCA-7)*, San Jose, CA, January 1999.

[7] B. Dutertre and V. Stavridou. A Model of Noninterference for Integrating Mixed-Criticality Software Components. *DCCA-7, Dependable Computing for Critical Applications*, San Jose, CA, January 1999.

[8] J.-C. Fabre, Y. Deswarte, and B. Randell. Designing Secure and Reliable Applications using Fragmentation-Redundancy-Scattering: an Object-Oriented Approach. *First European Dependable Computing Conference (EDCC-1)*, pages 21–38, Berlin, Germany, October 1994. Springer-Verlag, LNCS 852.

[9] M. Fischer, N. Lynch, and M. Merritt. Easy Impossibility Proofs for Distributed Consensus. *Distributed Computing*, 1(1):26–39, January 1986.

[10] J.A. Goguen and J. Meseguer. Security Policies and Security Models. *Proceedings of the IEEE Symposium on Research in Security and Privacy*, pages 11–20, Oakland, CA, 1982.

[11] J.A. Goguen and J. Meseguer. Unwinding and Inference Control. *Proceedings of the IEEE Symposium on Research in Security and Privacy*, pages 75–86, Oakland, CA, 1984.

[12] J.W. Gray. Probabilistic Interference. *Proceedings of the IEEE Symposium on Research in Security and Privacy*, pages 170–179, Oakland, CA, May 1990.

[13] J.W. Gray. Toward A Mathematical Foundation for Information Flow Security. *Journal of Computer Security*, 3–4(1):255–294, 1992.

[14] R. Kemmerer. NSTAT: A Model-based Real-time Network Intrusion Detection System. Technical Report TRCS97-18, University of California, Santa Barbara, June 1998.

[15] L. Lamport, R. Shostak, and M. Pease. The Byzantine General Problem. *Journal of the ACM*, 4(3):382–401, July 1982.

[16] B. Lampson. Atomic Tansactions. *Distributed Systems: Architecture and Implementation*, Volume 105 of *Lecture Notes in Computer Science*, pages 246–265. Springer-Verlag, 1981.

[17] J.-C. Laprie (Ed.). *Dependability: Basic Concepts and Terminology*. Springer-Verlag, 1992.

[18] W. Lee and S. Stolfo. Data Mining Approaches for Intrusion Detection. *Proceedings of the 7th USENIX Security Symposium*, pages 26–29, San Antonio, TX, January 1998.

[19] T. Lunt. A Survey of Intrusion Detection Techniques. *Computers and Security*, 12(4):405–418, June 1993.

[20] N. Lynch. *Distributed Algorithms*. Morgan Kaufmann, 1996.

[21] D. McCullough. Specifications for Multi-Level Security and a Hook-Up Property. *Proceedings of the IEEE Symposium on Research in Security and Privacy*, pages 161–166, Oakland, CA, 1987.

[22] D. McCullough. Noninterference and the Composability of Security Properties. *Proceedings of the IEEE Symposium on Research in Security and Privacy*, pages 177–186, Oakland, CA, April 1988.

[23] J. McLean. A Comment on the 'Basic Security Theorem' of Bell and LaPadula. *Information Processing Letters*, 20(2):67–70, February 1985.

[24] J. McLean. Security Models and Information Flow. *Proceedings of the IEEE Symposium on Research in Security and Privacy*, pages 180–187, Oakland, CA, May 1990.

[25] J. McLean. Proving Noninterference and Functional Correctness Using Traces. *Journal of Computer Security*, 1(1):37–57, 1992.

[26] J. McLean. Security Models. *Encyclopedia of Software Engineering*, J. Marciniak, editor. Wiley and Sons, 1994.

[27] C. Meadows. Using Traces Based on Procedure Calls to Reason About Composabiliy. *Proceedings of the IEEE Symposium on Research in Security and Privacy*, pages 177–188, Oakland, CA, 1992.

[28] J. Millen. Hookup Security for Synchronous Machines. *Proceedings of the Computer Security Foundations Workshop III*, pages 84–90, Franconia, NH, June 1990. IEEE Press.

[29] J.K. Millen. Covert Channel Capacity. *Proceedings of the IEEE Symposium on Research in Security and Privacy*, pages 60–66, Oakland, CA, April 1987.

[30] P. Neumann. Architectures and Formal Representations for Secure Systems. Technical Report SRI-CSL-96-05, Computer Science Laboratory, SRI International, Menlo Park, CA, May 1996.

[31] P. Porras and A. Valdes. Live Traffic Analysis of TCP/IP Gateways. In *Proceedigns of the 1998 ISOC Symposium on Network and Distributed System Security (NDSS'98)*, San Diego, CA, March 1998.

[32] A.W. Roscoe. CSP and Determinism in Security Modelling. *Proceedings of the IEEE Symposium on Research in Security and Privacy*, pages 114–127, Oakland, CA, May 1995.

[33] A.W. Roscoe and L. Wulf. Composing and Decomposing Systems under Security Properties. *Proceedings of the 8th IEEE Computer Security Foundation Workshop*, pages 9–15, Kenmare, Ireland, June 1995.

[34] J. Rushby. Kernels for Safety? *Safe & Secure Computing Systems*, T. Anderson, editor, pages 210–220. Blackwell Scientific Publications, 1989.

[35] J. Rushby. Noninterference, Transitivity, and Channel-Control Security Policies. Technical Report CSL-92-02, Computer Science Laboratory, SRI International, December 1992.

[36] J. Rushby. Partitioning in Avionics Architectures: Requirements, Mechanisms, and Assurance. Draft technical report, Computer Science Laboratory, SRI International, October 1998.

[37] P. Ryan and S. Schneider. Process Algebra and Non-Interference. *1999 IEEE Computer Security Foundations Workshop (CSFW12)*, Mordano, Italy, June 1999.

[38] F. Schneider. Implementing Fault-Tolerant Services Using the State-Machine Approach: A Tutorial. *ACM Computing Surveys*, 22, December 1990.

[39] A. Simpson, J. Woodcock, and J. Davies. Safety through Security. *Proceedings of the Ninth International Workshop on Software Specification and Design*, pages 18–24, Ise-Shima, Japan, April 1998.

[40] E. Spafford. The Internet Worm: Crisis and Aftermath. *Communications of the ACM*, 32(6):678–687, June 1989.

[41] D. Sutherland. A Model of Information. *Proceedings of the 9th National Computer Security Conference*, pages 175–183, Gaithersburg, MD, September 1986.

[42] K.G. Wika and J.C. Knight. A Safety Kernel Architecture. *Compass'95: Tenth Annual Conference on Computer Assurance*, Gaithersburg, Maryland, June 1995.

[43] M. Wilding, D. Hardin, and D. Greve. Invariant Performance: A Statement of Task Isolation Useful for Embedded Application Integration. *Dependable Computing for Critical Applications, DCCA-7*, San Jose, CA, January 1999.

[44] J.T. Wittbold and D.M. Johnson. Information Flow in Nondeterministic Systems. *Proceedings of the IEEE Symposium on Research in Security and Privacy*, pages 144–161, Oakland, CA, May 1990.

[45] A. Zakinthinos and E.S. Lee. The Composability of Non-Interference. *Proceedings of the 8th IEEE Computer Security Foundation Workshop*, pages 2–8, Kenmare, Ireland, June 1995.

Certificate Revocation the Responsible Way

Jonathan K. Millen
SRI International
millen@csl.sri.com

Rebecca N. Wright
AT&T Labs – Research
rwright@research.att.com

Abstract

Public-key certificates are managed by a combination of the informal web of trust and the use of servers maintained by organizations. Prompt and reliable distribution of revocation notices is an essential ingredient for security in a public-key infrastructure. Current schemes based on certificate revocation lists on key servers are inadequate. An approach based on distributing revocation notices to "dependers" on each certificate, with cascading forwarding, is suggested. Research is necessary to investigate architectural issues, particularly reliability and response time analysis.

1. Introduction

The more the Internet is used for important personal and commercial transactions, the more important are the basic security concerns of privacy and authentication of network communications, and an increasing number of organizations and individuals are affected. The fundamental tool for communication security is encryption. Encryption was largely the province of the military until the late 1970s, when the U.S. Data Encryption Standard (DES) was published for use in commerce and banking [2]; and public-key encryption, in the form of the Diffie-Hellman [3] and RSA [9] algorithms, was also invented. Public-key encryption made the key distribution problem easier, at least at first sight, since the key used to encrypt messages for a particular recipient did not have to be kept secret—it could be published freely. The corresponding decryption key was kept by the owner. This meant that courier services to carry secret master keys from one party to another were no longer necessary, and furthermore, for all pairs of n parties to communicate privately, only n rather than $n(n-1)/2$ keys had to be distributed.

Public-key cryptography first became easily accessible to the general public through a software package called PGP (Pretty Good Privacy), developed for UNIX and PCs and available for free [6]. It enabled users to generate their own public and corresponding secret keys, and put the keys to use with the RSA algorithm. If the sender and receiver of a message had the PGP software, it could be used either to send private messages or to authenticate messages with a digital signature. For digital signatures, the sender applies his own secret key to a message, and the recipient can confirm the identity of the sender by applying the sender's known public key.

Because public-key algorithms are typically slower than symmetric-key algorithms, public-key encryption is used primarily to distribute symmetric keys, and the symmetric keys are applied to the protected data using DES and other methods.

As RSA and other public-key techniques were judged over time to be as secure as established symmetric-key algorithms, their use spread to organizations and the government itself. The value of data protected by these techniques increased, focusing more attention on a problem that still remained with public key distribution: in order to ensure that encrypted data is only going to the proper recipient, and that digitally signed data is coming from the proper originator, the user of a public key has to be sure that it belongs to the right party. How can a public key be authenticated?

2. Public-Key Certificates

The immediate answer is to create a *certificate*, which is a signed message linking a public key to the identity of its owner. A certificate should be digitally signed by someone whose public key is already known, and who is trusted not to sign a certificate without confirming that the named owner actually possesses the corresponding secret key. In this way, a small number of public keys can be exchanged in a secure "out-of-band" manner, such as face-to-face or by secure courier; these keys can be "bootstrapped" to validate additional keys. This dependence of one key on another creates a public-key certificate infrastructure. There have been a number of proposals for the architecture of such infrastructures, ranging from an Internet standard for Privacy-Enhanced Mail (PEM) to the PGP-motivated informal "web of trust."

Note that a certificate might be issued either by an individual or an organization. An organization that signs public key certificates is called a *certification authority*. If an organization issues a certificate, it is usually because it conveys some privileges, such as access to an internal network, or to files in a certain category, or management authority on certain tasks. In this case the organization as well as the individual would hold the secret key. Most private organizations who have set up their own enterprise-level certificate systems, like PEM, make use of the X.509 standard for certificate format. Certificate dependencies form a hierarchy.

In PGP terminology, an individual who signs someone else's certificate is an *introducer*. There are no rules for the network of dependencies in the web of trust; it may have cycles, for example. The same certificate may have several signatures on it; in fact, multiple signatures are considered desirable, to increase the chance that someone who receives the certificate will find a trusted introducer among them, without having to trace back through a chain of certificates.

Public keys and their certificates may become invalid for various reasons. The secret key may have been lost or compromised. The owner's identifying information, which might include an Internet e-mail address or employer, may have changed. The certificate might have been used to enable organizational privileges which have been withdrawn by the employer. Some certificates have an expiration date, but if there is none, or if a certificate becomes invalid prior to the expiration date, there should be some way to revoke the certificate. Holders of a certificate must be notified that it is no longer valid, otherwise they will continue to use the same public key to encrypt messages to the owner, and accept signatures from the owner as proof of identity and associated privileges.

There is some logical structure here that needs careful investigation. The signature on a certificate is no good unless the recipient both trusts the signer and holds the certificate of the signer. If the signer's certificate is revoked, that does not invalidate certificates already signed, but new ones should not be accepted if they are signed by the revoked key. The timing issues can be subtle; a logic to support suitable policies was developed by Stubblebine and Wright [10]. Should revocation notices be accepted if they are not signed by the key in the certificate? In some sense, they need to be, since loss or destruction of the owner's copy of a key is reason for the owner to revoke it. These are general concerns about the principles of revocation, and they can be considered separately from questions about how to manage distribution of revocation notices.

Some of the questions that have to be asked about public-key certificate management, therefore, are:

- Was the key issued by the individual owner or an organization?

- Is the certificate signed by an introducer or a certificate authority?

- Was the key obtained from a server or via non-network channels?

- Does the key convey privileges or authority?

- What are the causes and consequences of revocation?

- How is the distribution of revocation notices handled?

In this note we focus on distribution of revocation notices, and how it can be handled in an environment where the other questions can have several possible answers.

3. Handling Revocation

Current proposed standards for revocation, such as in the Internet draft standard Public Key Infrastructure [7], involve *certificate revocation lists* (CRLs) maintained on key servers. A key server is a stable, reliable computer system accessible over the network that distributes certificates. To revoke a certificate, the owner sends the key server a *revocation notice*, which is a signed message identifying the certificate to be revoked.

Upon receipt of a revocation notice, the key server updates its CRL and no longer gives out the revoked certificate. Current certificate holders might be notified either with a "push" or a "pull" system. As an example of a "push" system, a key server could periodically broadcast its current CRL to a set of subscribers. A "pull" approach would be to ask a certificate holder who obtained the certificate from a particular key server to check with the key server periodically, or before using a certificate.

Any scheme involving periodic revocation updates, whether of a push or a pull nature, poses a risk due to the delay between the time the certificate is revoked (which may itself be some time after the cause for revocation took place) and the time of the update.

Push schemes are impractical if they have to broadcast an entire CRL update to a large number of subscribers. One can try to reduce the need for revocation by limiting certificates to brief expiration periods, but this approach leads to a more complex system that still requires a "suicide bureau" to maintain revocations due to key compromise, according to Rivest [8]. It also means that replacement certificates must be distributed.

Pull schemes require action on the part of the certificate holder. It is burdensome to check for revocation on every use, and often it is the owner rather than the certificate holder who suffers more from a failure to check revocation. The certificate holder might not always know who, or which server, to consult about the status of a certificate, particularly if there are several different kinds of certificates with different management characteristics.

For a key server that handles a large number of certificates and queries, there can be significant efficiency considerations for updating and accessing a CRL. Solutions such as such as Kocher's revocation tree [4] have been proposed for improved efficiency.

From a social point of view we want to acknowledge the fact that many certificates are issued by individuals, perhaps using PGP, and distributed without the use of a key server. Certificates might be posted on web servers to publicize them, but web servers typically do not support key server responsibilities such as CRL maintenance.

We need a better way to handle revocations. Some desired properties of a revocation scheme are:

- It should be workable for individuals.

- It should be "server-light," so that massive institutional facilities will not be required.

- It should be decentralized.

- It should support prompt revocation, given specified delay constraints.

- It should require only a realistic workload for those using the system.

- The workload should be allocated in proportion to the self-interest of users.

4. Suggestion: Dependers

One way to balance these goals is suggested here. The idea is to associate a list of "dependers" with a certificate. A depender may be either an individual who wants to be notified promptly of revocation if and when it occurs, or a server that should update its data base upon notification.

The basic advantage of a depender list is that it narrows the burden of notification to the minimal set of interested parties. It becomes practical, also, to perform push-style notification immediately, rather than delaying for a periodic schedule.

The basic depender concept is illustrated in Figure 1.

Notification would not be practical if the owner of a key had to notify everyone who had the key. Everyone with a copy of the PGP software, for example, has the certificate of the originator, Phil Zimmerman, and he would not and could not put everyone on his depender list.

The burden of notification can be distributed by requiring the depender list to cover only an immediate set of those who received the key directly, and invoking transitivity to cover the network. With some exceptions, we could make a rule saying that anyone who transmits a certificate should put the recipient on a depender list. That is, if A sends a certificate to B,

Figure 1: Dependers (RN: Revocation Notice)

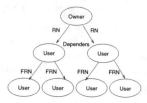

Figure 2: Cascading (FRN: Forwarded Revocation Notice)

then A puts B on A's depender list for that certificate, regardless of who owns the certificate or where it came from.

A cascaded or hierarchical architecture for forwarding revocation notices is illustrated in Figure 2.

The responsibility to maintain a depender list can be avoided in some cases by sending the revocation notice to a server. The server could operate on either a push or a pull model, implementing the push side as a forwarder of revocation notices, and, on the pull side, allowing users to query the status of a particular certificate. The server approach is illustrated in Figure 3.

The server approach is still decentralized in that different key owners may choose different servers on which to make their certificates available. Also, the server does not necessarily have to have a single combined CRL; it just has to be able to respond to queries about individual certificates, using information that may be stored in association with each certificate (or each user who might have a certificate).

Given the existing mixture of certificate management methods in the Internet, we will probably need a hybrid scheme that results from combining the cascading and server approaches, as suggested in Figure 4.

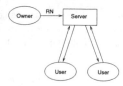

Figure 3: Using a Server

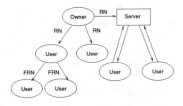

Figure 4: Hybrid Certificate Management

5. Implications

What would it take to implement a depender architecture? First, when a public key certificate is requested and sent from a holder to a user, the user has the option of asking to be a depender, and the holder has options of recording that dependency, or referring the user to a server or some depender who can forward the notice, or just refusing. This leads to a kind of protocol:

> A → B: Please send me the certificate of: ____
> B → A: (public key certificate)
> A → B: Please register me as a depender
> B → A: (Option 1) Okay
> B → A: (Option 2) Check the server at URL: ____
> B → A: (Option 3) Ask one of my dependers: ____
> B → A: (Option 4) No

Such a protocol would have to be implemented in some form by PGP and by certificate servers.

5.1. PGP Implications

PGP already has many commands for implementing various aspects of key and certificate management. It would not be inconsistent with its overall architecture to provide commands for adding dependers and for generating and revocation notices to them. Certificates are kept in data bases called "key rings;" the format of a key ring would have to be extended to hold depender information. Since revocation notices would be sent by e-mail, it would still be a task for individuals to respond to revocation notices by invoking the PGP command to process them.

5.2. Web Server Implications

Certificates are often posted by individuals on web pages on servers maintained by their organizations. The server itself may have no centralized awareness that some of its pages contain certificates. It is still possible, however, for a page containing a certificate to be updated automatically in response to a revocation notice. The notice could be sent in the form of an HTTP query invoking a CGI (Common Gateway Interface) script. CGI scripts are programs run by the server in response to queries similar to web page requests [1]. A CGI query specifies a particular script to use (an executable file in a CGI directory on the server) and gives it parameters relevant to the particular query, in this case a certificate ID. The CGI script can authenticate the request, access the web page containing the certificate, and erase it or mark it. Standard CGI scripts could be developed for this purpose, given conventions for the organization of web pages containing certificates.

5.3. Authentication Implications

In order to avoid spurious revocations, it is important that revocations be authenticated in some way. CRLs are typically signed by the server that issues them. In our case, we propose that revocation notices of an individual's public key should be signed, when possible, by the corresponding private key; forwarded revocation notices would maintain the initial signature. In this way, it can be determined that the revocation notice either came from the owner of the key and should therefore be trusted, or the revocation notice came from someone who knows the private key (or who knows how to forge signatures from that key), in which case the key is by definition compromised and should be revoked. One advantage of this method is that since the key used to verify the revocation notice is the same as the key that is being revoked, a user receiving a revocation notice will always have the capability to verify a signature to revoke any key in their key ring.

The only case where the above method is not be possible to use is when a public key is being revoked because the private key has been lost. In this case, here are three possibilities. One is that the user is required to first obtain a new set of keys and use these to authenticate the revocation message; this has the disadvantage of requiring the new key to be disseminated before the old key can be revoked. The second is to allow unsigned revocation notices; this has the disadvantage that it allows denial-of-service attacks by which anyone can arbitrarily revoke anyone else's keys. Finally, revocation notices could be signed in the same way that other certificates are, by some combination of servers and other individuals. In practice, a combination of the three may be the best solution, where the trust others will place in the revocation notice will depend on which keys have signed it.

5.4. Reliability Implications

A cascading scheme for forwarding revocation notices has the difficulty that it depends on the correct and prompt operation of individuals or servers. In general, one should assume that at least some of links in a chain of notices will be down at a given time. Hence it is necessary to develop architectures and dependency-creation protocols that build some redundancy into the forwarding hierarchy, so that it will be more reliable than the individual nodes. We will need analysis of the reliability of a planned architecture. Also, if reliability concerns are modeled in terms of delays rather than simply operation vs. non-operation, there can and should be analysis of the propagation time for a revocation notice.

5.5. Summary

Public-key cryptography is in widespread use for both individual and institutional applications. Public keys need to be certified for authenticity and for the authority behind any associated privileges. Certificates are managed by some combination of the informal web of trust and the use of servers maintained by organizations.

Prompt and reliable distribution of revocation notices is an essential ingredient for security in a public-key infrastructure. Current schemes based on certificate revocation lists on key servers are inadequate. An approach based on distributing revocation notices to "dependers" on each certificate, with cascading forwarding, has been suggested. This can be combined with enhanced web server and key server services in a hybrid approach. Research is still necessary to investigate architectural issues, particularly reliability and response time analysis.

References

[1] National Center for Supercomputing Applications, "Common Gateway Interface," University of Illinois at Urbana-Champaign, http://hoohoo.ncsa.uiuc.edu/cgi.

[2] National Institute of Standards and Technology (NIST), "The Data Encryption Standard (DES)," Federal Information Processing Standard 46 (FIPS PUB 46).

[3] W. Diffie and M. Hellman, "New directions in cryptography," *IEEE Trans. on Information Theory* 22(6), 1976, 644-654.

[4] P. Kocher, "On certificate revocation and validation," *Financial Cryptography*, LNCS 1465, 1998, 172-177.

[5] "Privacy Enhancement for Internet Electronic Mail," RFC 1421-1424, Internet Engineering Task Force (IETF).

[6] P. Zimmermann, *The Official PGP User's Guide*, MIT Press, 1995.

[7] C. Adams and R. Zuccherato, "Internet X.509 Public Key Infrastructure Data Certification Server Protocols," Internet Draft, PKIZ Working Group, 1998.

[8] R. Rivest, "Can we eliminate certificate revocation lists," *Financial Cryptography*, LNCS 1465, 1998, 178-183.

[9] R. Rivest, A Shamir, and L. Adleman, "A method for obtaining digital signatures and public-key cryptosystems," *Communications of the ACM* 21(2), Feb. 1978, 120-126.

[10] S. Stubblebine and R. Wright, "An authentication logic supporting synchronization, revocation, and recency," *Proc. 3rd ACM Conference on Computer and Communications Security*, March 1996.

[11] "The Directory-Authentication Framework," CCITT Recommendation X.509.

A Fault Tolerance Approach to Survivability

Paul Ammann   Sushil Jajodia   Peng Liu

Center for Secure Information Systems
George Mason University
{ *pammann,jajodia,pliu* } *@isse.gmu.edu*

Abstract

Attacks on computer systems have received a great deal of press attention; however, most of the focus has been on how an attacker can disrupt an organization's operations. Although attack prevention is clearly preferred, preventive measures do fail, and some attacks inevitably succeed in compromising some or all of particular systems, i.e., databases. We propose research into a fault-tolerance approach that addresses all phases of survivability: attack detection, damage confinement, damage assessment and repair, and attack avoidance. We focus attention on continued service and recovery issues. A promising area of research for continued service addresses relaxed notions of consistency. Expanding on the notion of self stabilization, the idea is to formalize the degree of damage under which useful services is still possible. A complementary research area for recovery is the engineering of suitable mechanisms into existing systems. We explain the underlying models for these research areas and illustrate them with examples from the database domain. We argue that these models form a natural part of a fault tolerance approach and propose research into adapting these models for larger systems.

1: Introduction

We propose three related ideas for addressing the defensive information warfare problem. Presented in Section 2, the first idea, which is neither novel nor universally accepted, is to adopt a fault tolerance perspective of responding to information warfare attacks. The second idea, which is presented in Section 3, is to rethink the notions of integrity and consistency, and to refine these notions to account for malicious activity and partial damage. The motivation is that damaged systems are often useful for certain services. Utility in the presence of damage is rarely formalized, but we argue that there is considerable benefit to such a formalization. The third idea, which is presented in Section 4, is to consider the engineering of recovery mechanisms into existing systems. Such re-engineering is a necessary part of incorporating a fault tolerance framework into existing systems because rebuilding systems from scratch is simply not realistic. We illustrate the latter two ideas with examples from the database context, and argue for research into how these approaches can be adapted to more general classes of systems. Some related work is described in Section 5, and we conclude in Section 6. We begin by describing the defensive information warfare problem, with an emphasis on the database perspective.

2: Fault Tolerance Perspective

Experience with traditional information systems security practices (INFOSEC) has shown that it is very difficult to adequately anticipate the abuse and misuse to which an information system will be subjected in the field. The focus of INFOSEC is prevention: security controls aim to

0-7695-0337-3/99 $10.00 © 1999 IEEE

prevent malicious activity that interferes with confidentiality, integrity or availability. However, outsiders (hackers) have proved many times that security controls can be breached in imaginative and unanticipated ways. Further, insiders have significant privileges by necessity, and so are in a position to inflict damage. Finally, the dramatic increase in internetworking has led to a corresponding increase in the opportunities for outsiders to masquerade as insiders. Network-based attacks on many systems can now be carried out from anywhere in the world. Although mechanisms such as firewalls reduce the threat of outside attack, in practice such mechanisms cannot eliminate the threat without blocking legitimate use as well. In brief, strong prevention is clearly necessary, but less and less sufficient, to protect information resources.

In response to problems with the INFOSEC approach, a complementary approach with an emphasis on survivability has emerged.* This 'information warfare' (IW) perspective is that not only should vigorous INFOSEC measures be taken to defend a system against attack, but that some attacks should be assumed to succeed, and that countermeasures to these successful attacks should be planned in advance. The IW perspective emphasizes the ability to live through and recover from attacks.

Information warfare defense does everything possible to prevent attacks from succeeding, but it also assumes that not all attacks will be averted at the outset. This places increased emphasis on the ability to live through and recover from successful attacks. Information warfare defense must consider the whole process of attack and recovery. This requires a recognition of the multiple phases of the IW process. These phases, which are essentially those of the traditional fault tolerance perspective [10], and the activities which occur in each of them are as follows:

Prevention: The defender puts protective measures into place.

Intelligence gathering: The attacker observes the system to determine its vulnerabilities and find the most critical functions or data to target.

Attack: The attacker carries out the resulting plan.

Detection: The defender observes symptoms of a problem and determines that an attack may have taken place or be in progress.

Confinement: The defender takes immediate action to try to eliminate the attacker's access to the system and to isolate or contain the problem to prevent further spread.

Damage assessment: The defender determines the extent of the problem, including failed functions and corrupted data.

Reconfiguration: The defender may reconfigure to allow operation to continue in a degraded mode while recovery proceeds.

Repair: The defender recovers corrupted or lost data and repairs or reinstalls failed system functions to reestablish a normal level of operation.

Fault treatment: To the extent possible, the weaknesses exploited in the attack are identified and steps are taken to prevent a recurrence.

Database Vulnerability

The goal of the information warfare attacker is to damage the organization's operation and fulfillment of its mission through disruption of its information systems. The specific target of an attack may be the system itself or its data. While attacks that bring the system down outright are severe and dramatic, they must be well-timed to achieve the attacker's goal, since they will receive immediate and concentrated attention to bring the system back to operational condition, diagnose how the attack took place, and install preventive measures. More successful in the long run might be attacks that, undetected, install plausible but incorrect data that misleads the organization to make bad decisions. This makes the organization's databases prime targets that must be carefully defended.

Although the IW adversary may find many weaknesses in the diverse components of an information system, databases provide a particularly inviting target. There are several reasons for this.

---

*For a recent summary with an emphasis on the database context, see [1].

First, databases are widely used, so the scope for attack is large. Second, information in databases can often be changed in subtle ways that are beyond the detection capabilities of the typical database mechanisms such as range and integrity constraints. For example, repricing merchandise is an important and desirable management function, but it can easily be exploited for fraudulent purposes. Finally, unlike most system components, many databases are explicitly optimized to accommodate frequent updates. The interface provides the outside attacker with built in functions to implement an attack; all that is necessary is to acquire sufficient privileges, a goal experience has shown is readily achievable. Advanced authorization services can reduce such a threat, but never eliminate it, since insider attacks are always possible, and also since system administrators are only human, and hence prone to making mistakes in configuring and managing authorization services.

Integrity, availability, and (to a lesser degree) confidentiality have always been key database issues, and commercial databases include diverse set of mechanisms towards these ends. For example, access controls, integrity constraints, concurrency control, replication, active databases, and recovery mechanisms deal well with many kinds of mistakes and errors. However, the IW attacker can easily evade some of these mechanisms and exploit others to further the attack. For example, access controls can be subverted by the inside attacker or the outside attacker who has assumed an insider's identity. Integrity constraints are weak at prohibiting plausible but incorrect data; classic examples are changes to dollar amounts in billing records or salary figures. To a concurrency control mechanism, an attacker's transaction is indistinguishable from any other transaction. Automatic replication facilities and active database triggers can serve to spread the damage introduced by an attacker at one site to many sites. Recovery mechanisms ensure that committed transactions appear in stable storage and provide means of rolling back a database, but no attention is given to distinguishing legitimate activity from malicious activity. In brief, by themselves, existing database mechanisms for managing integrity, availability, and confidentiality are inadequate for detecting, confining, and recovering from IW attacks.

3: Rethinking Integrity

Traditionally, system designers view integrity as boolean: a system either has it or it doesn't. In practice, of course, no real database enjoys complete integrity: invariably, a variety of factors conspire to make some information stale, missing, or just plain wrong. System design and analysis should recognize that real systems lack integrity, to some degree, most, if not all, of the time. Significant benefits flow from such recognition. Risk management techniques can identify the severity of different integrity loss scenarios, thereby focusing scarce resources on critical areas. A designer can deliberately sacrifice nonessential integrity under carefully controlled conditions to achieve other design objectives, such as performance, autonomy, availability, or security. Designers can achieve these objectives and still assure the preservation of essential aspects of integrity. Advanced applications can use explicit integrity markers on data to make integrity-dependent decisions. Powerful techniques can recognize and avoid impending integrity losses, or, failing that, recognize and contain damage and subsequently help restore integrity.

Systems model the real world—imperfectly, of course. A database that satisfies formally specified integrity constraints nonetheless diverges, sometimes seriously, from the real world. Many factors inhibit synchronization with the external world. Aside from the initial modeling problem, both the real world and the system evolve over time. Experience has shown keeping up with the evolution is time-consuming and error-prone. Of course, some systems evolve due to malicious activity. Attacker goals range from personal, such as fraudulently acquiring goods or services, to global, such as bringing down parts of the national information infrastructure. Designers need ways to address the incompleteness and inconsistency that crop up in real systems. We next describe one such approach in more detail.

Consistency in the Presence of Damage

There is very little work in formally specifying the degree to which maliciously damaged systems are still useful. Consequently, there is a poor understanding of precisely what it means for an attacker to damage a system. However, related work for systems that are not maliciously damaged offers significant promise for adaptation to malicious damage.

We propose the self stabilization model [5, 3] as a starting point for moving forward. Informally, a self-stabilizing system is guaranteed to return safely to normal operation following some abnormal interference. Viewing attacks as abnormal interference, the self stabilization model can be adapted to formalize a damaged, yet useful system. We illustrate this idea in the database context with a damage marking approach to delineate degrees of damage and repair, a notion of consistency built on the damage markings, a formalization of system behavior organized similar to self-stabilization, and the requirements for consistency maintenance that this approach places on transactions. We propose research to extend this model to more general systems than databases.

In the approach below explicit integrity grades—correct, acceptable, wrong but usable, unacceptable, and so forth—mark data. Which integrity constraints apply depends on the markings of the referenced data. Correct data should conform to the full set of integrity constraints; progressively more damaged data should conform to progressively weaker integrity constraints. Sophisticated algorithms identify integrity deviations, mark inconsistent data, track and contain the spread of inconsistency, inform users as to the reliability of query results, manage repair, and oversee a return to normal service. This fault-tolerance approach to integrity enables systems to survive information-warfare attacks [1].

Database Context Example

We mark data to maintain precise damage information during all phases of an attack. We adopt a four part classification; more complex schemes are certainly possible. The four markings are:

1. Red – damaged data that is unsafe to use,
2. Off-Red – damaged data whose use is nonetheless essential,
3. Off-Green – approximate data, and
4. Green – normal data.

Damaged data is untrustworthy; the value of damaged data is determined by the attacker. We assume that damaged data is incorrect and thus in need of repair. The damage in Red data is so serious, and the consequences of using Red data so severe, that the goal is to prohibit access to Red data.

Off-Red data is damaged, but the cost of prohibiting access to such data outweighs the cost of allowing access, auditing the spread of the damage, and subsequently recovering. One motivation for the Off-Red marking is if the damage is not mission critical. Allowing use of the Off-Red value permits transactions that read the damaged field to proceed. At the same time, use of the altered value clearly requires audit. One motivation for the Off-Red marking is a honeypot, where an attacker is deliberately allowed access so that information about the attacker may be collected.

Off-Green data is not necessarily correct. For example, an approximate value may violate an integrity constraint. The goal of approximate data is to allow on-the-fly repairs where the correct value is not known or available, but an approximate value satisfactory to the application is known. Off-Green values are never those supplied by the attacker, but rather replacement values for data damaged by the attacker. Backup versions are an example of approximate data.

Green is the marking for data where no damage has been detected. Of course, entries with undetected damage may be marked Off-Green or Green as well; there is no way in general of avoiding such a possibility. As in ordinary databases, data may also be incorrect for reasons unrelated to any attack, even if the data is marked Green.

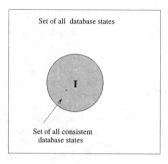

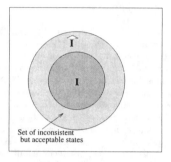

(a) Standard   classification of
database states

(b) Database states as classified in
our model

Figure 1. Classification of the Database States

Markings are possible at different granularities. At a very fine granularity level, the value for a single attribute in a tuple may be marked. Markings are sometimes more appropriate at coarser granularities, specifically tuples, attributes for tables, and entire tables. The integrity constraints can influence the choice of granularity.

We wish to provide an alternative to the standard all or nothing view of integrity constraints, namely, that a consistent database satisfies its constraints and a corrupted database does not. The starting point for such an alternative is to revisit of the standard notion of database consistency. We revise the definition for consistency to accommodate the color markings. Our main formal result is a syntactic protocol for transactions that preserves the revised notion of consistency.

Consistency for Database States

We define our notion of consistency with respect to integrity constraints. We define two sets of integrity constraints. The first set, denoted I, is the 'normal' set of integrity constraints. If all data referenced by an integrity constraint in I is Green, then we require the integrity constraint to hold. The second set, denoted $\hat{I}$, is the set of integrity constraints describing values that are acceptable, although not necessarily consistent with respect to I. Integrity constraints in $\hat{I}$ are required to hold for all data that is either Off-Green or Green. Since it is unreasonable to expect integrity constraints to hold for data supplied by the attacker, integrity constraints do not apply to Red or Off-Red data.

The relationship between I and $\hat{I}$ is shown in Figure 1. The ring denotes the set of all states that satisfy $\hat{I}$ but not I. The important part about Figure 1(b) is that the set of inconsistent but acceptable states is formally identified and distinguished from the states that are unacceptable. The advantage is that formal analysis can be used to investigate consistency in the presence of damage.

Definitions can be constructed so that the integrity constraints in $\hat{I}$ are (possibly) weakened versions of the integrity constraints in I. That is, if the integrity constraints in I are satisfied for some state of the database (regardless of the markings on the data), then the integrity constraints in $\hat{I}$ must also be satisfied for that state. Put succinctly, $I \Rightarrow \hat{I}$. Note that the closure property of self-stabilization [3], namely that activity stays within $\hat{I}$, is implicit in the model described here. We view the convergence property, namely that activity must return to I upon cessation of hostile activity, as too strong in general in the present context, and so do not include it. Clearly, for some systems, convergence may be possible.

Consistency for Transactions

In standard databases, normal transactions need only map consistent states to consistent states, where consistency has the usual definition. For the approximate values of Off-Green data to be useful, a normal transaction that accesses such a value must be prepared to maintain the extended notion of consistency. In fact, a syntactic protocol, called 'Normal Transaction Access Protocol', is proposed in [1] to meet this requirement. Details of the protocol are omitted here since the space is limited. Consistency preservation for transactions only forces the developer to consider the first two parts of the definition of consistency. Specifically, although the developer must consider the integrity constraints in $\hat{I}$ as well as those in I, the developer is not obligated to consider the large number of possible damage scenarios. This simplifies the developer's job.

Fault Tolerance Perspective Of Marking Protocol

Detection: Attack detection methods appear as detection transactions in our model. Although there are many possible sources for detection, the implementation of the detection in the database is through trusted countermeasure transactions.

Isolation and Reconfiguration: Isolation is achieved via the damage markings and Normal Transaction Access Protocol. Data with Red markings is completely isolated, and data with Off-Red markings propagates in a specific manner that can be audited. A possible way of propagation is specified in the Normal Transaction Access Protocol. Reconfiguration for damage to data in a database involves only changes in data access patterns, which the damage markings implement. For example, changes in the marking for a data item usually change the way transactions acess the item.

Damage Assessment: Damage assessment can be either automated by embedding damage marking policies in predefined detection transactions, or damage assessment can proceed with human intervention. In the latter case, the changes to the damage markings are still introduced to the database through detection transactions.

Repair: Repair can be achieved by a variety of methods, but all are mediated by trusted repair transactions. The values for the repair may come from expert humans, from derived data, from old versions of the database, from an explicit rollback to a prior state, and so on.

Fault Treatment: The damage markings do not address fault treatment directly; identification of the weaknesses the attacker exploits is a job that in general must take place outside the database. Nonetheless, the audit provisions for the Normal Transaction Access Protocol, as well as logs from the detection and repair transactions, should provide useful evidence for tracking down the attack.

Data Criticality Analysis: Promising techniques are available for data criticality analysis. For example, fault tree analysis [11] could be used to formalize arguments as to which data should be subject to marking with respect to a particular mission.

4: Recovery From Malicious Activity

Engineering fault tolerance into existing systems is a challenging undertaking; standard advice is that it is very difficult to accommodate fault tolerance unless it is planned for from the early stages of system design. Nonetheless, malicious activity is often directed against systems for which planning for recovery was not considered. Since it is simply not feasible to redesign these systems from scratch, adding provision for fault tolerance is necessary.

As a starting point we propose an undesirable transaction repair model [12]. Informally, an undesirable transaction repair model takes a set of committed transactions that are subsequently deemed to be undesirable and computes what changes to the existing state are necessary to remove their effects. We illustrate the approach below with a discussion of rewriting histories for purposes of repair in databases. A key difference in focus from traditional database research is that the undesirable nature of the transaction is unknown until after the decision to commit is made, with the consequence that an undo approach such as the nested transaction model is difficult to apply, and one is left instead with compensation as a general technique. This focus is well suited to both the problem of engineering fault tolerance into existing systems and to the problem of malicious activity in general. We propose expanding the model outlined below for more general systems than databases.

Compensation accommodates a loss of integrity by directly repairing damage [6]. Because other transactions may access or update the state after a transaction commits, syntactic undo methods do not apply to committed transactions. Instead a compensation transaction attempts to repair semantically the effects of an erroneously committed transaction, and possibly the effects of transactions that read from it. Some actions, such as dispensing cash or firing a missile, complicate or defy satisfactory compensation within a system. In the former case, a bank can compensate erroneously dispensed cash by establishing a loan, as in overdraft protection. In the latter case, compensation occurs outside the system, for example by courts or diplomatic means.

A semantic approach applies to the problem of restoring a database after the identification of a set of undesirable, but committed, transactions. The key transformation—which uses limited deviations from the specified integrity constraints—rewrites the execution history so that undesirable transactions appear as near to the end of the history as possible, thereby minimizing rework.

Since the general models for implementing recovery are well understood, the primary research needs are to show the feasibility and practicality of integrating recovery mechanisms into existing systems. The example we give in the database context suggests both feasibility and practicality. Even more interesting, the reasoning mechanism developed for rooting out undesirable transactions, denoted *can-follow*, has the property that it is more effective than the notion of commutativity that inspired it. The added power derives from the fact that the actions of some transactions are being discarded.

Rewriting Histories

For a serial history we augment the history with explicit database states so that the result is a sequence of interleaved transactions and database states.

In rewriting histories, the general goal is either to move bad transactions towards the end of a history or to move good transactions towards the beginning of a history. It turns out that the transformations do not necessarily result in a serializable history which is conflict-equivalent or view-equivalent to the original history [4]. The lack of serializability is justified by the observation that bad transactions ultimately must be backed out anyway along with some or all of the affected transactions. Hence the serializability of such transactions is not a requirement.

It turns out that rewriting histories for recovery purposes requires some care with respect to final-state-equivalence of histories. Two augmented histories are final-state-equivalent if they are over the same set of transactions and the final states are identical.

Keeping the final-state-equivalence of rewritten histories during a rewrite is essential to the success of the rewrite because otherwise even if the rewritten history is still consistent after the rewrite, the behaviors and effects of transactions may have changed, thus the original execution log may be useless. Moreover, the rewritten history usually does not result in the same final state. One approach to this problem is to decorate each transaction in an augmented history with special values for read purposes by the transaction [12].

The can-follow relation captures the notion that a transaction T can be moved to the end of a history past a sequence of transactions R if no transaction in R reads from T. The can-follow relation ensures that the cumulative effects of the transactions in R on the database state are identical both before and after T is moved.

5: Related Work

Database recovery mechanisms are not designed to deal with malicious attacks. Traditional recovery mechanisms [4] based on physical or logical logs guarantee the ACID properties of transactions – Atomicity, Consistency, Isolation, and Durability – in the face of process, transaction, system and media failures. In particular, the last of these properties ensure that traditional recovery mechanisms never undo committed transactions. However, the fact that a transaction commits does not guarantee that its effects are desirable. Specifically, a committed transaction may reflect inappropriate and/or malicious activity.

There are two common approaches to handling the problem of undesirable but committed transactions: rollback and compensation. The rollback approach, sometimes formalized in a nested transaction model [15], is simply to rollback all activity – desirable as well as undesirable – to a point believed to be free of damage. Such an approach may be used to recover from inadvertent as well as malicious damage. For example, users typically restore files with backup copies in the event of either a disk crash or a virus attack. In the database context, checkpoints serve a similar function of providing stable, consistent snapshots of the database. The rollback approach is effective, but expensive, in that all of the desirable work between the time of the backup and the time of recovery is lost. Keeping this window of vulnerability acceptably low incurs a substantial cost in maintaining frequent backups or checkpoints, although there are algorithms for efficiently establishing snapshots on-the-fly [2, 18, 19].

The compensation approach [6, 7] seeks to undo either committed transactions or committed steps in long-duration or nested transactions [9] without necessarily restoring the data state to appear as if the malicious transactions or steps had never executed. There are two kinds of compensation: action-oriented and effect-oriented [9, 13, 20, 21]. Action-oriented compensation for a transaction or step T_i compensates only the actions of T_i. Effect-oriented compensation for a transaction or step T_i compensates not only the actions of T_i, but also the actions that are affected by T_i. Although a variety of types of compensation are possible, all of them require semantic knowledge of the application. We do not rely on semantic information, but rather use the syntactic information of read-write dependencies. Although the semantic approach can be be very powerful, our goal here is to develop methods that integrate well with mainstream commercial systems, which currently do not support semantic models.

Information warfare has received attention in the database context. Graubert, Schlipper, and McCollum identified database management aspects that determine the vulnerability to information warfare attacks [8]. McDermott and Goldschlag [16, 17] developed storage jamming, which can be used to seed a database with dummy values, access to which indicates the presence of an intruder. Lunt surveyed a variety of intrusion detection methods [14].

6: Summary

We argue for a fault tolerance approach to survivability. Since no real system enjoys absolute integrity, corresponding models for these systems should explicitly address integrity losses. For example, damage markers make it easier to provide continued trustworthy service in systems under information warfare attacks, and inference methods can restore lost information. Rethinking integrity promises significant returns on the investment, and we argue for a research program that addresses this, organized around the notion of self-stabilizing systems. Likewise, reengineering existing systems to accommodate malicious activity requires the ability to determine the effects of undesirable actions and efficiently compensate for them, and we argue for a research program that addresses this, built upon successful work in the database context.

References

[1] P. Ammann, S. Jajodia, C.D. McCollum, and B.T. Blaustein. Surviving information warfare attacks on databases. In *Proceedings of the IEEE Symposium on Security and Privacy*, pages 164–174, Oakland, CA, May 1997.

[2] Paul Ammann, Sushil Jajodia, and Padmaja Mavuluri. On the fly reading of entire databases. *IEEE Transactions on Knowledge and Data Engineering*, 7(5):834–838, October 1995.

[3] A. Arora and M. Gouda. Closure and convergence: A foundation for fault-tolerant computing. *IEEE Transactions on Software Engineering*, 19(11):1015–1027, November 1993.

[4] P. A. Bernstein, V. Hadzilacos, and N. Goodman. *Concurrency Control and Recovery in Database Systems*. Addison-Wesley, Reading, MA, 1987.

[5] E. Dijkstra. Self-stabilizing systems in spite of distributed control. *Communications of the ACM*, 17(11), November 1974.

[6] H. Garcia-Molina. Using semantic knowledge for transaction processing in a distributed database. *ACM Transactions on Database Systems*, 8(2):186–213, June 1983.

[7] H. Garcia-Molina and K. Salem. Sagas. In *Proceedings of ACM-SIGMOD International Conference on Management of Data*, pages 249–259, San Francisco, CA, 1987.

[8] R. Graubart, L. Schlipper, and C. McCollum. Defending database management systems against information warfare attacks. Technical report, The MITRE Corporation, 1996.

[9] H.F. Korth, E. Levy, and A. Silberschatz. A formal approach to recovery by compensating transactions. In *Proceedings of the International Conference on Very Large Databases*, pages 95–106, Brisbane, Australia, 1990.

[10] P.A. Lee and T. Anderson. *Fault Tolerance: Principles and Practice*. Springer-Verlag, Wien, Austria, second edition, 1990.

[11] N.G. Leveson. *Safeware: System Safety and Computers*. Addison-Wesley, 1995.

[12] Peng Liu, Paul Ammann, and Sushil Jajodia. Incorporating transaction semantics to reduce reprocessing overhead in replicated mobile data applications. In *ICDCS'99: Proceedings 19th IEEE International Conference on Distributed Computing Systems*, Austin, TX, June 1999. To appear.

[13] D.B. Lomet. MLR: A recovery method for multi-level systems. In *Proceedings of ACM-SIGMOD International Conference on Management of Data*, pages 185–194, San Diego, CA, June 1992.

[14] Teresa F Lunt. A Survey of Intrusion Detection Techniques. *Computers & Security*, 12(4):405–418, June 1993.

[15] N. Lynch, M. Merritt, W. Weihl, and A. Fekete. *Atomic Transactions*. Morgan Kaufmann, San Mateo, CA, 1994.

[16] J. McDermott and D. Goldschlag. Storage jamming. In D.L. Spooner, S.A. Demurjian, and J.E. Dobson, editors, *Database Security IX: Status and Prospects*, pages 365–381. Chapman & Hall, London, 1996.

[17] J. McDermott and D. Goldschlag. Towards a model of storage jamming. In *Proceedings of the IEEE Computer Security Foundations Workshop*, pages 176–185, Kenmare, Ireland, June 1996.

[18] C. Mohan, H. Pirahesh, and R. Lorie. Efficient and flexible methods for transient versioning of records to avoid locking by read-only transactions. In *Proceedings of ACM SIGMOD International Conference on Management of Data*, pages 124–133, San Diego, CA, June 1992.

[19] Calton Pu. On-the-fly, incremental, consistent reading of entire databases. *Algorithmica*, 1(3):271–287, October 1986.

[20] G. Weikum, C. Hasse, P. Broessler, and P. Muth. Multi-level recovery. In *Proceedings of the Ninth ACM SIGACT-SIGMOD-SIGART Symposium of Principles of Database Systems*, pages 109–123, Nashville, Tenn, April 1990.

[21] G. Weikum and H.-J. Schek. Concepts and applications of multilevel transactions and open nested transactions. In Ahmed K. Elmagarmid, editor, *Database Transaction Models for Advanced Applications*, chapter 13. Morgan Kaufmann Publishers, Inc., 1992.

Author Index

Press Activities Board

IEEE Computer Society Publications

The world-renowned IEEE Computer Society publishes, promotes, and distributes a wide variety of authoritative computer science and engineering texts. These books are available from most retail outlets. Visit the Online Catalog, *http://computer.org*, for a list of products.

IEEE Computer Society Proceedings

The IEEE Computer Society also produces and actively promotes the proceedings of more than 141 acclaimed international conferences each year in multimedia formats that include hard and softcover books, CD-ROMs, videos, and on-line publications.

For information on the IEEE Computer Society proceedings, send e-mail to cs.books@computer.org or write to Proceedings, IEEE Computer Society, P.O. Box 3014, 10662 Los Vaqueros Circle, Los Alamitos, CA 90720-1314. Telephone +1 714-821-8380. FAX +1 714-761-1784.

Additional information regarding the Computer Society, conferences and proceedings, CD-ROMs, videos, and books can also be accessed from our web site at *http://computer.org/cspress*